Free Wind Home

A CHILDHOOD MEMOIR 1935~1948

Free Wind Home

A CHILDHOOD MEMOIR 1935~1948

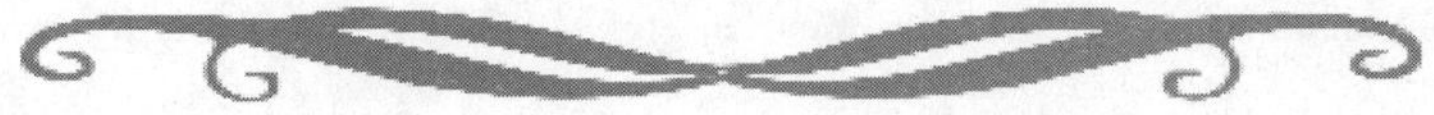

GARY L. SAUNDERS

BREAKWATER BOOKS LTD.
100 Water Street • P.O. Box 2188 • St. John's • NL • A1C 6E6
www.breakwaterbooks.com

Library and Archives Canada Cataloguing in Publication

Saunders, Gary L.
Free wind home: a childhood memoir, 1935-1948 / Gary L. Saunders.

ISBN 978-1-55081-231-2

1. Saunders, Gary L--Childhood and youth. 2. Newfoundland and Labrador--Biography. 3. St. John's (N.L.)--Biography. I. Title.

FC2174.1.S29A3 2007 971.8'03092 C2007-905895-7

Front Cover Photos:
(upper) Gary with his parents, Winnie and Brett, at home in Clarkes Head, Gander Bay, 1942;
(lower) View of Little Harbour, Fogo, looking north, late 1940s (Author's Collection).
Back Cover Photo: Courtesy David Quinton

We acknowledge the financial support of
The Canada Council for the Arts for our publishing activities.

We acknowledge the financial support of the Government of Canada through the Book Publishing Industry Development Program (BPIDP) for our publishing activities.

Printed in Canada.

To the memory of
my mother's father
Henry Eldred Layman (1875-1954),
who made barrels, and of her mother
Prudence (Waterman) Layman (1881-1927),
who loved Shakespeare

"Whoever writes about his childhood
must beware of exaggeration and self-pity."

– GEORGE ORWELL, *Such, Such Were the Joys*

"…memory is treacherous and books founded on reality are so often only faint reflections and sketches of all that we have seen and heard."

– NATALIA GINZBURG, *Family Sayings*

FOREWORD

When I entered Canada in the early spring of 1954 as an immigrant, I was told by the authorities to go to British Columbia. BC had lots of work for a professional forester, they said. But I insisted on heading for Newfoundland – my idea of true wilderness – and although they told me it would be foolish to do so, I traveled to St. John's in April 1954.

After a few months working in a greenhouse there, I was accepted as an employee in the forestry division of the provincial government. Here I met a young man, eighteen years of age, who was colouring forestry maps at the Department of Mines and Resources. Instantly I knew he was a person of extraordinary integrity, with a strong will to learn and an open mind.

At that time I had a limited English vocabulary, but I found in him an interested listener and an easy partner in discussions. He and I had many talks about nature, about forestry, about painting outdoors. It was he who introduced me to British and American poetry – and to Walt Kelly's comic strip *Pogo*.

This young man was of course Gary L. Saunders. When I was put in charge of the summer's forest surveying on the Avalon Peninsula, I was glad he had signed on as one of our crew. That summer Gary taught me a lot of practical things about living in the woods, such as how to paddle a canoe, how to handle a fly rod and how to make a proper bough bed.

He had learned all these things growing up in northeast Newfoundland. His father Brett Saunders was a real woodsman, who as a young man had often spent months alone in the woods. After stints working in Toronto and the United States, Brett made his living from the land, sometimes having plenty, sometimes going hungry, sometimes breaking through the ice at 30 below. He trapped, guided, carried freight and had many outdoor adventures. Over the years he encountered all kinds of beasts and birds, including bears prowling around his tent at night. After meeting both of Gary's parents I understood why their son became who he did.

During that summer of 1954 we became friends, and over the following years he was like a younger brother to me. I became devoted to him, as I felt he also became devoted to me. In 1959 I returned to Denmark. After that, Gary was my link to Canada – still, to my mind, the True North. Though separated by the Atlantic Ocean for more than forty-five years, we kept in touch by post.

Finally, in 1999, I decided to visit him at his "painting place" in Crow Head, Twillingate, a former cod-fishing centre not far from the birthplaces of his paternal grandfather and his mother. Twillingate is a fabulous landscape, even by Newfoundland standards, and it is Gary's place of "Innisfree."

We spent three weeks together there, painting icebergs and various other sceneries around Crow Head. It was a great experience, one which reconfirmed that he and I were kindred spirits still, sharing interests in literature, nature and many other things.

Gary always sends me his new books; I especially look forward to this one!

Hans Mandøe
Hvalpsund, Denmark, December 2006.

PROLOGUE

My childhood was an improbable mix of antique and modern, outdoor and indoor, freedom and constraint. At six I wanted to be a trapper, at seven a telegrapher, at eight a fighter pilot, at eleven Batman, at twelve an itinerant clergyman, at thirteen an artist.

It wasn't that I was watching too much TV; we had none. I was simply mirroring, as children will, the goings-on around me. Clarkes Head, my birthplace, was a sleepy 150-year-old village on the Gander River estuary in northeast Newfoundland. In 1935 it still had one foot in the nineteenth century.

Though Clarkes Head had had land-line telegraphy since the early 1880s and telephones by my time, our only physical links to the outside world were still by boat in summer and by horse and dogteam in winter. Our nearest hospital was an overnight trip away on Twillingate Island, a place all but inaccessible during freeze-up and break-up. We had neither electricity nor indoor plumbing. Our summer drinking water was unsafe. People still believed in toothache charms.

Of course such Third World conditions were common across rural North America in the 1930s, but change was coming. In Clarkes Head it came suddenly. Soon after 1939, we woke to find ourselves next door to one of the world's busiest aerodromes. Built in 1936, Gander Airport was waging furious twentieth century war by hurling new bombers across the Atlantic as fast as North America could roll them out. So on a dreamy Saturday afternoon I might watch old Uncle John Gillingham, a fourth-generation salmon fisher with a family licence from Queen Victoria, leisurely tending his home-knit net in his home-built punt. The next morning I might be wakened by the roar of Harvard trainers mock-strafing our village at rooftop level.

Home life reflected these polarities. My mother loved the city, my father the woods. She was from the bustling town of Fogo, a major cod fishing community of just over 1,000. While in high school she learned Morse code and by age seventeen was the youngest telegrapher in Newfoundland's postal service. Four years later she was assistant telegrapher at the Biltmore Hotel in New York City. She liked to boast, over a cup of tea, that Sir Thomas Lipton had been a client of hers there.

My father, to his credit, did give city life a try. When he met Gander Bay's new post-mistress he'd already attended Bishop Feild College in St. John's and worked in Montreal and Toronto. Smitten by the raven-haired Winnie in 1925, he'd followed her to New York, got a job driving street cars and married her there in 1927.

But for the Depression, they might have stayed in the States, but in 1931 they came home to ride it out. For Dad it was a relief, for Mom a comedown. It didn't help that the little country was nearly bankrupt, that malnutrition and disease were rife, that few good school teachers would brave the isolation.

In 1934, the year I was conceived, our desperate government suspended Newfoundland's hard-won, century-old democracy in exchange for rule by committee. "A rest from politics," they called it. My generation became political orphans for the next fifteen years.

Not that we minded. What do children care who runs their country? I thought it normal that we ate so much caribou and moose meat. That in the early years my father trapped all winter, often sleeping on fir boughs in a birchbark wigwam with a sled dog at his back for warmth. That he did so many odd jobs: catching and canning rabbits, ferrying freight and passengers, guiding anglers and hunters from spring to fall, even salvaging a downed

Hurricane fighter for the RCAF.

Nor did it seem unusual that my mother sewed or knitted much of our clothing, worked part-time at the post office, kept milch goats ("Cows harbour TB, my son"), boiled our summer drinking water; raked my scalp with a fine-toothed comb every September after school started.

Blissful in our ignorance, we contrived, most of the time, to be happy. We needed little entertaining. Long before I started school there was plenty to see and hear and do. We watched women knit sweaters, knead bread, make quilts, make fish, spin wool, put up wild fruit, clean lamps, pluck wildfowl.

We watched men split wood, make snowshoes, shoe horses, jig squid, skin otters, smoke salmon, mend kettles and roofs, build boats, run rapids. We listened spellbound to all their stories and where possible we aped their doings.

Grownups didn't mind. So long as we were respectful, did our chores, got to meals on time and didn't pester, they indulged us. "Leave the youngsters be," they said. "Lord knows they'll be slavin' soon enough." So saying, they bestowed on us a precious gift – the freedom to explore the natural world all but unhindered – though a whole village kept an eye on us. Little wonder that by age ten we were, like Kalahari children, accomplished naturalists.

Everyone has a childhood; why write about mine? Well, first, because it's mine, but also because for many years it has haunted me like a melody from the past. Only after I started jotting down recollections did I realise that, yes, my experiences were unusual and worth recounting.

What got me started was a brush with prostate cancer in 1995. Unaccountably, my surgery and slow recuperation uncapped a flood of memories. I was incontinent with memories. I started scribbling. Soon my scribbles filled a fat blue binder. That led to quizzing older kinfolk about the times we'd lived through, about the child I'd been. And I must have read a dozen memoirs.

Then I got better, put the binder away and all but forgot it. At sixty I was too young to be writing my memoirs anyway.

I did query my publisher. "Yes," said Breakwater's gutsy president Clyde Rose – sight unseen. "Send us samples when you can." I did. He liked them. "Take your time," he said. I did that too. It wasn't until 2004, during radiotherapy, that I really got down to it. Soon I'd filled a second binder. I organized all my notes. At sixty-nine I was surely old enough.

But waiting had its rewards. It let me see the forest for the twigs. It helped me understand Dad's frequent absences, Mom's mortal fear of germs, Grandma Saunders' ongoing concern for my immortal soul. It taught me new respect for my culture's lore and wisdom, and for how they were passed on.

Another reward was the new light being shed on child development. It showed the harm our market-driven, urbanized lifestyle was doing to children. It shocked me to learn of bylaws banning kids from climbing trees on their own property – or even from plucking a leaf! It troubled me that some "progressive" educators had eliminated school recess to save time. Most worrisome to me, a former educator, was the evident link between behavioural problems and a loss of contact with nature. Richard Louv, in his landmark 2005 study *Last Child in the Woods*, named the syndrome Nature Deficit Disorder.

What luck, I realised, to have been born when and where I was. A century earlier and I might have been a child labourer. Sixty years later and I might have been a bubble-wrapped suburban kid plugged into the electronic hive, all my free time scheduled for sports and lessons. And what luck to have known my father's wilderness before the snowmobiles and ATVs tore it up, my mother's world before the cod collapsed.

If my story has a hero it is she. Not that I'd meant to write about her. But in 1973, after I scripted "The Riverman," a CBC television production about my father, I promised to one day tell her story too. To my shame I never did. Imagine my surprise, then, when she quickly moved to centre stage in this work.

Yet it was only right she should have. My father risked life and limb to provide for us – but he was only doing what he loved. She, on the other hand, sacrificed a promising career in communications or music for our welfare. It was she who lit the winter fires and got my brother and me off to school. It was she who told me my first stories, who taught me to read and sing and pray. All she asked in return was that her boys escape the trapline, that we each "get nice clean office jobs."

If she was sometimes frantic with worry about my absent father, "not knowing if he was dead or alive," who could fault her? If she, diagnosed at forty-one with post-surgical grand mal epilepsy, sometimes railed at fate and at me, who could blame her?

Now that my story (and hers) is told, I see another hero emerging: the child at play. Childsplay, psychologists tell us, is the work which children intuitively do to ready themselves for adulthood. If so, then my generation apprenticed for the wrong century. Or did we? Now that the planet has a fever and cheap oil is on the wane, maybe the lore we learned will come in handy after all.

Gary L. Saunders
Old Barns, NS, Canada
August 2007

CONTENTS

Night Walk

If a bay boy can claim a hometown, mine would be St. John's. That was my thought while hiking up Cornwall Avenue in the city's west end one night in December 1994. I had come to promote a new book and had just spent the evening with old friends on Craigmillar Avenue. Now I was walking to lodgings some two miles away in the east end. From there I was to sign books in local malls the next morning.

I was on foot because the previous afternoon a northeaster had buried the city, plugging streets, stranding traffic and downing trees and power lines. Whole districts were still in the dark. Heavy rain had followed, collapsing a stadium roof. Now a cold front was sweeping in, freezing the whole mess. There was a fair chance my book signings would be cancelled.

What odds, I thought. For years I'd been meaning to revisit my childhood haunts downtown. Tonight I had the time. I was going that way. Why not do it now? Certainly the old city had never looked so immaculate. O holy night. "The Holy City," my poet host had called her, only half in jest.

Poets talk that way. But I knew what he meant. Nothing theological about it; more like aesthetic reverence. Neither of us had been born here; certainly no Pope had. He was a Labradorian lately come; I had merely sojourned here. Yet each of us had explored her steep streets and crazy alleys, roamed her storied waterfront, drunk her poetry.

My sojourns had never been this far west. The farthest west my family had ventured was Bennett Avenue, in 1946. Bennett lay just inside the invisible meridian dividing the propertied Upper Levels – "The Quality" – from the have-not Lower Levels, the tenement town where itinerant outporters clustered like puffins on a cliffside. Brazil Square, a little to the east, was its heartland.

Bennett was our first city address and our most respectable. The others, roughly one every two years for the next seven, were either rowhouse flats or rooms rented from relatives. We never owned a car, so where we lived was dictated by shank's mare and how much we could carry. Whatever couldn't be delivered free, we lugged on foot. For heavy bags of groceries this meant about ten blocks. Bookbags might get farther, but not if the snow was too deep. Such calculations dictated our choices. And of course the rent.

So much walking! St. John's was a walker's paradise. I'd tramped the older parts of New York, Toronto, Winnipeg, Vancouver, Victoria, not to mention Britain's London, Chester, Glasgow and Edinburgh. The city could hold its own with them all. Her every vista was enchanting. One could hardly get lost with Signal Hill and its castle for a beacon.

So many hills! A trip down Barter's Hill to Water Street and back was crippling for knees accustomed to gentler terrain. The first week was the worst. After that we could climb anything.

No wonder topography was on my mind that night. St. John's scenery was more like that of Fogo, my mother's outport birthplace, than of Gander Bay, mine. It smelled like Fogo too, especially the waterfront, which reeked of salt cod in summer and seal blubber in winter. Topology was on my mind as well, that interplay of geology and architecture and history which defines a place.

And the history! Ancient by North American standards, torched twice by French militias and razed three times by accident, then re-built on the smoking ashes in fire-trap housing that would burn again. Variously called "the slum on the hill," "the fishiest of modern capitals" and "the fifth province of Ireland," St. John's was home to the sealing fleet, it was a longtime rendezvous for fishing fleets local and foreign, a repair depot for the government's Alphabet Fleet, a cauldron of political and religious strife, Canada's Little Europe.

Topography and topology and time.

Approaching the intersection on Hamilton Avenue, I emerge from a matrix of tree shadows into open moonlight – and deeper snow. Here, snot-green slush has filled the few footprints, which are rapidly gelling into ankle-wrenching craters. Now it is two steps forward and one back. Once, I go arse-over-kettle. Part of me now wants to turn around, go back to my hosts and beg a night's lodging. Then I hit on a better gait – the bow-legged, forward-leaning lurch of a sailor on a reeling deck.

The westerly is becoming a gale. Leafless branches are clashing in the dark, showering shell ice and clots of snow onto the sidewalks. Now and then a lighted lamp or candle glimmers behind closed drapes like a campfire winking in the forest. I have a fey sense of mushing behind sled dogs through a wilderness, as my trapper father did years ago.

But this is no wilderness. Above the *crunch-slosh, crunch-slosh* of my boots, I hear the wind fluting and keening among telephone wires and chimney pots. The music calls to mind Peter Pan's statue in Bowring Park a mile or so west. I should have gone to visit him; another time perhaps. It's already past eleven o'clock. My B & B may close at midnight. So with the wind at my back, tacking from sidewalk to mid-street and back, avoiding the drifts and keeping my trim, I sail east past Cornwall Heights, Shaw Street and Symonds Avenue.

Puffing along, primed with good food and good talk and good whisky, half-wishing I lived here still, I feel grateful to St. John's. Except for a year in Toronto in my mid-teens, no other place had so fed my youthful imagination. It was here I first heard the lovely cadence of an Irish brogue, performed my first act of vandalism, was terrorized by a street gang, read my first comic book, saw my first movie in a real theatre, climbed a square-rigger, learned some Norwegian, began seriously to draw and paint, bought my first real book, loved a girl who wasn't a cousin. And tonight, thanks to a Twillingate doctor, a chance blizzard and my Craigmillar friends, I was home.

At LeMarchant and Hamilton, the westering moon breaks through the storm wrack, casting my crab-like shadow on the snow banks ahead. Then the cloud swallows the moon and my shadow, and I am one with the wind, the trees, the snow, the moon, the darkness, the Holy City.

I hadn't always felt that way about St. John's. That first winter, living on Gilbert Street, I'd hated it. Of course my parents had good reasons to move: health; schooling; steady work; but to me it seemed senseless. Why abandon a place where we had miles of pristine ice to skate on, skyfuls of clean air to breathe, and a wilderness to ramble in – for this? Bennett Avenue hadn't been too bad, but Gilbert Street seemed pinched and sordid. My mother railed at the sooty rain that soiled her clean laundry. My eyes thirsted for river water, my feet craved landwash.

Jaywalking along, the wind at my back, I'm making good time. Bennett can't be much farther, I think; somewhere on my left perhaps. Each step sharpens the sense of delicious familiarity. In the strobe-like play of light and shadow, long-forgotten images surface like trout in a still pond. Wasn't there some sort of low building near the corner? A creamery perhaps? Painted pale yellow? The building seems to be gone, but there, at the corner of a street, is a sign saying "Bennett Avenue." And far up Bennett, where it veers west and uphill, stands a long, grey silhouette that should be St. Michael's Collegiate, the school I briefly attended in 1946 and where Calvin, my older brother, completed Grade 11. Midway between the school and the corner should be the house where we lived with Mr. and Mrs. Andrews that spring and summer when Mom was recovering from surgery.

Part of me wants to explore the street and school grounds, but tonight is not the time, not when I've forgotten to confirm my B & B reservation. I trudge on. Wasn't there, on the same side, a blocky, two-storey structure of glass and pebbled cement? The Cornwall Theatre? With a large circular window out front? My parents took me to a movie there, my first in a real theatre.

There it is, window and all. I peek in. The ornate lobby is divided into work spaces. Where the ticket booth had been is now crowded with desks, typewriters and filing cabinets.

Several blocks ahead, a ragged lattice of lights hangs above the housetops – the Grace Maternity Hospital. They have managed to get auxiliary lighting for the middle floors. Another memory swims to the surface. Hadn't Mom's sister Beatrix and her husband George lived somewhere near here that spring and summer? An image of a sunlit kitchen flits across my mind. I recall breakfasting with her during my mother's stay in the hospital. Uncle George had just got a job with the Merchant Marine. Again, no time to linger, except to glance down the curving tunnel of Pleasant Street, glimpsing the harbour in its deep tureen of hills. Pleasant Street; something about the name tugs at me, but I pass on.

A few more blocks east, on the opposite side, is another constellation of lights, another ship, slightly taller, adrift in the ocean of darkness. It is Saint Clare's Mercy Hospital, the one where my mother had her hysterectomy. Closer to St. Clare Avenue there are people moving, breaking trail like me, company at last.

I try to picture my mother lying up there sleepless, surgery only hours away, scared that the cyst or tumour or whatever will be cancerous; dreading the knife but no more so than the foolishness she is liable to spout under ether.

"People curse like troopers, you know."

Leaving the glare, I am once more immersed in gloom. Even so, the cityscape is ever more familiar. That street sloping steeply up from the southwest must be Patrick, I think, and the one angling in from the south would be Springdale, where I took Grade 5 in 1947. And, a bit farther east, on the same side, is the top of Casey Street – Casey's Hill we called it.

Casey Street and the streets below defined my first winter in St. John's. And despite my initial impressions, they were where I began, at last, to feel at home. This was the chimney-potted nursery where the city midwifed me out of my 19th century world of wood stoves and kerosene lamps and moose meat, and into the 20th century.

Gilbert Street isn't visible from the top of Casey, but I can see the familiar silhouettes of chimneys and dormers stepping down, tier by tier, to the glimmering harbour and the black South Side Hills beyond. Ghostly moonlight plays richly over the angularity of snowy roofs and shadowy alleys, the accidental glinting cubism of skylights, ladders, fire escapes.

Casey Street draws me down. Reservation or no, locked out or no, I must see Gilbert Street. Maybe the house is still there. What was its number? From some deep well of memory the number forty-seven floats up. And now I recall how Pleasant Street fits in: a long walk, Mom's youngest brother Harry, a walk that warmed my heart.

One row house looks very like another. At first I can't find number 47. I remember the colour was foxy, like our house in Gander Bay, but how many times has it been painted since? No matter; by moonlight they all look grey anyhow. And there have been renovations: a dormer here, a doorstep there, window boxes hung. The only thing I know for sure is that it was on the harbour side, halfway between Casey and the next street – whose name I have forgotten. I settle on one, it looks possible; but I must go.

I dodge back up Casey and resign myself to walking the last mile or so to Prescott, hoping they still have a bunk for me. On the way I chuckle at my fear of the John Street gang, my consternation over school nicknames, my happy hours playing Batman after supper in these shadowy alleys. I remember Saturday matinees and reading comic books by the hour. Had my Gilbert Street friend Bobby Chafe told me back then that I'd be poking around our old haunts a half century later, I'd have said, "My son, you're cracked!"

As LeMarchant merges with Freshwater Road and Parade Street, my first job comes to mind. At seventeen, newly graduated from Grade 11 in Gander Bay, I'd been hired as a checkout boy at Ayre's Parade Street Supermarket, likely the first such store in the city. Later I'd worked in their produce department, walking every weekday from 49 Pennywell Road where we rented a flat from Mom's cousin Mabel Cull and her husband Len.

Just past Parade, where Harvey Road takes in, I pass the old Department of Mines and Resources building where I'd spent the winter of 1953-54 colouring forestry maps before heading out to survey woodlands all summer on the Avalon Peninsula with Hans Mandøe. That winter my family had lived on Hayward Avenue to the northeast. I'd begun to paint landscapes and was winning small prizes. My most ambitious was *The Last Mile*, a watercolour depicting in tender detail a lone trapper mushing home with dogs and komatik over open muskeg in a turquoise dusk. It expressed my yearning for home: wind-bent tamarack; tufted marsh grasses poking through snow; the dogs' panting weariness; snowshoes I'd watched my father make in our kitchen. It was the best thing I had yet done and it won a medal and my parents were proud, especially, I think, my father.

Suddenly, looming vast against the driven clouds, the twin spires of the Roman Catholic Basilica come into view, and, not far beyond, on the harbour side, the old Nickel Theatre with its green cupola topped with delicate wrought iron.

In my hurry to reach my B & B before midnight, I hardly notice Bannerman Park and Colonial House. In the first I'd often walked during my last summer in town, admiring the leafy trees and the girls. In Colonial House I'd had my first painting displayed a few years later in a Newfoundland Arts and Letters competition. Approaching Prescott House, I hardly give a thought to nearby Cochrane Street where I'd taken a night course at Reg and Helen Shepherd's Newfoundland Academy of Art.

Prescott House was open. I fell into bed and, full of childhood memories, slept like a ten-year-old.

Born!

"I didn't know much, but I knew everything I had to know."

– ALBERTO MANGUEL, *After Carthage*

Sometime in February 1934, in the downstairs bedroom of a weathered ochre and green frame house in the village of Clarkes Head, Gander Bay, northeast Newfoundland, my father Brett, thirty, impregnated my mother Winnifred, twenty-nine, for the second time in seven years that I know of. Seven years is a long time, but it was the Dirty Thirties and they were poor, but not careless. In a different milieu I might have had more siblings, another brother perhaps, a sister or two, a larger family constellation.

As it was, of the millions of his spermatozoa which perished that night in a vinegar douche, the whip-tailed wriggler on which my genes were riding succeeded, like a salmon surmounting a cascade, in swimming upstream through the cervix and into the waiting uterus, there to meet and pierce and lose itself in the enormous moon of that month's ovum, which otherwise would have let go and perished in my mother's monthly rag in the kitchen stove. Instead, it took root, grew a placenta and prospered.

And when, nearly ten months later, on the snowy night of November 23, 1935, the midwife finally eased me from my mother's body, sticky with blood and amniotic fluid and going blue for lack of oxygen because my face was smothered in a filmy caul, I was like a pink squid washed up on an alien shore. For three dozen weeks I'd floated in a tropical sea, first plastered on the placenta, then free-floating like an astronaut on a coiling tether; suspended in pink darkness and total silence save for the muffled drumbeat of my mother's heart somewhere above, the steady susurration of her breath, the tidal flux of fluids to and from that tether, which fed and cleansed my exploding blastula of cells.

Thus suspended, blind as a cave fish, I knew neither sunrise nor moon-set, gravity nor weather. My single outer constant was the Voices, remote and strange like the singing of whales. The way I heard best was by thrusting out my feet and arms for better purchase and pressing my spine against hers. Sometimes a high-pitched third voice joined in – my brother's. Often I heard the erratic trumpeting of my father's snoring. Sometimes many voices danced in counterpoint.

As my body expanded, it bumped hers more often. I could feel the thrust of a table edge as she kneaded bread, the pull and pinch of garments, the occasional, dizzying, lurching descent from the vertical when she fell and caught herself, the gradual slowing of her burdened movements as I continued to expand. The most alarming sensations came with the draining of my world, followed by irresistible spasms of compression and relaxation and the triphammer beating of her heart, thrusting me down and down and down to emerge at last into the dry, cool, bright, harsh, weightiness of my mother's world.

Terra incognita.

I knew nothing of the bed, the room, the faded orange and green box of a house that would be my nest for the next eleven years, of the cart path that followed the winding estuary and petered out where the River lost its sweetness in the salt cold Labrador Current.

I knew even less of the saw-toothed, many-islanded triangle of rock and forest and bog to which my forebears had boated from southern England three and four generations ago: Tizzards and Watermans and Laymans on my mother's side; Gillinghams, Porters and Saunderses on my father's. Some of them, like migrant salmon, left their storm-lashed islands and the serfdom of merchant princes for the balsamy woods. They found these woods as rich in salmon and caribou, fur and timber, as the ocean was rich in cod and seals.

But all I knew was feeding and voiding, warmth and cold, dry and wet. Nothing else had anything to do with me, contentedly sucking my mother's nipples day and night.

No odds to me that on February 11, 1934, the month of my conception, my country's sovereignty had been signed away; that all Newfoundland babies born that year would have to wait fifteen years for a country to call their own. Political orphans.

Orphan or no, I did have kin. Unknown to me, blood aunts and uncles and cousins lived up and down the road. And I had a seven-year-old brother sleeping upstairs, aware of my first mewling cries. The only person I yet knew on the planet was my mother, lying exhausted and sweaty in bed beside me, forehead swathed in cold face cloths placed by her mother-in-law Mary, who was tending us now the midwife had left. Mom had weeks of recuperation ahead.

By all accounts, mine was a hard birth. "She was *so* big," her sister Beatty would say. "We both had narrow pelvises." Although Mom's pink complexion and solid figure – "I was always chubby before the children came" – suggested vibrant health, she was anaemic and the pregnancy had taxed her. And it had not gone as planned. My brother's birth in Buffalo had not been easy, but at least there was a doctor on call. Women's childbed fever was a constant worry with home birthing; that and complications. She'd lost her infant sister Alma in 1919. Mary had lost her first child, Gordon, after only six days in 1902.

That was why, in her third trimester, my mother arranged to go to Fogo. Even if the town's promised cottage hospital was a year away, at least the town had a doctor and a nurse. Moreover, her sister Frances lived there, also her younger brother Tom and his wife Carrie and her widowed father. Carrie had neither chick nor child, but Fanny and Jabez did, and would welcome her. Therefore she would have my father take her in the passenger boat, and have him fetch us home before the winter storms set in.

That was her plan.

But Fogo Island was four or five hours' steam away, and the North Atlantic is notoriously fickle in the fall. Near the end of October, a week or so before her calculated date, they chanced it. For a woman prone to seasickness the voyage wasn't easy. Once safely there, however, with my father heading back home, she relaxed a little.

Two weeks later I still hadn't come. Embarrassed, fearful of being stormbound away from home, or, worse, marooned in Fogo all winter – Mom wired for Dad to fetch her home. A week later, back in Clarkes Head, she felt the first pangs, slow but sure. I can imagine the dialogue:

"Brett! Wake up!" (elbowing him in the ribs). He groans and rolls toward her. "Brett (she pronounces it 'Britt'), you better get Aunt Sis. My contractions started an hour ago; they're comin' steady now."

Aunt Elizabeth Peckford was the nearest practising midwife. She was no relation, just one of many honourary aunts and uncles in that place and time. She lived across the bay at Harris Point, a fifteen-minute canoe trip. There was no causeway then, no cars.

"You're sure?" he mutters, striking a match and squinting at the alarm clock. After midnight. "Not another false alarm?" There had been several.

"No," she says testily, gasping as a spasm grips her. Fully awake now, he swings his feet onto the cold canvas floor. He lights the kerosene lamp, he lodges it on the sideboard and twists the knob until the flame is low, then pulls on a heavy mackinaw shirt over his long underwear. He heads for the kitchen, buttoning as he goes, breathing deeply to stay calm. Seven years since he's done this…easy in Buffalo, just call the doctor, grab a taxi to the hospital. Still, he and his six siblings were all born at home. But according to Winnie this baby was already weeks late.

He was in the kitchen before he heard her shout: "Britt, my son. You forgot your pants. I'm not *that* far along." This would become a family joke. He hurries back, dons his khaki Home Guard breeches and shrugs into his suspenders. In the kitchen he grabs a lantern and lights it. A pause to haul on his thigh rubbers, another to grab his parka off its peg, another to put fresh wood in the stove, and he is out the gate. Head down in the raw east wind, he strides to his parents' home five minutes away to rouse his mother. That done, and Mary safely in the foxy house, he grabs a blanket and tarpaulin for Mrs. Peckford and hurries down to the wharf. Reaching the wharf, he unties the canoe and, grunting with effort, launches the heavy craft, stern-first, into the choppy waters. A two-handed shove with his river pole propels it along. In one motion he replaces the pole on the thwarts, sets the aging outboard's controls, spins the starter wheel and is on his way. Canoe and man are soon lost in the first snow squalls.

Twenty minutes later Winnifred and Mary hear the hum of his motor. In the cuddy, bundled under the tarp, sits the sleepy midwife. God willing, he thinks, things will be all right now.

It was the caul, that troublesome tatter of amniotic sac that kept me from bawling as a newborn should. Like Dickens' David Copperfield, I was born with such an impediment, which, says the author in a footnote, "[is] taken as an omen that [the child] will be lucky in life and never drowned." The trouble was, my good luck film was suffocating me until the midwife peeled it off. What followed was the strangled cry my brother heard.

Years later I would learn that Calvin came downstairs the next morning and said, "Mommy, Daddy, last night I heard my lost kitten meow. Did she come back?" My father had made away with the little stray after it shit in his slipper.

"She's gone, my son," he said, pulling the boy close, "but come see what we've got for you. A baby brother."

Poor Calvin.

Instead of a furry kitten with green eyes he saw a red-faced monkey with moist black hair noisily sucking at his mother. He must have been disappointed; I would have been. Especially when our mom was so weak she lay in bed for ten days afterward, drinking nothing but tea and scarcely eating.

But there I was, his little and last brother, conceived in a lull between two disastrous world wars, born at the tail end of an economic depression into a bankrupt former colony governed by a committee, born between forest and sea into a community built on lumber, salmon, furring and guiding, whose population six years hence would still number only 324, of whom most still had one foot in the 19th century, born to a woman who loved the city and a man who loved a river.

The Foxy House

It was just a little frame house, the house I was born in, barely a storey and a half, three rooms downstairs and two up, two windows to a side downstairs, one per gable, and a stovepipe for a chimney. It had a lean-to kitchen on its north wall, and, to the west, a tiny porch that opened onto a two-inch plank deck which, though the North Atlantic was an estuary away, we called "The Bridge."

Small and makeshift though it was, it was my childhood home. And though its clapboard seemed always thirsty for paint, it was well built. It had good lines. Unlike your typical squat-roofed outport house, it had that steep Change Islands look. In fact my grandfather-to-be, Frank Saunders, who hired the carpenter, was a Change Islands man. A bookkeeper by trade, he'd arrived in Gander Bay via Twillingate and Lewisporte around 1899, seeking land and a business of his own. He married a local beauty, Mary Gillingham, and went on to become the sawmiller/shopkeeper of Clarkes Head.

But he'd never meant the house to be lived in. It had started out as one of several storage buildings – "stores" they called them then – more like something you'd see hunkered on a wharf than smiling behind a white picket fence. The place just happened to be empty in March 1931, when my parents and baby brother arrived home from Away.

Having lived four years in the States – Boston, New York and Buffalo – and having spent a winter near Huntsville, Ontario, they had come home to ride out the Depression. It was a harrowing journey for a young couple and a toddler: two days and a night by train to North Sydney, with changes in Montreal and Truro, Nova Scotia; thirteen hours crossing Cabot Strait in the S.S. *Kyle* in a 60-mph gale that sickened everyone but Captain Tavernere, his crew and Dad; stuck overnight in a snowdrift near Kittys Brook on the high and windy uplands of the Gaff Topsails of western Newfoundland, and, finally, an overnight horse and sleigh ride from Lewisporte across Dog Bay Neck to the bay. But the three of them arrived home safe at last and thankful.

And since they planned to stay, they needed something to live in, something warmer than Grandpa's drafty summer cabin in by Clarkes Brook. Since they had no money to build new, and since Clarkes Head had nothing for rent, the warehouse got the nod. They couldn't very well live on the wharf, but relocating was never a problem in Newfoundland. Newfoundlanders and Laradorians launched houses as casually as shifting a trunk across a room. Over land, over ice, over water – it was all the same. To them it was like launching a skiff or a schooner, just more cumbersome. It was almost a social event.

All you had to do was send out word and name your date. On the appointed day, usually in winter, dozens of men converged on the structure with stout manila ropes and long timber skids. Sometimes they brought horses; always there were children and dogs. All they asked was that the stove be cold and the flue be dismantled (brick chimneys were rare so this was seldom a problem) or at least stuffed with rags to stifle the soot; that crockery, lamps and other breakables be removed to safety and that doors and windows be closed.

So that April, before the ground thawed, a crowd of men moved the store body-and-bones up the road to a vacant corner of Grandpa's meadow. It was done by levering it up onto long timber skids, tying a stout hawser to the sills and heaving in unison. Once the haulers had taken their places along the rope, some leather-lunged fellow started a traditional launching shanty:

Oh we'll do our Jolly Poker,
We will 'aul an' 'eave togedder
An' we'll do our Jolly Poker,
Do!

On the last word, the crowd would bow as one beast and the house would lurch forward a few inches – or not. If it didn't, which was rare, more men would be summoned, or horses hitched, until it did move. To move Grandpa's store took only a few dozen stout fellows. And they hadn't far to haul. By slow stages the groaning structure lurched past the wharf and up the narrow road. The hardest part was getting it up the slight grassy knoll opposite the alder bed. At one point they had to use rollers. From there they eased it up onto a prepared foundation of peeled juniper posts – good for thirty years at least – sunk deep in the gravelly ground.

"Whoa!" shouted the foreman at last. A bit more jimmying, a swift inspection for broken windows and stuck doors and the men went home. No question of pay. Grandma would have served mugs of hot tea, some jam bread or fruit cake. Neighbourliness, you'd do the same for me.

It only remained to make the store livable. A carpenter – likely Willy John Torraville of Victoria Cove – was hired to build on a kitchen and porch, floor the loft, put in a stair, partition off rooms. The rest my father could do himself. By early summer the vacant store had become a house. By winter it had become a home.

My father, never fond of city life, home after three years spent in the clatter and smoke of New York and Buffalo, first driving streetcars, then selling insurance, surely breathed a sigh of relief. For the time being he'd help Pop in his store, cannery and sawmill. He'd clerked in Toronto and Buffalo; he had some ideas of his own. But father and son never did see eye to eye; if need be he'd run the passenger boat. Beggars couldn't be choosers. Anyhow, it was only a stopgap until he could afford a river boat and motor of his own. Then he'd ferry passengers up and down the River and guide sports in between.

As for Winnie, the young Fogo telegrapher who had met him when she came as postmistress in 1925 and wed him in New York two years later, leaving the States must have seemed a step backward. But in Buffalo she'd had a baby and couldn't work, and Brett's Prudential customers often couldn't afford their payments. To stay there any longer might have meant standing in bread lines and eating in soup kitchens.

Anyhow, with her mother's recent death she was needed closer to home. She doubted her father Harry Layman Sr. would ever re-marry, and her youngest sister Beatrix was scarcely fifteen. And, who knew, the local post office might still need her services now and then. At least here they'd never go hungry. Her woodsman Brett would see to that. The land and water teemed with game and fish. Timber and firewood were plentiful. Only a layabout could starve here. Besides, the air was sweet and the nights as quiet as church.

My parents' new home stood midway between Point Head to the west and Clarkes Brook to the east, between woods to the north and the estuary to the south. It was oriented to the road, the road to the shore and the shore to the great geological fault lines running northeast and southwest.

From their southwest gable window they could see the River glimmering two miles away. From the other they could see down the bay past Webbs Island and Gander Bay Island out toward the Notre Dame Bay archipelago. Eastward lay fifty miles of unpopulated wilderness clear to Cape Freels. Westward lay 180 miles of sparsely settled wilderness clear to Bonne Bay. On the whole, not a bad place to be. Or to be born into.

Every old house has a past; ours had a past we could smell. At least my mother could, or thought she could. Not all the time – only when the wind was in easterly and the glass was falling. Then she'd wrinkle her small beak of a nose and say, "Can you smell it? That pissy smell?"

"No," I'd say, five years old but sniffing manfully. What could she mean?

"Well *I* can," she'd say, breathing hard through her nose, a sure sign of displeasure.

"Smell what, Mommy?"

"Fox, my son. Fox." And she'd dart to the porch, seize scrub-brush and pail, slosh in hot water from the kettle and cold from the rain barrel, grab a bar of Sunlight soap and punish the floorboards yet again.

Small children, even at the best of times, find it hard to grasp adult meanings. Foxes? I knew what they were: small red-brown dogs with bushy white-tipped tails. My trapper father brought dozens of fox pelts home every winter from the country. I even knew the different kinds: red, cross and patch. And I'd seen him skin them, seen their pelts stretched on boards, drying behind the stove.

Our house had a foxy colour, a faded ochre yellow; but that couldn't be it. She must mean there were foxes *living* somewhere in the house. After all, she could smell them even if I couldn't. Foxes, roaming the house while we slept! The notion both pleased and alarmed me. For months afterward it stuck to my mind like a bur to a dog.

Noticing my puzzlement, Mom looked up from her scrubbing, flicked a lock of black hair from her damp forehead and panted, "No, no, my son, not living *with* us. You see, long before you were born, even before Calvin was born, Grandpa Saunders had a fox farm. He fed them salmon guts from his cannery in summer and rabbit meat in winter. In summer they were kept in outdoor pens, but wintertime the mother foxes needed a warm place to have their babies. So he rigged up a storehouse with cages. That storehouse became our home. This home."

When this had sunk in I said, "Why didn't he have cows or sheep like other farmers? Do foxes give wool?" I was always a great question asker.

"'Twas for their pretty fur, my son. Do you remember my green coat with the fur collar?" I nodded, and she went and got it from the bedroom closet. "Bought this with my first salary check in New York," she crooned, holding it against her bosom and stroking it. I remembered it well. She used to scoop me up and let me bury my face in its rust-red collar. It had a real fox's head too – shiny black nose, life-like greenish-yellow glass eyes, pointy black-edged ears and all. The fur rode high around her shoulders, the nose almost touching the white-tipped tail.

"Your most expensive fur came from the silver fox. It was black with silver tips. One pelt might fetch over a thousand dollars! That got Grandpa Saunders interested. So he enquired about fox ranching in Canada and bought shares in a Nova Scotia company that had a farm at Garia Bay on our south coast. They sent him a boy silver fox on the steamer – I believe it was the *Clyde* – in a special wooden crate. Now all he needed was some wild vixens and–"

"Vixens?"

"Girl foxes. Local trappers used to smoke them and their babies out of their winter dens into *brin* bags and sell them to breeders like him. Grandpa bought three wild vixens and he was in such a hurry to get started that he did a right foolish thing."

"What was that?"

"He didn't wait for them to get used to each other. Right away, he put that lovely silver fox in the pen with those three wild vixens."

"Why?"

"So they could start making baby foxes right away."

"How?"

"Never you mind. Don't you want to know what happened?"

"Yes, but–"

"Well, those vixens killed that beautiful silver fox, killed him and ate him! That was the end of Grandpa's fox farming. Except for the three females, which he kept until their fur was prime in November and then sold them. And that's how we came to have live foxes in our house."

"But, Mommy, tell me more about the foxes making babies…"

"Enough fox stories for one day! Run outside and play!"

I considered asking Dad for a pet fox of my own. But, much as Mom liked wearing a fox pelt round her neck, I felt sure she wouldn't want a real fox running round her house.

When I reached age seven or eight, big enough to be seriously teased, Calvin told me there was a bear living in my parents' bedroom closet. The closet was beside my bed. I laughed at the time, but soon I began to stay up as late as possible. One day, to make amends, my brother made me look inside the closet. "See?" he said. "No bear." I wasn't convinced. What if it was a very slim bear hiding behind the coats and pants?

So he took me there at night. He got me to hold his three-cell flashlight while he removed all the garments, hangers and all. Then he pulled me inside the closet. While I stood trembling with fear, he shone the powerful beam into each corner. All I saw were shoe boxes, some old Eaton's catalogues, some Christmas decorations and Dad's half-empty bottle of Christmas rum. No bear and no bear poop. Slowly my fear subsided. Of bears, at any rate.

Then one dark night that summer, watching raindrops travel down my window panes, I saw a fox face, plain as day: whiskered, white-throated, ears alert, eyes like fire, looking straight at me. It was only small, yet seemed like a great wolf. I screamed and dived under the covers. My parents rushed in to tell me there was no bear. I was ashamed to tell them what had really frightened me.

After they left, I glanced back at the window. Nothing. For weeks afterward, I needed a lamp to get to sleep. Next time it rained I checked the window again; still nothing. The fox face never came back.

Years later I learned that Grandpa had kept a female red fox for a pet when my brother was a toddler. He said the fox, whose name was Purb, had the run of the house, trotting about on her dainty black feet like a crackie. She was fed table scraps and dried capelin. Sometimes Grandma gave her a cake of hard bread to gnaw on. One day she noticed the vixen bounding upstairs with some in her mouth. After Purb returned, Grandma investigated. That fox, like a pregnant dog burying bones in the garden, was stockpiling food in the attic! Later, several kits were born there.

Calvin's story intrigued me. Foxes can often live twelve to fifteen years in captivity. So the face I saw that night *could* have been Purb's.

At this time I still slept in my parents' small bedroom. It had two four-paned windows, one facing east, one south, which by day lit up the pale flowered wallpaper and canvassed floor and the glossy white wooden ceiling. There was also a large mirror on a natural pine dresser by the west wall, which further brightened the room. When ill, I'd lie in bed and watch the play of coloured light and shadow on the exposed ceiling beams. On sunny summer mornings the shadowed sides glowed warm green from the grass outside; wintertime they were pale blue. Once when measles laid me up for a week I watched the light from each window travel round the room from right to left as the sun travelled across the sky.

Lying in my spindle bed I faced east. But I could never watch the sunrise. The reason, odd though it sounds, was that my mother was such a nervous sleeper. The slightest sound – a cat meowing in the night, a bird skittering across the roof at dawn, Calvin clumping down the stairs – would rouse her. So did the sunrise. She hated summer sunrises. They came too early to suit her. "Just as I'm settling into my best sleep," she'd moan. Indeed, by the time school let out in June, daylight came as early as 5:30 a.m., and the sun not much later. (We had no Daylight Savings Time until World War II.)

As if that weren't enough, summer was also milling season. My Uncle Harold, who owned the sawmill, had a winter's cut of logs to saw by September. Sharp at 7:00 a.m., his sawyer, Uncle Hezekiah, would dance up the mill steps and yank the bell rope. The brass ship's bell gave, I thought, a very satisfying *clang.* Then Harold would start the big diesel engine. This was even noisier, like muzzle-loaders going off on New Year's Eve, each blast coming faster and faster until the ground fairly shook. Then the whole mill with its maze of spinning pulleys and slapping belts would come to thunderous life. And when the first log hit the headsaw, what a terrible, plangent wail filled the morning, what a glorious racket. To me it was the very sound of summer. Not to my mother it wasn't. That sawmill ruined her mornings for five months every year.

Whereas nothing could be done about the sawmill, she could, as it were, stop the sunrise. She put up dark window blinds and pulled them every bedtime. At least this gained her another hour and a half. So I never got to see the rising sun. Too bad for me. Sunrise was my favourite time. Sunsets saddened me, still do.

I did try to raise the blind a crack and peek. It is shocking the racket one small boy can make with a spring-loaded window blind. The noise, to a peacefully snoring adult, is like a gunshot, or the end of the world, or both. The problem is with the ratchet. To release it you have to pull the blind down a notch, and, holding onto the string, let the blind ride back up until the spring-loaded metal pawl finds a new ratchet to hold it. I only needed a few inches to see the sky. But if my arm got tired or my mother turned over in her sleep, I'd panic and let go.

WHIRRCRASH!

A few catastrophes like this and I learned to do without sunrises. I learned to look through the blind instead. This wouldn't work in broad daylight, when the sun was far too high, too brilliant. But at its rising, when the golden light hit the window square-on, it pierced that flimsy painted fabric as if it were a leaf.

So here I am at first light, eyes wide, hands behind my head on the pillow, waiting for my light show. I imagine the sky over Webbs Island going from grey to purple to orange over the sleeping waters. As the sun rises, a slender violet cross appears on the opaque blind, a perfect likeness of each sash and mullion. Within this stark armature, the blind's criss-cross weave and the glass beyond are projected in exquisite detail, down to every bubble and mote and speck in all four panes. And as the eastern sky warms from orange to gold, the dark green blind flushes from deep viridian to kelly green to lily pad yellow.

Now a movement catches my eye. A chilled housefly, warmed by its tiny greenhouse, begins a sleepy shadow dance; combs its head, face and feelers with jerks of its forelimbs. Hoists first one hind leg and then the other over its transparent wings and strokes each firmly fore and aft. Starts and revs its tiny motor, startling the dreaming room. My mother stirs but does not wake. Now the early-bird fly lifts off, only to blunder into the blind an inch inside, which rouses several other flies, which one by one repeat the performance.

I'm wide awake now. My bare feet thud on the night-cool linoleum (or canvas as we call it). The chamber pot hides under our washstand behind a little door. A person would never know it was there. I need both hands to lift it; last year I couldn't even do that and had to use the slop pail. Peeing, my eyes are on a level with Mom's white porcelain pitcher in its matching fluted bowl, a fixture in rural Newfoundland homes. Towel, face cloth and soap dish dress the altar of hospitality.

Apart from peeing in the chamber pot, my brother and I never touch these things. They are for Company. Even when we're late for school and the kitchen wash pan is busy, they're out of bounds. In my mind this elevates the status of every guest – school principal, midwife, stranded bush pilot, sportsman, politician. The night before, the fluted pitcher is ceremoniously filled so the guest may bathe in private. Winter guests even get warm water delivered in the morning; left overnight it might freeze and crack the costly pitcher. Meanwhile the rest of us wash as usual in shuddering cold rain barrel water at the kitchen washstand – or at least we did until we got the new range.

Our bedroom door opens onto a short hallway with a steep stair on the right and the front door opposite. The stairs are somewhat dangerous, especially for sleepwalkers, as I would find out some months later when I was promoted to an upstairs room. On my first or second night up there I had a dream. In the dream I was walking across to my brother's room, perhaps to get a book. In reality I was stepping across the open stairwell, only to wake in a crumpled heap below.

Although my midnight tumble left me unharmed except for bruises, it rattled my parents enough to bring my bed back down until I outgrew sleepwalking. I protested that I wasn't as bad as the Gander Bay man who woke one winter night to find himself a half mile in the woods dressed only in his underwear. But my tumble was worrisome all the same. Having my own sunrise window would have to wait.

It had been exhilarating though. Besides uncensored sunrises, the upstairs room afforded a higher view of the wharf, shop and bay. Better still, Calvin's room housed my parents' modest library. At that age only the pictures captivated me, but I spent many happy hours flopped on my belly by the west window feasting on them.

The hall door was almost never opened except to air the house in spring. It had a large pane of pebbled glass which the storm door blocked all winter. But in summer, with the outer door removed, a flood of amber light would pour in. Even rainy days seemed sunny then. On truly sunny days the effect was dazzling. The amber colour of the glass turned the next room, the parlour or "inside room," greenish purple, giving it an undersea look, a storybook strangeness. Otherwise the room was ordinary: floor covered with worn linoleum in a faded pattern, ceiling painted white like the bedroom, floral wallpaper. Yet for me, this room had six attractions: an upright stove; a drop-leaf table; a sewing machine; a pedal organ; a radio and a colourful wall map.

Our cast iron upright stove stood on the left as I entered. Every summer Mom gave it a fresh coat of aluminum paint to prevent rust and make it shine. Once a Fogo coal stove, it now burned mostly wood – but only in winter or when company came. As soon as the sides heated up the new paint would start to smoke. The room would fill with oily fumes and someone would have to open a door or two.

The stove had a fretted removable dome, topped with a metal maple leaf. I coveted that ornament. At least once a week I'd tug at it in passing. Though loose, it never let go.

The stove door was special to me. It was round on top with three small openings like church windows through which the flames showed, tinted brownish like an old photograph. When the stove was lit, I liked to sit on the floor and watch the fire flicker in those windows. Dad said they were made of mica, a mineral, whatever that was. I knew it wasn't glass, but why didn't it burn? Fire fascinated me utterly.

Opposite the stove stood my favourite table with the embroidered green and gold tasselled cloth. I always paused to touch its Persian arabesques, which even on sweltering days felt cool. I also liked the cloth because its skirts brushed the floor and concealed my secret hideaway. Under there, with the wall behind me and two hinged oak boards and two thick legs in front like tree trunks, I felt secure. With sunlight streaming through the tassels it was Tarzan's jungle. Here I passed many dreaming hours. Here too I had my first chew of tobacco, which made Tarzan deathly ill for fifteen minutes and put him off tobacco for many years.

On the table stood a heavy green glass pitcher. Around it, like chicks around a mother hen, was a flock of heavy matching tumblers. All the pieces were embossed with wild strawberries. I ran my fingers over them so often I would know them in the dark. Their lime-green colour made even our tea-coloured brook water seem delectable.

The Singer sewing machine wasn't always kept on the table, but that was where Mom used it. Normally she kept it in a round-roofed wooden case like a little dog house. When the top was off I liked to watch its intricate machinery move to the rhythm of her sewing: the bobbins, the lever, the twinkling needle. Best of all I liked the look of contentment that suffused her eyes when she sewed. The machine's industrious whir, like the organ's somber largo and the stove's crackle, was part of the symphony of home.

Just past the table, high against the same wall, stood Mom's pump organ. Sturdily made of stained oak, it likely came from Fogo too, where as a girl she took music lessons. I couldn't reach the keyboard; it was kept covered against dust and grubby fingers anyway, but sometimes Mom would lift me onto her lap and coax my stumbling fingers through "Baa, Baa, Black Sheep" or "Twinkle, Twinkle Little Star."

I preferred to help her pump the pedals or work the swinging knee levers that controlled air flow from the bellows. The best thing was to sit on the circular stool and spin it. I liked the giddy feeling and the way the seat lifted me ever so slowly on its well-oiled screw. I was the pilot of a bush plane taking off – something we saw fairly often in Gander Bay. One day I spun too far. My landing was noisy and dented the floor if not the chair. End of organ privileges for a while.

The radio was so important it had its own table. It sat in the corner opposite the organ. In all of Gander Bay there were only five or six radios when I was small. Ours had a shiny brown wooden cabinet with tiny pointed church windows in front like the stove door's. There was a knob for turning it on and off and dials for finding different stations and for making the sound go up or down.

I was never to touch these dials for fear of "running down the batteries" and "wasting juice." That would cut us off from the BBC news. The BBC sent us news of The War, which was a big fight somewhere far away. My parents and Grandpa Saunders hardly listened to anything else. It seemed to me that winning the fight depended on having strong batteries, on the radio's not losing its strange crackly voice.

I hoped the fight would soon be over. People kept saying batteries would be cheaper then, which would mean we could listen to other things, things like music and people telling stories and jokes and laughing. They said there would even be shows about *Family Herald* and *Weekly Star* comic book characters like Superman.

The kitchen was the only warm room in our house. Wintertime we practically lived there. It was the locus of eating and conversation and quarrels, of neighbours' visits, of mending and darning, of knitting and quilting, of minor household repairs. It was nursery, bakery, scullery, reading room, homework carrel, cobbler's bench, barber shop (winter only; summertime it was, "Outside with you and your hair!"), outpatient clinic, storyteller's loft, even an occasional dance floor.

Here on any given day or night a child might witness bread making, cooking, knitting, dressmaking, crockery and kettle repairs, the cleaning of lamps, guns, timepieces (with a feather dipped in kerosene), the piecing of quilts, hooking of mats, filling of snowshoes. It was where my brother and I took our weekly baths in winter, and I suppose our parents bathed there too though I never saw it. For a time during The War, when cash was very scarce, it was a brewery and pub.

The furnishings were simple: on the high side an oil-clothed table, on the low side a daybed and in the opposite corners a washstand and wood box. In between, against the windowless east wall, stood Mom's gleaming Bridgewall range. Nearly as tall as I, with a gun-metal top set off by ivory enamel, it dominated the room.

The stove was made in Ontario. Around the time I was born, my father had been the company's local agent. They paid him $10 per sale. But at $120 apiece – four months' wages – sales were few. Grandpa Saunders bought one. So did Uncle Harold and Max Gillingham and possibly his brother-in-law Roy Reccord. And us.

But the Bridgewall was a superior stove and worth its price. Unlike the old-fashioned, similar Waterloo, Maid of Avalon and Ensign step stove models then in use, and the Home Comfort it replaced, it could hold a fire overnight. This was thanks to what the company called its "airtight technology" – one of the first kitchen ranges of its kind. Its 700 pounds of fire brick and metal kept our small kitchen cozy all night. In an uninsulated frame house this was no small luxury. Our bedrooms might freeze but our kitchen stayed warm.

In a small way this costly stove compensated Mom for the many other inconveniences she endured. She liked to enumerate its virtues: a steady baking heat; an oven temperature gauge; a wide upper warming oven for rising bread or drying mittens; a three-gallon hot water reservoir; easy-to-clean surfaces; special kettle-sized and pot-sized lids for quick boiling; even a pull-out ash pan. My father liked the fact it got by with less firewood.

For all its virtues, the Bridgewall gave me a nasty gash on the head. The stove had two nickel bosses the size of a man's little finger to hold up the open oven door. With the door closed, they stuck out like little horns. Perhaps to celebrate the stove's arrival, my father laid shiny new canvas on the kitchen floor. It was grand for sliding on, much better than the old canvas. One day, diving headfirst on my belly, I went farther than expected. My head hit one of those horns, sending spatters of bright blood across the lovely linoleum. It gave my parents a fright and me a fine bump. And healthy respect for kitchen ranges.

The daybed was a low leatherette couch, a place to lie down when tuckered, but not tired enough for bed. It was also where company sat when our four chairs were full. And one winter it would become my grandfather Layman's bed.

The table was the brightest spot. "Dark colours make a room look so dismal," my mother always said. Every year she'd pester Grandpa Saunders to order colourful oilcloth. If he didn't, she would order the gayest print she could find in the Eaton's catalogue: I recall one that was snowy white with yellow and red triangles.

Our table was like a bird: it migrated north and south. Summers it usually stood against the cooler north wall. Winter found it against the warmer inside wall. And since this was where all our close work was done, the overhead oil lamp followed these peregrinations, bracket and all.

At night the room was lit only by this lamp. It sat in a swivel bracket that was painted gold. To spread the light, a concave circular blown glass mirror hovered behind. A foot or so over the glass chimney, Dad hung a horizontal tin circle to protect the ceiling from soot and fire.

The lamplight was dim, but compared to a candle it was bright. I liked its amber glow, and the whiff of kerosene. When we couldn't find the flashlight or its batteries were dead, it lit our way to bed, pantry, attic or chamber pot.

Our simple wooden chairs were repainted every summer. During my toddler years, they must have had four coats, each a different bright hue. By late winter all these earlier coats would be showing through and I liked it better that way.

The washstand was a busy corner. Since the bedroom basin was out of bounds to all but guests, we all washed our faces and hair there. Mom, in her war on germs, also insisted we scrub our hands before each meal and after using the toilet. Under the stand, Dad kept the tools he used for small repair jobs, his hammer, screwdriver and so on.

Opposite the stove was the door to the porch. It was low; my five-foot-eleven-inch father sometimes forgot to duck, and skinned his forehead. The porch contained our water barrel and pantry. The covered barrel, also painted green, seemed huge to me at age five, but in fact held only ten or twelve gallons, enough for a few days' cooking, drinking, dish-washing and laundry. Grandpa Layman made it for us. He used the cooper's trick of converting a damaged and leaky larger barrel to a whole and tight smaller one; oak was too dear to discard. Mom cherished his present as long as we lived in the foxy house. After my father installed the rain barrel for laundry and floor washing, the porch barrel needed filling less often.

Beside the barrel, on a nail nearby, hung a dipper for drinking. On the low bench under the lone window, nestled one inside the other, was a pair of 2.5-gallon galvanized buckets for fetching water from Clarkes Brook. All our drinking water came from that brook. Our land was too low for a well.

The pantry was both cold room and larder. It held our flour barrel and bread box, plus shelves for canisters of sugar, oatmeal, molasses, tea and such. There were also bottles of moose, caribou and rabbit in season, jars of blueberry and bakeapple jam, and, sometimes squashberry jelly, a favourite of Dad's. For Christmas Mom would lay in raisins, dried apricots and candied citrus peel for cakes. These were hard to resist, almost as good as the fruitcakes she made from them. Occasionally there were apples and oranges too. One year there was even a coconut and a pineapple that Dad brought home from somewhere. Because no one had ever seen the like, they were shown off and discussed before being eaten.

To keep everything cool in summer and unfrozen in winter, my father stogged the porch walls with dry sawdust. If I kicked the outside clapboards it fell out like golden snow. The porch also served as a milking parlour for Mom's goats, but that's another story.

Beyond the porch lay the Outside World. During my first few months it was a winter world. Had I been born a Beothuk baby I'd have been out in it right away, riding in my mother's parka hood, swaddled in rabbit skins, feeling wind on my cheeks, snow on my eyelashes, sun in my eyes. Not being so lucky or unlucky, I had to wait a while for my mother to recover. Then we were out in it, bundled to the eyeballs. And before long, the snow was melting and the world warming up again. Then we were out there every chance.

All Outdoors

"I imagined the world had stood from everlasting to everlasting. The dust and stones of the street were as precious as gold; the gates were at first the end of the world. The green trees when I saw them first…ravished me, their sweetness and unusual beauty made my heart to leap…"

– THOMAS TRAHERNE, *Centuries of Meditation*

Dawn. A charm of birds. Like a lazing trout I drift up from dreams into its roseate glow. Knuckle my eyes to loosen the grit which the Sandman sprinkles on us while we sleep. Flex my arms and legs like a swimmer under the blankets until my elbows and kneecaps tingle. Clench and unclench my fists to relieve the night cramp.

Six years old now, I'm allowed to get up as early as I want and even go outside, so long as I don't bang doors and wake the house. I swing my bare feet onto cool canvas, pad to the washstand, drag out the heavy chamber pot, fumble with my nightshirt, make water. I always aim to the side, so as not to tinkle and wake my mother. She says to sit on the pot like she does – "quieter and less pee on the floor" – but Daddy always pees standing up, holding the pot to himself, so I do the same.

I shed my nightshirt and shiver into my day clothes: cotton shirt, wool sweater, short pants. In the kitchen I turn on the tap from the outside rain barrel, splash my face and hands in the basin and towel them dry as my mother has told me and *told* me. "Wash those hands!" She is death on germs.

Into the porch for a drink of water. I tilt the lid off the green barrel, unhook the dipper and gulp thirstily. We're not supposed to drink from the dipper, but I'm in a hurry. I duck into the dark pantry, twist off a crust of bread and smear on some jam. Breakfast in hand, I unlatch the outer door and step out into another summer day.

Far as I know, every outport youngster goes barefoot summertime. Footwear is for church and school and winter. This morning my feet rejoice in the dusty sun-warmed planks of our bridge. Every knot and fissure is familiar. Bare feet only hurt for the first couple weeks – and you never get wet socks. By July, my soles are so leathery I can tread on anything except glass shards and broken clamshells. Yet I can still feel things underfoot. Blindfold me and I can still tell gravel from grass, plank from boulder, sand from silt. If, while wading, I step on a baby flounder, I can usually catch it before it wriggles free.

I see Uncle Hezekiah, Grandma Saunders' brother, striding down the road. Must be nearly seven o'clock. As he disappears into the mill I hear him humming to himself. He is Uncle Harold's sawyer and is always up before me. A robin distracts me and I forget to brace myself:

Clanggg!

It's the sawmill's brass bell. Hezekiah rings it to warn people that the mill is about to start sawing. In the silence before Uncle Harold gets the big black diesel engine going I finish chewing my last mouthful of bread and calmly inspect the day. What to do? And where? Wharf and sawmill are out of bounds; I am too young. Grandpa's shop isn't open yet and anyhow I don't have even one penny. All that's in my pocket is a pebble and a piece of string. Perhaps after I water the dogs and feed the hens my mother will give me one to buy some candy.

That leaves garden, landwash, cove and brook. If Uncle Harold's forge was open I might dodge over to watch him shoe a horse or cast bright new babbit bearings for the mill's pulley shafts to run on. But he's under the mill, checking all its belts and pulleys, getting ready to start the diesel.

After chores, I opt for the garden. It's nothing special – no flowers or even potatoes, just a fenced rectangle of grass with a grey rock here and there. Like Arabs who picture Paradise as any well-watered place, we Newfoundlanders call any fenced plot with more grass than rocks a garden.

Gander Bay gardens are much bigger than Fogo gardens. Ours holds not only our house, woodshed, cellar and a potato patch (some years), but also, at the rear, a hen pen, goat barn and three dog houses. It is so big that if Mommy stands on the bridge holding a plate of crumbs and calls, "Here, coopie, coopie," the hens take two or three minutes to half-fly, half-run to her. It would take me longer than that.

After watering our sled dogs I linger to play with Spot and Jack and Gelert. It must be hard for them, being tied up all summer like that. But they keep warm and dry in their molasses puncheons. Dad laid the barrels side by side in the lee – Dad called it *lun* – of the goat barn for shelter.

Today I feed them flatfish my brother has pronged specially for them. Then I let the goats out the back gate to graze wherever they want. I would spend longer with them, but this year they have no babies.

On the way back I visit my boat. It is really a rock half sunk in tall grass between the path and the Sawdust Road fence. It is pale grey, flecked with glassy black crystals. Dad's geologist friend called it a "glacial erratic," a stone dropped by melting ice thousands of years ago. I see it as a small grey skiff plowing through green waves.

I pretend I am in Grandpa's green skiff. It has no engine though; I am its engine. Making it go is my job. Sometimes I pole it along like my father does his river canoe. Sometimes I hum it along like an outboard motor. Sometimes I sail it – but my mast always falls over. Mostly I whack it with a junk of birch to make it sound like the green skiff's old make-and-break engine.

One way or another I get around: across the bay to Salt Island; up the

River as far as tidewater; down the bay as far as Victoria Cove, even to Tims Harbour and any other handy place grownups talk about. I played boat by the hour from ages three to six. Sometimes my mother, going to the barn to feed her nannies, asks me where I'm off to. As I babble away she notices my socks – no long pants for me yet – are torn at the knees again. I tell her my boat's rough *gunnels* (gunwales) are chafing them away, and it is getting too small to kneel on.

Now I have a new boat. My father brought it from the shop. At first it smelled like tea, a nice smell, but the rain washed the scent away. He says, yes, it was a tea chest, and came lined with lead sheeting, but he removed it to use for window flashing to keep the rain out of our woodshed.

This new boat sits between the woodshed and kitchen, waiting for me to make a trip. It is made of five thin sheets of a brown tropical wood, cross-braced inside. The corners are strengthened by tin strips fastened with roundhead nails. Stencilled on two sides of the tea crate are black letters which my father says spell "Product of Ceylon."

Daddy moored my new boat where he did so my mother can see and hear me through the kitchen window. For a time I missed my rock and went back to it every few days; now I hardly ever do. The new one has more room and its tall sides seem more real. Mommy likes it because my stockings need less mending.

My favourite thing about *Product of Ceylon* is the engine. Drumming on the thin wood with a stick causes echoes to bounce off the walls on either side. The sound is just like the *put-put-put* of a fisherman's four-horsepower Coaker inboard engine. At full speed it is deafening, like going through the Fogo canal. For half-throttle I bang my fist, like knocking on a door. For dead slow I just pat the wood with my palm.

In the new boat I venture farther each summer, out around Cape Farewell to Horwood, out past Noggin Cove to Carmanville. I go north to the Indian Islands and even to Fogo and Twillingate. Every place I've heard of, even St. John's, I try to get to. It is a very good boat.

But today I don't linger. I decide I'd rather play along the landwash with a friend. The borderland between high tide and low is good for exploring at any season, especially in summer and especially after storms. We never know what we'll find. A length of new rope? Some strange creature like a billfish or a squid? A giant red jellyfish? A schooner railing?

This week Frank is my friend and Everett my enemy. We're all cousins; but that is how it is. Next week it may be the other way round. As I reach our front gate I notice Frank's younger sister Susie playing in the yard. I sing out across our two fences and the road: "Frank 'ome?"

"'E's across the bay with Daddy," she cries in her high voice. I think, well then, I'll go alone. No question of inviting a girl, even Susie. Besides, her mother needs her. I open our gate. The shortest way is to the right, past the forge and around the pile of fresh edgings or crip that the mill pours out week by week and which Uncle Harold burns only on wet days.

That is the way to the cove part of the landwash, our favourite wading place – but only on sunny afternoons at low tide. That's when the shallow water is at its warmest. This early in the day it will be cold. So I turn left, cross the road to the wharf and go down the three steps to the beach.

The sand on this beach is different. Most of our beaches have brownish sand that is sugary underfoot. This sand is dark blue and silky underfoot. Daddy's expert friend says it eroded from a soft rock called oil shale. Our wharf is built over a whole cliff of this, and because it is layered like the pages of a book, and also set on edge, the rain and frost pry it apart flake by flake. It is these flakes, he told Daddy, and Daddy told me, that collect behind the wharf like drifting snow and build the beach. Indeed the cliff is nearly gone. But the wharf's wooden cribwork is strong and its boulder ballast is heavy so I am sure it will last forever.

This blue sand floats. I saw it myself. It was after a hot day with no wind. The tide was rising and as it came in it lifted the flakes one by one like tiny rafts and floated them about. Rocks aren't supposed to float – but oil does. I figure it's the oil in them. From this I learned that the phrase "Sink like a rock" isn't always true. However, when I touched them with my finger tip, they did. Like Peter on the Sea of Galilee they remembered what they were and sank.

Grandpa's shop stands farther east, halfway between the wharf and Clarkes Brook. It juts out over the beach on juniper pilings rammed deep. The tan-coloured poles are bearded with green slub below the tide mark but dry and smooth above. Under the shop it is cool and dim even on a hot day. But my friends and I never linger; Grandpa's shop toilet is overhead to one side and he doesn't want us down there. We only come to hunt for carbon rods from discarded batteries. The carbon is black and soft and good for drawing on light-coloured rocks and boards. If my grandfather happens to hear us, he roars, "Outta there, you sleevens!" and even if we've been doing nothing wrong, we skedaddle anyway, laughing.

Moseying on toward the brook, I pass a smaller building up on stilts – the old cannery. Here Daddy and his brothers used to put up salmon and rabbit to sell in St. John's. You had to de-bone the meat, pack the flat one-pound tins, boil them for so long, punch a hole to let out steam and quickly solder the hole shut. If any of the cans puffed up they were culled. The good tins had a piece of paper glued on. Calvin told me it read: "Frank Saunders & Sons, Clarkes Head, Gander Bay." I felt proud.

Beyond the cannery, the beach broadens to include a gravel bank held back by a jumble of boulders, some as tall as me. They look as if a crew of blind giants started to build a wall and gave up. The colours are brick-red, olive green, gunmetal blue, tawny yellow, and every kind of grey. The pale ones sparkle with glassy crystals like those in my boat rock. The finer-grained ones look duller, but up close they're mottled with black and grey, criss-crossed with veins of milky white rock that Dad calls quartz. This tumbled wall marches up and down the landwash, a fence against the sea, a border of rugged beauty.

It is a good place to look for wolf spiders. I often poke at the flotsam and jetsam with a stick, hoping to flush one out. Big and hairy and sand-coloured, they chase down sand fleas, pouncing like cats on mice. They are impossible to catch even if I want to, which I don't, because they can bite painfully.

We never find fossils. But my brother once found a stripy red and black rock hereabouts, very heavy. When he showed it to Grandma's step-brother he cried out, "Oh my son, you're some lucky!"

"Why, Uncle John?"

"Because you've found a thunderbolt!" Calvin kept that meteorite for years.

The most we ever find is a lump of coal or a bit of fool's gold. Clarkes Brook is the place to look for coal. "Oh, that's just a piece washed down from some old lumber camp," is what most grownups say. But Uncle Harold knows better. He says he has seen, a mile up the brook where the pond empties out, a whole seam of coal.

Fool's gold is found in smaller rocks along the beach. It really does look like gold, once you clean it up. Before that, it is just rusty greenish cubes stuck in the rock like raisins in a cake. Unlike real gold, it crumbles if you hit it. And the shine doesn't last. But my father says the Red Indians prized it because, if they struck a piece against a piece of flint, it would throw sparks. Their word for it meant "firestone," he said. My ears pricked up at that. I thought, one of those in my pocket and I'll never have to steal matches again.

So when Ted Reccord, a cousin home from the States for summer holidays, found this turnip-sized chunk one day, I coveted it. We were swarving along the landwash, Frank and Everett and I, when he sang out, "Look what I found!" The rock was fair studded with iron pyrite crystals. I made out it was nothing. But Ted's grey eyes searched mine and he knew better. Scooping it up, he took off home to Aunt Carrie's. Thanks to my greed we never even got a good look before he scravelled it off to California somewhere.

Clarkes Brook was the farthest I ever went east along the landwash before age eight. People said it was named, like our village, for an old-time shipbuilder. In summer the brook didn't look like much. Its shallow waters whispered through alder and spruce glades and cascaded tamely over blue-black shale ledges. In April, though, it was a ferocious little river, deep and swift enough to drive logs down, sluicing under the bridge with a roar that shivered the timbers. In the 1920s my grandfather drove pitprops down it, corralling them at its mouth for shipment overseas. And when Dad was small, Grandpa had a water-powered shingle mill there.

I knew because the rusting turbine was right there, half buried in sand and cobbles, a stout shaft, two fathoms long with a whorl of iron cups at one end and what they call a crown gear at the other. The water to run it, said my father, came from a dam one quarter mile upstream at Steady Water. It came down a gently sloping wooden flume that Uncle Hezekiah, "always good at ciphering," laid out using only a plumb line and a ball of twine to calculate the slope. The flume crossed the road ten feet up and dropped its water into a tall wooden box where the turbine stood, gear end up. The water's weight and pressure turned the shaft which turned a smaller gear inside the mill which turned the saw which sliced the logs into clapboard and shingles.

Every workday morning, he said, a mill hand walked the flume to start the flow, and every evening he shut it off in order to "keep a head of water" behind the upstream dam to power the mill. As a boy my age, my father had walked the flume himself. Except for that rusty turbine you'd never know a mill had been there.

Another oddity by the brook was a long grey curved thing that looked like a piece of bleached driftwood. It was really a whale's rib. By the time I was old enough to wonder how it got there, it was gone. The bone was as tall as my father. A whale that big could easily have swallowed him, I'd think with a shudder.

That is one half of my landwash.

The other half is west of the wharf, where the cove begins. It is so safe in summer that our mothers often leave us alone there to play. Shallow and warm, enclosed by the wharf on one side and Point Head on the other, it is our wading pool. While at full or new moon it is too deep in the middle, at low tide it barely comes to our waists and the rest of it is dry, save for the wandering rivulets from Cow House Brook.

I love that little brook. It comes out of the woods behind Uncle Joe Gillingham's hayfield, runs under a bridge and passes right by his house. Walking along it after supper in the summer, I often hear Joe and his friends playing 45s, laughing and pounding the table with every winning hand.

At very low tide it turns into a watery tree. On reaching the cove it divides into a thousand twiggy branches that dawdle here and there across the wide delta in delicate dendritic riffles, depositing a smidgeon of silt here, undercutting a miniature river bank there, forever veering as if reluctant to lose itself in the sea a few yards on. Yet when the inevitable happens, the melding is seamless. One cannot tell which is which. The only clue is a subtle steepness in the little waves that come cats-pawing in over the rippled silt on the sea breeze that always sets in after a hot day. The whole performance always moves me to tenderness. A river my size. A doodle of God.

Here and there along the landwash lie stranded logs from Uncle Harold's boom. For this is where, on the mill side, he keeps his winter's cut. To prevent the logs from drifting out the bay he corrals them with a floating fence of long peeled poles chained end to end and secured to rock-filled cribwork piers offshore. From this corral a boatman shepherds groups of logs to the ramp where a spiked "green chain" hauls them up to the wailing saws.

Sometimes, on fine Sunday afternoons at high tide, we also see young men running across the logs, pretending to be river drivers, daring each other, trying not to wet their good shoes and pants. My parents have ordered me never to try it. They say the heavy logs could easily crush me, but I admire the young men anyhow and can't wait to do the same.

Meanwhile, I search the stranded logs for lumps of frankgum – hardened spruce resin – to chew. Whoever has a pocket knife pries the glassy knobs free and hands them round. One day, picking at a splendid knob, I got a sharp piece in my eye. At first the pain was bad, but it faded when the resin melted and washed out. We don't talk much after we find frankgum; we're too busy chewing. There's a trick to it. First you have to gnaw the knob to a sandy powder, then tongue it into a lump, without swallowing, until it bonds. After a spell of chewing, it turns first into grey, then pink, chewing gum. It tastes fresh and leaves my teeth and gums squeaky clean. It is our only toothpaste.

But it's the wading we mostly come for. Not on the mill side, though, because the bottom there is ankle deep in muck and slime, the residue of years of fallen bark from the thousands of logs that have jostled here since Grandpa started the mill in 1938. At low tide on hot days the sulphur reek is sickening. Our sea water is never as clear as Fogo's. Fogo water beyond the stageheads is so clear and green, so deep, that looking down I sometimes feel a giddiness and dread. Down there is Davy Jones' Locker, where drowned sailors go. Clarkes Head water is more the colour of weak tea, a tint it receives from the peat bogs that sponge up the rain and meltwater that feed the Gander River on its 100-mile journey from the southern uplands of Newfoundland island to us.

Nor is our water as salty as Fogo's. Theirs is so salty it bites the tongue and stings a cut. Ours is so fresh it is almost drinkable, especially at low tide. That is why so many different creatures, creatures from both ocean and river, can live in it: flounder and sculpin; sea trout and salmon; eels and mud shrimp and sand worms.

Often after wading, we follow the landwash west to Point Head to explore its tidal pools. Point Head is made of the same dark blue shale as our cliff by the wharf, only higher and steeper. Eons of waves have cut a bench which is submerged at high tide and dotted with tiny ponds which often hold stranded fish at low tide. In twos and threes we choose a pond and flop beside it with our chins inches from the limpid water. By parting the weedy fronds, I can see everything with great clarity. I can even see the sand-coloured shrimp on the shrimp-coloured sand. But to catch one is another matter. It is much easier to catch the brownish side-swimming scuds that hide under rocks along the landwash.

What we really want to catch are barnystickles. Pairs of those minnow-sized fish nest under the fronds like tiny birds in trees. We have no dip net small enough to catch them, but by cupping a hand underneath we can sometimes flick one out. "Come 'ere quick!" someone shouts, and we huddle to inspect the catch. Barnystickles have big eyes for their size and saucy upturned mouths. The males sport flaming red, opalescent bellies, like mud trout in October. Sometimes I take one home in a jam jar full of bay water, but they always die.

Only the foolhardy grabs one outright. They have several long sharp spines: three or more along the back fin and a longer pair by the front fins. The fish can raise them all in an instant. It was our sincere belief that if you broke one of those barbs under the skin and it festered, your hand would swell enormously and drop off.

One time I saw a school of glass eels going by. We call them that because their bodies are transparent. With the sun high over my shoulder I could see their hearts and stomachs and every little bone. Calvin said they were elvers coming home from the Sargasso Sea, thousands of miles away, to become regular eels in Cow House Brook.

Winter transforms the landwash. No more quicksilver sheets of water, no more dry sugary sand, no more warm, limpid pools. Instead, we have this stark landscape of white, umber, jade. But grownups don't seem to notice. All they seem to see is youngsters drowning under the ice. When the ice is making or breaking they seldom let us out of their sight.

People have drowned falling through the ice, it is true. One winter morning on my way to school I saw a knot of grownups staring out the bay. Out there in the waste of white I saw a dark speck. At length, the speck became a horse and sleigh with two men plodding behind. Nothing unusual in that, but as I turned to go, something glinted on the sleigh. I waited and wished I hadn't. It was a body, lashed in a tarpaulin. The tarp was coated with ice, as if they had used it to pull him out. They were bringing him for burial in the only cemetery around. I had nightmares for a week. The worst involved Frank and me. I was crawling on my belly over ice, trying to reach his outstretched arm but failing because a powerful vortex kept dragging him under. I'd wake with pounding heart, his voice still in my brain, echoing fainter and fainter as if from a long tunnel.

By late October we check the shore nearly every morning on our way to school. Though I have seen plenty of new ice, the actual freezing process puzzles me. One evening, determined to see it happen, I linger over a puddle. At first there is only my reflection on the still water. Then, as darkness falls, I become aware of arrows of ice, feathered on one side, where nothing but water was before. At that moment I hear my mother's treble voice calling me to supper. Next morning the puddle has a crystal roof, and I am none the wiser.

We call such new ice "*sish*," from the sound it makes when wind blows on its broken surface, or when a boat passes through. Sish ice usually vanishes by mid-day, even with no wind. But when the nights are cold enough, in sheltered coves it creates polished sheets of black ice too thin to walk on, but tantalizing to contemplate.

To test its strength we bounce small rocks across. An echoing *ping* is good, but not if little jets of water follow. When we get a hollow *pong* without water, the ice is at least half an inch thick. Two or three more frosty nights with no snow and it's likely ready.

Of course our parents say no – because it isn't thick enough to bear *them*, and we respect their judgment and experience. They know that *slob ice* – ice with snow in it – cannot be trusted. They know that freshwater ice freezes faster than seawater ice and is more brittle. They know that new saltwater ice is rubbery and seems strong, but gives less warning. They know that estuary ice is the most unpredictable of all. That is why they always say, "Better safe than sorry."

So we wait some more.

At last the suspense is unbearable. "Nothing ventured, nothing gained," we whisper, quoting another grownup saying. We find some hidden spot with a shallow bottom and chance it. It is worth a tongue-lashing, a wetting even, to creep out on clear ice as if on glass and to kneel carefully and, shading your eyes from the glare of sky and snow, peer down into that dim crystal world of moon snails and worm tracks and summer-green eel-grass, waving in slow motion. Whatever the weather up here, down below it is tranquil. It's a wonder we haven't drowned. And this isn't the only risk we take. I like the *frisson* of danger. It is safe enough if you know what to watch and listen for and aren't foolhardy about it. When I see a grown man or woman tip-toeing across two inches of black ice, I have to laugh.

Long after the shore ice is considered safe, the estuary isn't. The river channel is always last to freeze. As late as February we can see its ribbon of menacing black water. People eye it daily, the way Fogo people eye the sea. In an emergency, one could still cross by boat; but getting in and out is tricky, especially after dark.

At last the channel's ocean end begins, like a wound healing, to close. This is the riskiest time of all, especially after snow. Fresh snow masks the thin spots and hinders further freezing.

By Christmas, the whole bay is catching over. However, no sensible person would risk treading it so early. They remember how young Ward Snow of Wings Point drowned. One dark night in January, after a dance, he was walking his girlfriend home across the Bay to Georges Point. Fresh snow had covered the trail, so they wandered a bit. Not far off the Point, minutes from shore, they both fell in. He heaved her onto solid ice, but the effort exhausted him and he perished. A similar miscalculation would put a Norseman aircraft through the channel ice in 1945.

Grownups on both sides are anxious now; it has been weeks since they could cross by boat. Southsiders need to buy things at our two shops, things they can't get at home. Uncle Harold needs to start hauling his Barrys Brook sawlogs to the landings for the spring drive. People on both sides miss their kinfolk.

So people wait until after New Year and then some. What they really want is for George Harris of Harris Point to cross. For years he's been the first to do so and people have come to expect it. One day his neighbours will notice him ambling toward the woods with an axe. When he comes out with an armful of var tops, they know the time has come; they spread the word.

Mr. Harris generally chooses a calm overcast day. He needs to hear the slightest crackle and he doesn't want shadows or snow cover. On such a day he takes his axe and his evergreens and sets out. A few steps, a chop or two, a marker tree left behind. A few more steps, another tree, another chop – the blade falls through! He changes course. And so on, from Harris Point to Grandpa's wharf, like a bloodhound on a trail, he makes his deliberate way. He will continue to play this bellwether role until he can no longer walk.

Perhaps he too was born with a caul.

A bay is not like an indoor rink that freezes once and for all. Week by week the icescape alters. Every twelve hours the tidal flux lifts and lowers the great sheet, even the thickest part as much as half a fathom through.

Early on, while the shore ice is still thin, the taller rocks punch through at low tide, shattering the ice like dropped platters. In time the rocks develop conical hats of ice, open at the top – *ballicaders.* Floating or aground they can swallow small children. We are never to climb on them and we obey, for now.

The ice has a voice but its bark is worse than its bite. On sunny days, as surface layers expand, it thunders. This opens large *rents* or cracks that wander for miles, fill with water and freeze overnight. At evening the ice shrinks and thunders again. Thunder underfoot. At first it makes me jump but I get used to it. Rents pose a different sort of danger. When the weather is too mild for them to re-freeze, ice water sluices up through the seams. Suddenly there's a lake where none was before. Someone out skating, or taking a short cut after school, can easily be cut off from shore and have to wade or swim.

It happened to me once. I was wearing wooden stock skates tied to laced-up, rubber-bottomed logans. It must have been new moon or full moon because the water near our wharf was gurgling up so fast it frightened me. I tried to cross on skates, but got one stuck in a crack and nearly fell and had to go back. By the time I got both icy skates untied, water had ponded right and left. It wasn't the getting wet I minded – home was only minutes away – so much as the disgrace of it. "Pride goeth before a fall," my grandmother would say. Wet or no, I should have crossed right away. Instead I kept looking for a dry place. Always, it flooded before I got there. I trotted along in the gathering dusk, holding my skates, a desperate figure. I ended up wading through thigh-high ice water. A good lesson.

Obedient as we tried to be, by February we dare each other to jump the rents. We slide down the slopes of larger, bigger, ballicaders at low tide. And of course we skate. Not hockey skating – we have no tradition of it – but we skim to and fro, chase each other, enjoying the speed, the wind in our ears.

Anyhow, homemade skates won't do for real hockey. The stock skates we wear are hand-carved little boats of spruce or pine keeled with old files. An old file is devilish hard and brittle, so your father or grandfather has to first heat it white-hot in an alder or charcoal fire and hammer one edge smooth on an anvil. Then, having curved the sharp tang up for safety, he'll dunk the steel in a pail of water like you would a new horseshoe. "To temper the steel," he'll say, meaning to soften it just enough so it won't break, so it can be sharpened.

Slotted into the wood, which he'd drill crossways, fore and aft with a gimlet to thread leather thongs through, the skates score the ice with a lovely hollow sound. But because the blades are scarcely half an inch deep, leaning too low lets the wood touch the ice and sends the skater arse over kettle.

Also, in damp weather the thongs soften and stretch, loosening the skates. Those problems were solved for me at age eleven when I was given a pair of Star skates from Nova Scotia. They were a good two inches higher. I never wore stock skates after that.

One afternoon I get a surprise. My grandfather appears on skates. He is wearing lace-up boots with very long blades – over a foot long. Speed skates, he calls them. Now everyone expects the portly, fiftyish gentleman to fall, and I'm embarrassed to watch.

Far from falling, Grandpa is as graceful as a gull in flight. There by the wharf, in front of an admiring crowd, hands behind his back, scarf billowing behind, he executes several turns. I feel at once proud and humbled. My grandfather, already ancient in my eyes, skating better than any of us! Then my father tells me why: "In his twenties Pop was a speed skater of some note in Change Islands and St. John's." Grownups are full of surprises. Later I wonder whether it was Grandpa's skates my father used when he skated to Fogo to fetch a new sled dog from his father-in-law.

Spring transforms the landwash yet again. Everywhere, the ice is breaking instead of making. It happens first along the shore. The sun, beaming slantwise on the lanes of shallow open water, on the pebbled beaches and humped boulders, begins its inexorable warming. Tiny creatures, scuds and sandworms and clams, yawn and suck and wriggle. Beach fleas and wolf spiders walk stiffly about.

By May the beaches are cumbered with slabs and pans that litter the wet and steaming strand like beached white whales, bleeding their lives away. A little sadly, I creep under the largest to marvel at its dimpled grey-green porcelain ceiling and inhale its dank Arctic breath. I fancy myself a Bob Bartlett or a Roald Amundsen, famous explorers grownups talk so much about. Fear comes and I scamper out.

Each high tide sets all this afloat. Every cove is full of jostling navies. Nothing is so seductive to an outport boy. This seduction we call copying – as in following a leader – and its object is to stay dry while leaping from pan to pan as long as humanly possible. What could be more enticing, for ten-year-olds and up, than a sport which marries floating, speed and risk, demanding daring, judgment and quick reflexes?

The trick is to spot, while running, a sequence of pans big enough to bear one's weight and, having spotted them, to dance over intervening pans to reach them. Mad bursts of speed with sudden stops, reliance on instinct not thought; that's the ticket. A wetting is no disgrace. Socks and pants can be dried by the school stove. But a ducking means going home in disgrace, with punishment to follow. Girls admire the sport but seldom play.

Fortunately for grownups, copying pans is very seasonal. Every day the pans are smaller. Wind and wave and tide jostle the navies around, rounding their corners, breaking their backs on sunkers. One morning we can find nothing large enough to stand on anywhere. The next day even the small pans have vanished, leaving behind only soggy beaches and an endless sheet of trembling, beckoning water.

Winter has officially ended.

Indoor Play

I approved of all weathers, good or bad. Bad was good because then I could play indoors for a change. Waking to a blizzard's howl, I burrowed under the covers and dreamed of hot porridge. Waking to the stutter of rain, I considered what to do with myself. It felt good to be warm in bitter weather, to be dry in a weeping world. Bad weather turned our house into a trusty galleon riding out a storm at sea. It spiced the ordinary with danger and isolation. After age seven, when I started school, my feelings wavered. School was fun too; I did not want to miss it.

The first resort for indoor play was crayons. I loved their sultry smell. Secretly, I'd swipe them across the hot stove to sniff the melting wax. I loved their rainbow colours, especially the blue and orange and yellow, and what they did together.

A storm lasting two or three days took more ingenuity. For my natural habitat was outside. Two days and our house began to shrink. Parents grew cranky, especially when my brother and I fought; and the storm got on their nerves too. The walls closed in.

Playing with my locomotive engine was good for an hour. So was thumbing through the Eaton's catalogue. I liked looking at comics, especially *Tarzan* – the drawings were so good. I spent many hours on Calvin's bed poring over our few picture books. Watching my mother work her sewing machine was engrossing. So was watching my father mend a kettle or make new snowshoes.

We had a few board games, but we had no gramophones, no electronic pastimes – no electricity for that matter. Georges Point had it for a dozen years when the big Phillips steam mill supplied the hamlet from its own generator, but that ended soon after 1900. On the other hand, almost every home could make its own music. There was nearly always someone who could play the accordion, fiddle, harmonica or spoons. My mother played the organ at least once a week, mostly hymns but also popular tunes like "You Are My Sunshine," "Don't Fence Me In," and Art Scammell's "Squid Jiggin' Ground." Sometimes she sang and we joined in.

Then there were the storytellers. Grandmothers and grandfathers, uncles and aunts, with time on their hands and heads full of history. By age six or so I was a professional listener. After bedtime my favourite listening post, at least until they moved my bed upstairs a couple years later, was a heat register cut into my parents' bedroom. This foot-square, wood-framed, glassless window let hot air from the kitchen flow into our often wintry bedroom.

It also conveyed kitchen smells and above all noises: clash of stove lid, crackle of wood in the stove, clatter of dishes, creak of the table as my mother kneaded bread. Through it I could also hear the comforting murmur of adult voices in easy nighttime conversation. That register became my Keatsean casement, a casement opening not onto perilous seas but onto local lore and culture, a window onto family history, onto adulthood. Here began my unofficial education.

But the casement was high. In order to hear properly I had to stand on the head of my iron bed and, keeping my fingers out of sight, grip the wooden ledge. This brought every syllable crisply to my ears. I could even hear the kettle's quiet song. In that posture I would cling, like a sailor to the ratlines of a ship, until either my feet went *dunch* or my eyelids fluttered.

Much of what I heard puzzled me. What did they mean: "Love child," or "She's in the family way," or "He's his aunt's boy"? Equally puzzling were sayings like, "So poor they've na'r pot to piss in nor no window to throw it out." Other expressions were easier: "neither fish nor fowl," "in over the mish," "athwart the bay." I heard local names like Caseys Angle, The Ballast Bed, Floatin' Tart Steadies, Bread 'n' Cheese Rock as well as the names of more distant places such as Farewell Head, Indian Islands and Fogo. They were all grist for my mill, my growing vocabulary.

The best storytellers were retired rivermen and trappers. They were my Homers, my Chaucers, my Shakespeares. The minute my father got home from an expedition, oldtimers drifted in to "hear the news." By news they meant the high or low state of the River, the scarcity or abundance of fish and game, the success of his labours, the latest fur prices. The news varied with the season.

"Much salmon in Joe Batt's Pool?"

"Be the deer [caribou] crossin' at Big Gull yet?"

"Is the muskrat thick on Millers Brook?"

Then they'd launch into the anecdotes. "Do 'e mind the time…?" Winter evenings were the best. Then the storytellers settled back, lit their pipes and launched into long narratives of fall birding expeditions to "The Outside" – meaning Notre Dame Bay – of salmon catching or caribou hunting on the River, of feats of strength and harrowing escapes.

"Do 'y mind the time, in 1912, when the forest fire come down in back o' Bellmans and Clarkes Pond an' clear through to Dog Bay waters? The time poor Stan Gillingham nearly perished?"

"Yis, b'y. 'E was workin' on the Horwood Lumber Company drive up to Dog Bay Brook that spring when the fire roared down on they. 'Twas all they could do to get clear of it, my son. Spent the livelong night up to their necks in a pond, splashin' water on each other and duckin' their 'eads to keep their hair from catchin' fire. The knapsacks they dropped on the shore, all their grub and gear, was burnt to ashes…" And Dad would respond with a story of his own.

All this came to me on that warm kitchen breeze. Like windblown aspen seeds in springtime, the stories settled gently in my soul and struck root, blossomed into thickets of meaning, forests of metaphor. They wove a tapestry of family and communal life in which I could become a thread, a pattern. They let me glimpse the hinterlands of history. My fingers might ache, my toes go numb; yet I listened for dear life. I seemed to know it could not last. Indeed, within a year or two my family would embark on a series of peregrinations which would take us to St. John's and back three times, to Lewisporte and back, to Toronto and back. Necessary travels all – but fatal to the sense of continuity children need to make sense of their careening world.

In November 1940, my father lived out a tale of his own. While hunting moose on the Northwest Gander for our winter venison, he accidentally put a bullet through his thigh. Had he been alone he would have died there. To make matters worse, Mom was in Twillingate hospital for an ulcerated stomach. Before leaving home they had arranged for Aunt Beatty, then living in St. John's, to come and look after Calvin and me. Years later, in a letter to me, my aunt recounted her role in the drama:

> "They brought your Dad into the house, his hunting partner Howard Thistle and the Game Warden did, and he looked like a ghost, lifeless. Scared me half to death. 'Hello Beatty,' he said, cool as a cucumber. 'Don't be frightened. I only shot myself. How are the boys behaving?' That was the extent of our conversation. His underwear was soaked in blood. They had to peel it off his thigh where the bullet went through."

Howard had brought him seventy miles downriver, an overnight journey. Grandpa now wired his son-in-law Roy Reccord in Victoria Cove to bring the motor boat at daylight. Beatty made him comfortable that night and the next afternoon they made Twillingate. Mom knew nothing of all this until Dr. Olds came in on rounds. After checking her over he grunted, "Like to see your husband?"

"Of course, Doctor," she said. "But Brett is up on the Northwest moose hunting."

"No more he isn't."

"He isn't? Then where…?"

"He's right here in Twillingate hospital."

"Oh no," she cried, "Doctor, don't tell me he's shot himself again!?"

"Afraid so. But don't worry, he'll be fine. He's a very lucky man." After breakfast I'll have Mr. Ings, the orderly, wheel him in so you can talk. Go easy on him; he's lost a lot of blood. I'm gonna keep him a few days just in case. You can go home together." Without further explanation he moved to the next patient.

That evening she got the full story, or as much as Dad cared to tell her. How the rifle had accidentally discharged, sending the heavy bullet through his thigh; how Howard, World War I veteran, had waded in deep ice water to reach him, twisted a tourniquet, got him aboard the canoe, took him to a nearby camp, lit a fire and kept him warm all night. How, starting at dawn, he'd motored and poled and paddled Dad for two days to Clarkes Head. How Roy had brought him the rest of the way, another day's journey.

The only other thing that saved him, Dr. Olds said later, was the bullet's path. An inch one way and it would have smashed his thigh bone, making it impossible for him to walk back across the island to where Howard found him. An inch the other way and it would have severed the femoral artery, bleeding him to death in minutes.

What he didn't tell her until later was that while hunting he'd seen a fine muskrat swimming under the ice and had tried, by waving the rifle butt over it, to turn it toward open water where he could kill it with the axe; how he'd lost his balance and thumped the rifle butt hard enough to set the gun off. It was Harold's Remington 44.40 pump action, the one with the tricky safety catch. "I never knew when it was on and when it was off," Dad always said.

As for me, I must have been asleep when they came and when they left. My blessed aunt, frightened as she was, must have smiled and for my sake pretended nothing had happened. My parents were away, that was all, and they'd be back in a week. Meanwhile, she dressed and fed my brother and me and read and sang – so I was content. All I could ever recall was her bathing me on the kitchen table, and her towelling me dry and tickling me and how in our glee we splashed suds all over the oilcloth and the floor.

But in my father's mind the accident was no blank. He often told us about it:

> "I made two or three quick steps – thought maybe my leg was broken, I didn't know – but I could walk all right. So I left to walk across the island, back to where the canoe was. On reaching the other side I felt giddy, sort of weak, like I was going to faint. I lay down. Then I took to shivering, shivering and shaking pretty hard. After that was over I hauled off my rubber, poured out a pint or so of blood, and got my pants down to look at the hole in my thigh where the bullet went in. The hole was big enough to

> put my little finger in. A bit of pink muscle was throbbing in and out…
>
> "So I hollered out to Howard, and finally he came out of the woods just across the River. But I had the boat…and it was about 200 yards away, down at the other end of the island. To reach me he had to wade in that ice-cold water to his waist…We had no pain killers with us, not even rum."

Aunt Beatty never forgot any of it either, including her miserable trip downriver the week before, her first in a Gander River canoe:

> "I almost froze to death. Your father brought lots of warm clothes, long hip boots, socks, whatever; but I had to sit still in the centre of the boat. I stayed with you until March, when George got back to St. John's. To catch the train I had to go to Lewisporte. So I went with the mail carrier Moses Downer across Dog Bay Neck as far as Boyds Cove. From there, Uncle Arthur Waterman, my mother's brother, took me to Lewisporte over the ice to Loon Bay by horse and sled and from there by road to the railway station."

The one bright spot was my birthday. Amid all that confusion and pain, she made me a birthday cake. As the three of us sat at the kitchen table and I blew out the five candles, my wish was simple: "Bring Mommy and Daddy home safe again."

That must have been the winter we ate too much moose. For Howard did manage to fetch Dad's kill home before the ravens got it. Moose to us was little better than horse meat. My father always complained when Mom cooked it too often. That winter, however, he'd limp out and saw off roasts for supper, trimmings for stew meat, a bone for soup. We even had moose steaks for breakfast.

Normally we ate caribou, a much finer venison that came with its own sweet cooking lard along the animal's back. This was our basic winter protein, that and the odd brace of rabbits, a scattered meal of turr and, of course, salt cod. By late November we always had two or three quarters of tender doe meat freezing in the woodshed alongside one of moose; that year we ate only moose and the scattered black duck. By the time the venison ran out, winter was almost over. Then we dined on salmon, trout and the odd muskrat.

Storytelling, music, snatches of radio, gossip, homework – these more than filled our indoor interludes. I never felt deprived. I would be a young man before I noticed, in a 1940s photograph, how shabby my clothing was, how much swankier my parents' New York photographs were.

By age seven my parents had taught me to read. This opened up new vistas in our meagre upstairs library. Now I not only scanned the pictures, but could decipher some of the captions and text. The English children's annual *Chatterbox*, with its masterful engravings, had captivated me since age five, even though the scenes of cricket and fox-hunting and ivyed mansions meant little to me. We also had *The Boy's Book of Trains and Ships*, a Penguin guide to World War II aircraft, a Buck Rogers novel and a medical guide. *Trains and Ships* was my favourite because of its photographs of speeding locomotives, of great steamy vaulted railway stations and ships' engine rooms with gleaming pistons and toiling firemen. Its best feature was its cover: a full-colour painting of the passenger liner *Mauritania*, plowing through sunlit seas, black smoke billowing from her four rakish funnels.

The Penguin guide, likely published for the Home Guard, had a paper cover, salmon-coloured with white borders and black text. Inside, it bristled with black silhouettes of aircraft, top view and side view, with descriptions of each, much like a modern birding handbook. By comparing those silhouettes to a real plane flying overhead, said Dad, we could tell whether it was one of ours or Hitler's. To show us how, he looked up the Harvard Trainer, a type of plane which often flew over Gander Bay from the base in nearby Gander. He also showed us the Hurricane and the Catalina Flying Boat, two airplanes we already knew. I spent many rainy afternoons during the war thumbing through that guide, praying I might spot a German Messerschmidt. Still, pictures were far less interesting than the real thing. With Gander Airport only twenty-five miles due south, we were no strangers to military aircraft – although we seldom saw bombers, which were flown directly to Britain.

By far the most intriguing book, at least at first, was our medical guide. When a quick riffle through its pages revealed diagrams of human anatomy, male and female, I shut the bedroom door, took it over to the window and sat myself down to discover the meaning of life or at least of male and female bodies.

That book was a disappointment. The woman's thing looked nothing like what a five-year-old cousin had recently shown me for a penny. And certainly my *toppie* (penis) looked nothing like the thing in the picture. If it had, I would have been alarmed. The pictures were about as erotic as those Penguin silhouettes. What I craved were actual photographs, photographs of live bodies, undressed bodies, especially female bodies. Even the Eaton's catalogue was better. At least in Eaton's undergarment section you saw, or thought you saw, shadowy aureoles and hints of nipples, and even, if you held the pages at a certain angle, tantalizing hints of pubic hair.

Downstairs, my favourite reading was cartoons and comics. *The Family Herald* featured a black-and-white cartoon page called "Juniper Junction" about a lanky old farmer who owned a tame bull moose that never shed its antlers. I fancied he – the farmer – looked like Uncle Hezekiah, except Hezekiah never wore a peaked railroad cap.

The moose, like me, was always getting into scrapes. The farmer would harness him to a buggy and he would knock over an outhouse. Or snag his antlers in a clothesline and canter off with bloomers and bed sheets flapping.

Folded into the tabloid were *Toronto Weekly Star* comics in rainbow colour. My brother and I each had our favourites, and our parents had theirs; *Blondie & Dagwood* was one. Still, we had to grab them quickly, before they were used to light fires or clean lamp chimneys.

My favourites were *Li'l Abner*, *Dick Tracy* and *Tarzan*. I used to copy them in pencil. Abner lived a backwoods life like mine. Dick was a city man who toted a .45 automatic and wore this amazing two-way wrist radio. He was easier to draw: yellow felt hat, belted yellow raglan with the collar up, half-closed, heavy-lidded eyes, clenched pointy jaw. Al Capp's Abner and Daisy Mae were harder; and anyhow I found his drunken drooping evergreens silly, a city slicker's notion of a spruce.

Tarzan was wonderfully drawn. He had everything going for him. What child doesn't, at some point, envy the orphan's freedom? I know I did. With Dad away so much I got a double dose of fathering from my brother. Once, around age eleven, I even ran away – a quarter mile in the woods, in fact – but got hungry and came back for supper. But Tarzan! Orphan scion of an English Lord, raised by apes in the African jungle, friend of elephants and chimpanzees, who, armed with nothing but a knife, slew nasty crocodiles and rogue lions. I also admired his bulging biceps, washboard abdominals and rippling deltoids and hoped to grow some of my own.

So, from the start, I loved John Burroughs' imaginary jungle world as seen by the artist, whose name I hardly noticed. Instead I patiently copied his delicate contour lines and curved cross-hatchings, his lifelike textures and animal anatomy. Often this was frustrating, because he used India ink and a fine-nibbed pen while I used pencils that needed constant re-sharpening. But he taught me the rudiments of drawing muscles and animals.

We had radio – though severely rationed. Even after the war we had to "save the batteries" for the *Gerald S. Doyle News* and, more important, the BBC news. Joey Smallwood's weekly "Barrelman" commentary had ended in 1943. By then we listened to music too, mostly Irish groups like The McNulty Family from VOCM out of St. John's. By age nine or ten I knew such ballads as "Far Away in Australia" and "The Wild Colonial Boy" by heart, as well as sentimental ditties like "A Mother's Love is a Blessing" – "For you'll never miss a mother's love/Till she's buried beneath the clay…" – and humorous songs like "Mrs. Fogarty's Christmas Cake."

Late at night there was cowboy music from Wheeling, West Virginia. But listening to such music was considered, even after the war, at best a luxury and at worst an extravagance. However, Newfoundland songs, being patriotic, were exempt from these strictures. After the war, with cash and batteries easier to come by, they let us listen to *Superman* every week, and sometimes even *The Shadow*, my brother's favourite. Calvin could intone its opening tag, "*Who knows what evil lurks in the heart of man? The Shadow knows…*" so realistically he sent shivers up my spine.

Eventually, during and after our sojourn in St. John's and my discovery of comic books, I also got to listen to *Superman*. By now he was like an old friend. As such I introduced him to my real friends, the ones who had no radios. By then, too my parents were listening to American comedy shows, some of which they had heard in the States: *Amos and Andy, Jack Benny* and *Mary Livingstone*, the puppet show *Edgar Bergen and Charlie McCarthy* and *Fibber McGee and Molly*. CBC we seldom heard until 1951, except for the King's Christmas message. By the mid-fifties my parents would seldom miss *Don Messer and His Islanders* out of Prince Edward Island.

One Christmas, Santa gave me a toy telephone. Black vinyl, half-size, it looked exactly like the latest rotary phones in the Eaton's catalogue. When I dialed, it rang like the telephone in the local post office up the road where my mother worked part-time. But hers was only an old-fashioned wooden box with a separate ear piece and a hand crank. However, she had an office with a desk and a typewriter for transcribing telegrams and a telegraph key for sending and receiving them. She taught me some Morse code. She also had a cabinet for filing papers and a safe for money.

Once I had the phone, I wanted an office too. For a desk she lent me the inside room table, first removing the beautiful cloth and her water pitcher set. From the office she brought a half-used telegram pad and some scrap paper and lent me an old pair of scissors and a bottle of mucilage. For invoices I pounded a nail in a block of wood.

I was in business. Perched on the organ stool with a thick cushion for height, rain pattering against the windows, telephone at my elbow, I imagined myself on the 100th floor of the Empire State Building, Boss of Everything. I sorted mail, paid bills, fired off important telegrams and business letters to Hitler and Churchill, answered myself on the phone. To handle the growing volume of mail, I scissored cardboard folders from corn flakes cartons and folded my precious papers in them against the next stormy day.

Next to that toy telephone I prized my Viewmaster, another Christmas gift. It was an updated version of the two-handed parlour stereoscope which had startled Victorian ladies and gentlemen with its illusions of depth and solidity in sepia photographs of the Eiffel Tower and the Matterhorn. But my plastic Viewmaster presented all this and more, at the flick of a lever, in natural colour, using tiny paired transparent images mounted in a rotating cardboard disk. When I held the picture to a sunlit window or a lamp, the back-lit image glowed with stained-glass brilliance.

It took me to the pyramids, to Arizona's Grand Canyon, to Hawaii's Waikiki Beach, to India's Taj Mahal. There were no Canadian scenes in this American invention, let alone any from Newfoundland and Labrador; still, these jewel-like Kodachromes transported my picture-starved imagination.

The nearest thing to it was Uncle Harold's spyglass. I was playing over to Frank's one hot day when he fetched his father's brass telescope for something to do. "Come see this," he said. Opening it, he steadied it on the fence, trained it on a yellow spot at Main Point and twirled the eyepiece. I put my eye to it. The yellow spot exploded into a sawdust pile and a sawmill, French's sawmill down in The Bight. The heat made it shimmer. I vowed to have a telescope of my own some day.

When my first Viewmaster slides got scratched and finger-printed, I tried making my own discs from waxed paper and crayons and a corn flakes box. The Viewmaster rejected them. My sympathetic parents ordered new scenes. Decades later, in college and visiting them at Christmas at their new house in Gander, I found my old toy carefully stored in a bedroom closet. On a whim, I inserted a disk, walked to the window and had a look. How little it took to please us then.

Although we had no gramophone, my father's parents did. It was a handsome thing in dark mahogany, two feet square and as tall as I, with a cabinet below for 78-rpm records. It might have been a Victrola. It stood in their dim cool parlour against the south wall, near a window overlooking Grandma's rose garden and fence.

When I got old enough – eleven or twelve – she sometimes let me play the records, some of them. Wind the crank, open the lid, lay the thin black platter on the turntable, lower the needle – "gently now" – into the spinning record's outermost groove, click the "On" switch.

Grandma chose the records for me. Mostly it was British music hall songs by Harry Lauder and American ballads from the Depression years. Among those was "Bum Songs No. I and II." Mr. Lauder's rolling Rs confused me at first, as did his Scottish dialect, so different from ours.

> O, I belong tae Glasgow, dear ol' Glasgow toon;
> But there's somethin' tae matter wi' Glasgow,
> For 'tis spinnin' r-r-ound and r-r-ound…

I preferred the "Bum Songs." They were about ordinary people down on their luck. And while much of their irony and social commentary went over my head, I got the drift. I especially liked "Hallelujah, I'm a Bum," to the tune of William Paton Mackay's 19th century gospel hymn:

Oh, I like Jim Hill, he's a good friend o' mine,
That is why I am hikin' down Jim Hill's main line;
Hallelujah, I'm a bum,
Hallelujah, bum again,
Hallelujah, give us a handout
To revive us again.

Another one, set to a faster beat, went like this:

Oh lady, would ya be kind enough
To give me somethin' to eat?
A piece of bread and butter,
And a ten-foot slice o' meat?
A piece o' pie or custard
To tickle me appetite,
For lady, I'm so hungry,
I don't know where to sleep tonight…

But the one I played most was "The Big Rock Candy Mountain," written, Grandma said, the year my brother was born. Fragments still come back to me:

In the Big Rock Candy Mountain
You never wash your socks,
And little streams of alcohol
Come a-tricklin' down the rocks;
The bulldogs all have rubber teeth,
An' the hens lay soft-boiled eggs;
There's a lake of stew and of whisky too,
You can paddle all around 'em in a big canoe
In the Big Rock Candy Mountain.

And several more verses in the same vein, ending with,

Oh, I'm bound to go where there ain't no snow
When the rain don't fall and the wind don't blow
In the Big Rock Candy Mountain;
I'll see you all this coming fall
In the Big Rock Candy Mountain.

While the irony escaped me, the fantasy didn't. What rural boy could resist such romantic metaphors of the unfettered life? They were, after all, childhood fantasies, pure and simple. Except that, while I went home to fresh milk and hot cookies, these men bedded down hungry under some railroad trestle.

War

When the three-week Falklands spat broke out between Britain and Argentina in April 1982, I found myself unaccountably glued to the radio and television. I even started buying daily newspapers I'd seldom bought before. And when the British Navy sank the Argentinean troop ship *General Belgrano* with hundreds of sailors lost, I almost cheered. But when Argentina destroyed HMS *Sheffield*, I was outraged.

And ashamed. What was happening to me? Why should a small conflict half a world away engage me so, keep me awake nights? Then it dawned on me: I had grown up with a war that involved British ships and planes and, ultimately, British soldiers landing on hostile beaches. The Falklands was a microcosm of World War II – and likewise being played for keeps.

As a small child I thought war was played on a map. *The* Map, we called it importantly, for it covered the wall above the radio and bristled with brass thumb tacks that sparkled on fields of pink and green and yellow ink. The tacks were regiments that moved to and fro, sometimes with glacial slowness, sometimes with swift purpose overnight. After age five or so I realised this was no game my father and grandfather played night after night by the radio.

This war, whatever and wherever it was, was urgent and serious and worthy of all attention. It was impossible to ignore the look of fear in my parents' eyes, the cloud of oppression that had settled over our home after September 1939. Sometimes the cloud lifted but always it returned, a dangerous storm that would not go away. And it wasn't just about remote and incomprehensible places like Poland and France and Italy. It also had to do with England. Our England.

But how to help? I couldn't even picture their war. *The Family Herald* had very little coverage. All I had to go on was that Penguin aircraft handbook in the attic and the radio's nightly crackle of voices, sounds and static from the BBC World news on my way to bed. That, plus the doleful tolling of London's Big Ben and the urgent voice of newscaster Matthew Halton. Not that his newscasts made much sense to me, even when static didn't drown them out.

So those sounds, not The Map, became the war for me. If anything, they were more frightening than any picture could have been. I heard phrases like "fire-bombing," "Panzer divisions," and "V2 rockets." I heard unfamiliar names like Hitler and Mussolini and de Gaulle, Dunkirk and Trieste and Monte Cassino. To gauge what it all meant, I studied my parents' and Grandpa's faces. Their expressions of shock and dismay and exultation told me more than Halton's often garbled words.

As the war dragged on, I began to link the news with the thumb tacks. BBC news and wall map and thumb tacks and worried faces – that, to my childish mind, was the war. And after I saw my first yellow Harvard Trainers flying practice sorties, my first Catalina Flying Boat rumbling overhead, I began to visualize what bombing and strafing might be like, what an aerial dogfight might be. Likewise, after our Fogo kinfolk started seeing the flames of dying ships at night, "sea battles" took on new meaning. Now *The Family Herald* began to show more pictures of planes and warships, such as the troop ship *Prince of Wales* sinking in Hong Kong or somewhere, with tiny figures leaping off her leaning flank like ants.

I began to comprehend. Something somewhere was terribly wrong. And my parents, who knew everything and could do anything, seemed helpless to halt it. Nothing so frightens a child. World War II was ruining my life.

This is how it was. Every weeknight after supper, if Dad was home, Grandpa Saunders would open the porch door, wipe his shoes on the mat, greet us and come in. Hitching the rocking chair closer to the radio without blocking the parlour door, he would ease his bulk into it. Sometimes he'd hang up his pepper-and-salt cap first; more often he'd sit down with it on. Then he'd fold his hands across his ample belly and await the latest developments.

Meanwhile, Dad would flick on the radio and fiddle with the dials until he picked up London and the BBC. First came the stately *bong, bong* of London's Big Ben, powerful as an army marching. Then came the gravelly voice: "This is Matthew Halton reporting from London." I had no idea where London was, even when my father showed me on the map, only that it was a long way from us. It *sounded* far away, especially with the static's staccato bursts, like gunfire, as if bullets were whizzing by poor Mr. Halton as he spoke.

In fact, most of the time he seemed to be speaking from a small noisy plane, battling squalls of snow or rain or sand, his voice forever fading and my father forever rescuing him by frantically working the dials. Then the BBC would tell us what the Germans and the Allies were doing to each other and where, what the Italians were up to in Africa, what battles had been fought, what ships had been sunk, who if anyone was winning. When the broadcast was over and the radio switched off, Grandpa and Dad would sit silent for several minutes, deep in thought. Then, in hushed and earnest tones, they analyzed what they had heard: Rommel in North Africa, air battles over southern England, bombs over Coventry, Panzer divisions swarming across Europe like ants over a picnic blanket. Gravest of all were the increasing U-boat kills off our shores.

Meanwhile, Calvin and I would be sitting at the kitchen table, he doing homework (or trying to), I eating a night lunch of goat's milk and toast. Mom would be mending or knitting or making bread or helping one of us. Leaving for bed, I waited to hear some word of hope. It seemed to me the war's outcome depended on these two brave men with their radio and map and pins. The sudden fall of France all but defeated them. Mr. Churchill's impassioned speeches and Mr. Roosevelt's "Fireside Chats" buoyed them wonderfully.

They seldom argued, but when they did my heart sank. Grandpa would heave himself up out of his chair, tug at his cap and storm out. If this kept up we'd lose for sure. Or if Grandpa dozed during the broadcast, as he often did, snoring softly, I felt sorry for my father, fighting all alone. The moment the radio went silent, Grandpa would start in his chair, mumble apologies and sheepishly ask what was new.

That was how it was for five years. Night by night, shoulder to shoulder with Mr. Halton, with Mr. Churchill and President Roosevelt, my father and grandfather kept the enemy at bay. It was all they could do. Dad was thirty-five when the war started and Grandpa sixty-three.

Sometimes I worried about our batteries. Often they seemed dangerously low. Moreover, The Map had so many pinholes, so many bomb craters that it was in danger of falling apart. If it did, or the battery failed, what would become of us? My only solace was Big Ben. Its wind-baffled chimes seemed the very epitome of embattled *good.* A German child would have heard it differently of course. But I was only three generations removed from Dorsetshire and, small as I was, my blood was up.

My mother, at work in the adjoining kitchen, must have heard all of this, all the broadcasts and the war councils. If so, she said little. It wasn't a woman's place to talk war talk. She was just thankful her family was safe. But like hundreds of women all over the island and in Labrador, she knit mitts to send overseas. Hers were finger mitts. Any Newfoundland wife knew you couldn't properly shoot a gun without them.

By age eight I wanted to be a fighter pilot. It was only natural. Living between two wartime bases, Gander and Botwood, both of them minutes away by air, I saw a lot of warplanes. Gander had become, since its completion in 1936, one of North America's busiest airports. Every month it ferried hundreds of new Hudson and Lancaster bombers across the North Atlantic, a feat unimaginable a few years earlier. And it was training pilots. Botwood was only a small seaplane base, yet it played a crucial role in hunting Nazi submarines. U-boats had now become alarmingly successful, sinking iron ore carriers at anchor in Bell Island, sinking our Nova Scotia ferry S.S. *Caribou.* St. John's strung a torpedo net across the Narrows just in case.

The planes I loved most were the Harvards. They came in different colours. Ours was a cheerful buttercup-yellow and I thought it altogether lovely. Though it wasn't sleek and powerful like the Hurricane and Spitfire, the real fighters, its engine and metal propeller made a glorious racket. Sometimes one would pass low enough for us to see, as it banked for another pretend strafing run, the goggled pilots, trainee and trainer, flashing grins from their double cockpit.

"Just young bucks trying to scare the yokels," my father muttered. Perhaps he was right. They did come mostly on Sundays. And we certainly looked like yokels, half-dressed, hands clapped over our ears, staring skyward open-mouthed. One pilot so angered my father that he slung a rock at the plane. Dad had a powerful arm and a sure aim. He had gunned enough ducks and turrs on the wing to know about leading his target. He was so sure the rock hit home that he felt immediately remorseful. Hitting a plane going nearly 400 miles per hour, he said, could do great damage, especially if you struck the prop. It might even bring the plane down, perhaps onto someone's house, killing who knew how many. He never did that again.

But I exulted in those great hurtling yellow birds, whose deafening roar sometimes made you piss yourself with mingled delicious fright. Oh, I would be a pilot all right!

It was the livestock Dad mostly wanted to spare. The bigger the animal, the more terrified it was. Our hens, though wary of hawks, hardly looked up. Goats and sheep might bleat and charge about but soon calmed down, but horses went berserk. At the first sound – and they heard them far sooner than we – they whinnied and bolted. As the terrible noise grew, they galloped full tilt at the fences, reared, pirouetted and galloped again.

One day I tasted their terror. I was up on Point Head wharf, fishing for eels alone, when a low thundery rumble came from the northeast. I could see nothing in that direction except Gander Bay Island and some clouds, but soon the sound took on the wind-baffled drone of a large airplane. Then I saw a great grey whale of a thing, new to me, with a stepped belly slung low under a single wing carrying two huge engines. The aircraft was coming so low I thought it might land.

As it was downwind, at first the sound seemed too small for the plane. But as the aircraft crept nearer the sound peeled off layer after layer. I dropped my fishing pole, covered my ears and dived down among the timbers and ballast rocks. Then the sky swiftly darkened and I heard the loudest noise of my life, louder than Uncle Harold's sawmill in full career, louder than the spring ice leaving Clarkes Brook, louder even than midnight muskets on New Year's Eve. The very rocks rattled under my knees. I could not have borne it a minute longer; but suddenly the sky brightened, the roar dropped an octave and the monster was fading into the west and I was still alive.

Later, when I told him, my father smiled. "Yes, I heard it too. That was a Catalina from Botwood. One big ugly plane."

The other bright spot in the war was gimmicks on or in cereal boxes. My favourite was the Airplane Ring. The picture showed a fighter zooming through the air. If you pressed a secret lever, said the advertisement, the plane would fly.

For a child raised on war talk it was irresistible. All next week I gobbled corn flakes; it seemed unpatriotic to send the coupon without first doing so. I saved my box top, got an envelope and stamp and mailed it off. For a week I hardly slept. At last the parcel came. Its smallness surprised me. Finding the ring among the shredded wood excelsior wasn't easy either. The plane was crudely made and nothing like the picture. The ring did fit my finger, however, and the plane did fly, after a fashion, when I touched the secret lever. But it never flew straight. And I couldn't take it outdoors; it was too easy to lose. A week or two later it went missing anyway. My first lesson in false advertising.

I decided it was better to make my own planes, even from snow. At least they had heft and range and flew where I pointed them. We buzzed the school playground with them during recess. If an enemy shot off a wing you could fix it directly, in flight if need be. Or build a better model next time.

Like most outport people then, we worried about spies. Strangers were automatically suspect. At Twillingate hospital an Austrian-born nurse was forced, by gossip, to resign. It didn't matter that she had fled the Nazis when they annexed her country in 1938. After all, she had a strong "German" accent. The Home Guard must be watchful. Suspect planes were to be reported by telegram to the Royal Canadian Air Force in Gander or Botwood. The enemy was rumoured to be setting up coastal radio transmitters to track shipping off our coasts – which later proved to be true.

As the war spread into Asia after Pearl Harbour, there was a risk that older men, even my father, would be called up. Harvey Francis had enlisted. Elam Gillingham was serving in the Navy. Reg Peckford, brother of Joan, whom I so admired from Grade 2, was in the regular services. Two Webb brothers from Victoria Cove were in training and one had already been killed in some dock accident overseas. Uncle Don had enlisted right away, at age eighteen, and was serving with Colonel Jack Turner's Newfoundland Forestry Corps in Scotland, cutting pitprops to shore up Britain's coal mines to keep her warships warring until they could be converted to diesel. Eldred Snow served in the Corps as well. And our Calvin was nearly old enough.

But at last Japan surrendered and it was all over. Uncle Don and some other local veterans came home in December 1945. I remember admiring his khaki uniform, its bright buttons and insignia. A special commemoration was held at the school, I think during the Christmas concert. We rehearsed for weeks.

My role was to march around reciting "When Johnny Comes Marching Home" and to brandish a sword at the end. I'd insisted on covering the wooden blade with tinsel. When I unsheathed my sword the tinsel came off and people laughed. Disgraced, I beat a quick retreat, but people clapped anyway.

My only other war effort was in Grade 3 when I served as treasurer for our tiny Red Cross group. They issued us white, inch-wide metal buttons. This licensed us to collect money for the soldiers overseas. My job was to record the amounts in a special little ledger and report to the weekly meeting. Then our president handed the money over to the teacher for mailing to St. John's or wherever. It was a serious business. Even at ten I felt its burden. The soldiers and nurses "over there" were depending on us for bandages and medicine.

Grandpa's third son Aubrey never went overseas, instead he worked at the Argentia naval base on the southern Avalon for most of the war. It was there he caught pneumonia, which led to TB, which led to his spending most of 1945-46 at the Sanatorium in St. John's. After he returned home I never knew, given my mother's dread of TB, what to say to him.

One bright March day, leaving the shop, I saw him sitting outside his parents' house wrapped in blankets. He was taking the fresh-air-and-sunshine-cure which doctors prescribed in those days before antibiotics like aureomycin became locally available. Timidly, I approached this little-known uncle whose beak of a nose so resembled my father's. To make conversation, I pointed to the cloudy pale brown liquid he was sipping.

"Is it Cocomalt?" I said.

A smile crinkled his hazel eyes. "No, my son, 'tis cow's milk mixed with blackstrap molasses. Tastes awful but they say it'll build up my blood. They also makes me drink cod liver oil."

"Me too," I said. Then he asked me how old I was now, how I liked school, and when we were leaving for St. John's. It surprised and touched me that he knew about my mother's impending surgery. After that we were always friends.

SCHOOL

"Calvin," I shouted across the classroom on my first morning at school, "can I have some paper?" The whole room fell silent. Some older students tittered. My brother, several seats away, rolled his eyes. I was baffled.

It was September 1942, the year the Commission of Government passed a law that all healthy Newfoundland children between the ages of seven and fourteen must go to school. Not that my parents wanted to keep me out. I already knew my letters – at home I had a porringer with the alphabet printed round its wide rim – and I could read. I could also count to ten and knew my colours.

All I needed was some paper to prove it.

Miss Payne regarded me over her glasses, then cleared her throat. "Young man," she said, "we don't talk out loud without permission. And younger pupils must use slates"– she pointed to a stack beside her – "which I'll be handing out soon. There's a war going on."

"Yes ma'am."

My brother, fourteen, walks me to school that first day. We both have bookbags, but mine is empty. I am wearing a brown wool sweater against the morning chill, short pants over my best knee socks, leather shoes and a cap. The first part of our walk, as far as the church, is familiar: mill, wharf, shop, my grandparents' house and Uncle John's on this side of the brook; Ralph Peckford's and church and belfry on the other. Beyond that I've seldom been, except in winter by horse and sleigh, to visit Dad's only sister Aunt Marion and her husband Roy in Victoria Cove five miles away. The school seems far but he says it's only a quarter mile.

Presently we come to a high-fenced garden with a house beyond. I ask what the tall pickets are for. "To keep bad boys from stealing the apples," says Calvin. He points to two bushy trees dotted with fruit. "Henry George and his sister Mary Ann sell them for fifty cents a dozen. The yellow ones are nearly ripe." My mouth waters. We rarely get apples except at Christmas, when Grandpa buys a barrel or two of shiny red ones from Nova Scotia. They come wrapped in white tissue. "People say George loads his shotgun with rock salt and hides in the tall grass after dark."

We walk in silence past the little house and between a long fenced meadow and tall evergreens. In the distance a round-roofed white building appears. I've seen it before, from Grandpa's wharf. "That's the school," says Calvin. I feel at once excited and nervous.

We cross a plank bridge over a small brook. "Where do that path go?" I ask, nodding toward a wide grassy path that angles into the woods to our left.

"To the cemetery."

"Cemetery?"

"Graveyard. Where they put dead people. You ask too many questions."

"Who…?" But we're already turning the fence corner into the schoolyard, a grassy field which sheep have cropped short over the summer. The school is four times as long as our foxy house and twice as wide. Behind it is a woodshed, also painted white. Some boys and girls stand around the porch waiting.

After a while a woman steps out and rings a handbell. The sound is high and urgent and echoes from the woods across the road. We all file into the small porch, which has a woodbox and a water barrel on one side and a line of coat hooks down the other. The barrel has a dipper like ours but the barrel isn't painted green.

The classroom has seven tall windows on the bay side and a long blackboard on the other. In between are four rows of unpainted wooden desks with an empty row in the middle for the big black box stove. At the far end is a platform reached by three steps on either side. Up there is Teacher's desk. On it I see the gleaming, black-handled brass bell. The stove is cold because the day is warm.

Miss Payne assigns me a desk one row from the windows. Seeing the water helps to calm my thumping heart. Another comforting sight is the neat white outhouse by the landwash – for my bladder is getting tight. Far to the left, out of sight, is Burnt Point with its lone pine and tiny fenced graveyard.

She calls our names and ticks them off in a flat ruled book she calls "The Register." We are mostly Gillinghams with a sprinkling of Peckfords, Francises, Days and Collinses. My brother and me are the only Saunderses. There is a blonde girl Calvin's age named Joan Peckford, very pretty, and her brothers Ralph and Gordon. Closer to my own age there's Viola, Clifford, Nellie and my best friend Everett. Cousin Frank won't be starting until next year, and Susie a year or so later.

Miss Payne hands out the promised slates to the first graders. She walks with a slight limp because, they say, she once had polio. The slates are small wood-framed rectangles of thin stone, like our shale but harder and smoother. And we each get a pointed stone pencil. "When you go home," she says, "ask your mother for a rag and a small jar for water to clean your slate with." She shows us how. The wetted slate darkens suddenly, then fades back to its normal grey.

Then we each receive a reader. The book's paper smells faintly like Dad's yellow oilskins. The stories in it are all about two children named Dick and Jane and a small dog called Laddie. There are many pictures. One of them shows a dog chasing a ball. Another shows Dick waking up and stretching, just like me, with a smiling sun winking in the windows at him. Dick is luckier than me; he has his own sunrise window.

Teacher says we won't be reading from this book just yet. Instead she carefully prints the ABCs across the top of the blackboard in block letters and small letters, shuffling awkwardly sideways as she goes. Her chalk breaks once but she picks up the pieces and continues. Then, while she supervises the older pupils, we in turn copy the letters onto our slates.

Our stone pencils tap and skreal. The marks we make are pale compared to her white chalk letters. She limps about, checking and correcting. My printing is worse than at home, where I can work on paper. After recess, we work on the smaller letters – "lower case," she calls them – then it is time to go home for dinner. The afternoon sessions are much the same. Day one of my new life.

After that, weekdays took on a new rhythm, an indoor-outdoor rhythm, one with more walking – four trips a day, a mile in all – and more sitting, plus the challenges of hand printing, spelling, adding and subtracting.

I learned the other rules: no going to the toilet without asking, no chewing gum in class, no spit-balls, no passing notes, no pulling girls' pigtails. In the grades that followed, we would tackle times tables, harder words, the tables of distances and weights and measures: "three feet equal one yard, two yards one fathom, 1760 yards one mile, two pints equal one quart, four quarts one gallon, four pecks one bushel." We repeated the names and distances of rivers until we knew them by heart, and the capitals of the countries of our mother country's vast pink Commonwealth. Eventually we practised penmanship, using real ink and long-handled nib pens. Always, in the background, we heard the older students murmuring at their work.

At home we struggled with homework on the lamp-lit kitchen table: Calvin with algebra and geometry and kings and queens and English literature; I with arithmetic and spelling. On such a night early in the school year, while she had us captive, Mom would check us for head lice.

She'd sit us by the stove, set the lamp close and examine our scalps. If she found even one louse, out came the carbolic soap and the fine-toothed comb. It was a double-edged comb, one side with close-spaced teeth for eggs and nits (baby lice), the coarser side for grown insects. A double-edged sword. As the comb raked my scalp I'd hear her exult: "Ahh! Got the little bugger!" and another louse would pop and sizzle on the stove. "Sit still now," she'd mutter, "I haven't done the back of your head!"

It wasn't all work in the round-roofed school. The building was also a community centre. Once a month or oftener, it overflowed with grownups. There were sales of goods, suppers, dances and Christmas concerts.

My parents took me to my first "time" at an early age, well before I started school. It was usually a meal followed by a dance. They were nights of happy uproar, of steaming plates of salt beef and vegetables or soup, of coats piled on side tables, of accordion music and the *whumpa, whumpa* of dancers shaking the floor and jiggling the lamps. After dancing, panting for air, they smelled of sweat when they sat close to you. Always there were tipplers huddled in the porch. Later in the evening there was often a fight, which we all enjoyed until a strong man or two separated the brawlers. Then everyone trudged home happy and shivering in the suddenly cold air.

In Grades 2 and 3 we had a man teacher. Everything about Mr. White seems blurred except that he was tall and pale and sometimes strapped the older boys. Seeing them weep and wring their hands was very sobering. He used a long horsehide strap, glossy from use, which he kept in his top desk drawer. It was about two inches wide and two feet long.

"Hold out your right hand!" he'd bark as the class went mute. "Your other right hand!" No one dared snicker. "Palm up!" Down came the whistling leather – *Thwack!* All the smaller pupils flinched.

Cunning older boys devised tricks to lessen the pain. They learned to extend the hand ever so slightly, which made the blow fall partly on their coat sleeve. Others, less adept, got it on the fingertips, which was worse. Some even drew back all the way at the last instant, making him slap his own leg. But Mr. White knew all their tricks and whacked them all the harder.

One boy dared to curse his tormenter. Mr. White bellowed like a bull and fairly flung him off the stage. I can still see, as if in slow motion, the boy's red-shirted form diving off the platform, still hear him crash against the nearest desks. Somehow he caught himself, and, grinning insolently, walked to the porch, put on his coat and stomped out. He never even took his bookbag. You had to admire that. We heard he went to work in the lumberwoods.

In slack times I eavesdropped on the lessons of the upper grades, especially the grades just below and above my brother's. *His* lessons I was already acquainted with from homework. What were the others learning over there? Often, listening in, I'd forget my own work and be chastised for daydreaming and have to rush to catch up.

Home was better for second-hand learning, especially when my brother recited. Rote learning was our main method then. Between supper and bedtime I heard a lot of Grade 9 and 10 history and geography that way.

I liked the poetry best. I can see him now, his blue and red *Canada Book of Prose and Verse* open in one hand, pacing between kitchen and parlour, learning Macaulay's "Horatius":

'O Tiber! Father Tiber!
To whom the Romans pray,
A Roman's life, a Roman's arms
Take thou in charge this day.'
So he spake, and speaking
Sheathed the good sword by his side,
And with his harness on his back
Plunged headlong in the tide…

Here, he paused to blow his nose. To my astonishment his eyes were brimming with tears. I was on the edge of my chair for the next few stanzas:

No sound of joy or sorrow
Was heard from either bank;
But friends and foes in dumb surprise
With parted lips and straining eyes
Stood gazing where he sank.

And when above the billows
They saw his crest appear,
All Rome sent forth a rapturious [sic] cry,
And even the ranks of Tuscany
Could scarce forbear to cheer.

Another week it would be Longfellow's "Hiawatha," or Tennyson's poem about the Lady of Shalott, that beautiful, sad weaver who had never left her enchanted loom until a certain knight rode by. I think we were both in love with her and envied Lancelot:

A bow-shot from her bower-eaves,
He rode between the barley-sheaves,
The sun came dazzling thro' the leaves,

And flamed upon the brazen greaves
Of bold Sir Lancelot.
A red-cross knight forever kneeled
To a lady in his shield,
that sparkled in the yellow field,
Beside remote Shalott.

Thus, without really trying, or even reading the books, I too learned snippets and skeins of Wordsworth's "Lucy Gray," Campbell's "Lord Ullin's Daughter," Sir Walter Scott's "The Lady of The Lake," Bliss Carman's "The Master of the *Scud*." I even picked up some of Tennyson's "Le Morte d'Arthur," harder going, darker, full of strange words, dismal yet thrilling, like being in church:

And slowly answered Arthur from the barge:
'the old order changeth, yielding place to new,
And God fulfils himself in many ways,
Lest one good custom should corrupt the world.
Comfort thyself; what comfort is in me?
I have lived my life, and that which I have done
May He himself make pure! But thou,
If thou shouldst never see my face again,
Pray for my soul. More things are wrought by prayer
Than this world dreams of.'

Next to eavesdropping, the best thing about school was recess, that interlude of freedom and fresh air when we dived outside to play, largely unsupervised, for fifteen minutes morning and afternoon.

Even at school there were few organised games for boys. Our fathers knew hardly any. Unless some sports-minded teacher coached us after school or on weekends, how could we learn? In later years one teacher would show us how to play "cat," a cricket-like game played with a six-inch stick for a ball and a shallow pit for a wicket. It was fun and fast, with base-running and throwing and yelling. Risky too, for we wore no pads or helmets, and a speeding stick could bruise a kidney or pop an eye.

Anyway, that was for the older boys. We youngsters were more or less left to romp and race and beachcomb until the bell rang. However, crying was investigated and fights were reported and stopped. Having an older brother helped – even if he was more interested in girls.

Girls were far better organised than we, especially in the warm days of spring and fall. Some drew a double cross of squares in the gravel with a stick and played hopscotch. Others brought a length of clothesline and trooped over to the bridge by the cemetery path to skip rope. On fine days we'd see them over there, hopping one-foot, two-feet, pigtails flying, dresses billowing, rope slicing the air, taking turns on it without missing a step. Or we'd hear their high voices raised in a traditional ring dance: wheel and curtsey, bow and kneel. A favourite was "The Farmer in The Dell." After choosing a girl to play the farmer – they preferred a boy, but who would venture? – they'd chant:

> The farmer in the dell,
> The farmer in the dell,
> Heigh-ho, the dairy-o,
> The farmer in the dell.

Then the farmer would reach out and tag someone – "The farmer takes a wife, the farmer takes a wife" – and pull this person inside the circle and twirl her about while the rest chanted, "Heigh-ho, the dairy-o, the farmer takes a wife." After this, the wife would take a child, the child a dog, the dog a cat, the cat a mouse, ending with:

> The cheese stands alone,
> The cheese stands alone;
> Heigh-o, the dairy-o,
> The cheese stands alone.

Often, with hardly a pause, they'd reform the ring, double the beat and launch into another:

> Georgie Porgie, pudding and pie;
> Kissed the girls and made them cry
> When the girls came out to play,
> Georgie Porgie ran away!

Or we'd hear a bit of history:

King William was King George's son,
All the royal races run;
On his breast a star he wore
Pointing to the Governor's door.
Come choose to the east
Come choose to the west,
Choose the very one you love best.
If she's not there to take your part,
Choose another one with all your heart…

A couple would sink down facing each other:

Down on this carpet you must kneel
As the grass grows in the field
Kiss your partner, kiss her sweet,
You may stand upon your feet.

When we tired of our haphazard play, we might sidle over to watch. The few times I tried skipping alone, my feet got tangled. So nimble on the ice pans, so clumsy on the rope. As for the ring dances, they were mostly about boring things like kissing and matchmaking and plighting and trothing. Yet now and then one of us, saucier or more smitten than the rest, would join the girls. Then we'd dodge on, making out we had better things to do. But secretly we admired the girls for their fleetness and skill – where did they learn all that? – and for the fun they could squeeze out of a bit of clothesline and thin air.

By late October that air was getting nippy. Trudging along the road with our bookbags, we went out of our way to scuff through fallen leaves and stamp on frozen puddles. By the time my birthday came in late November we could slide on the ice. On such mornings, though the school stove would have been lit an hour before by an upper grade boy assigned to do so for that month, the classroom would still be chilly when we arrived at nine o'clock.

By early December, especially on overcast afternoons, we needed to light the lamps. These were kerosene lamps mounted between the windows on swinging brackets, each with a reflector like ours at home. Again, an older student was assigned the job, a girl this time. "Now you be careful with those glass chimneys!" said Teacher, "and don't be turning the wicks too high and soot up the glass!" And the lamplighter, looking very important, would glide along each wall, a box of Seadog matches in one hand and a tall stool in the other, touching flame to wick, flame to wick. As a reformed arsonist, I envied her the job.

Once the lamps were lit, I always saw an astonishing sight: the undraped windows turned teal blue! But as my eyes adjusted to the amber light, the illusion faded.

The week before Christmas would find us huddled round the stove each morning, warming our scrammed hands and toes. Some of us wore coats until recess time. After dinner the classroom was always warm as toast. On mild snowy days we stamped boots clean outdoors and lined them up in the porch. The teacher let those who wanted warm them by the stove before heading home.

The Christmas concert is coming. On the Saturday before, men wrestle a big fir tree onto the platform and wire it upright. By Monday morning our classroom smells like the woods. A girl is asked to sweep up the trail of green sprinkles the tree men left. We grab a handful from the dustpan and drop them on the hot stove to enjoy the balsamy smell of blasty boughs. We spend hours snipping and twisting red and green crepe paper into garlands for the tree. We finish decorating it with coloured paper cutouts and small white birthday candles glued to cardboard squares cut from cereal boxes.

And we practise for the concert. The first year all I had to do was hold one of the letters to spell out C-H-R-I-S-T-M-A-S. It is important to hide your letter until Teacher nods; then you flip it, hoping for right side up.

On the big night we stand on stage and shuffle our feet and scratch ourselves and gaze about like surprised hens. Several letters, mine included, come out upside down. But since only the audience and the teacher know, we revel and blush as they applaud. Older pupils recite longer pieces alone. Some sing songs accompanied on the accordion by a brother or an uncle; we have no piano. Most of us on stage want to get it over with so Father Christmas can bring our presents.

Finally, sitting with my parents again, we hear the distant tinkle of his sleigh bells, followed by a loud thumping on the door. Someone opens it – and in he strides, scarlet in his baggy suit and black belt, holding his white beard in one hand and his sack in the other. "Ho! Ho! Ho!" he booms in a strangely familiar voice, "Happy Christmas!"

Clumping on stage, he lowers his brin bag of presents and asks how many youngsters have been good. "All of you? Well, well!" One by one he calls our names – How does he know us all? – and one by one we troop shyly forward for a little gift.

All too soon it is over. A flurry of waving and goodbyes and he is gone for another year. Happily we trudge home with our families – happier if fluffy snow is falling. Dad stokes the fire. Mom makes hot cocoa. I go to bed and, with the real Christmas only a week away, try to sleep.

We were a patriotic and pious bunch – or made ourselves out to be. We started every school day with "God Save the King" (wondering, some of us, what "long train run over us" could mean), and ended it with the Lord's Prayer. When the minister appeared on one of his visits we stood at attention, listened politely and sang some simple hymn: "Fair waved the golden corn/In Canaan's pleasant land," or "There is a green hill far away/Without a city wall." (I could never understand why a hill needed a wall. None of ours did.)

While we never outwardly criticized those rites, sometimes we murmured against them. One afternoon when Teacher said, "Now bow your heads quietly for the Lord's Prayer," Clifford leaned over to me and whispered, "My neck don't scroop." On the playground we could be more blasphemous:

> I don't care if it rains or freezes,
> I am safe in the arms of Jesus;
> I am Jesus' little lamb,
> Yes, by Jesus, yes I am!

Or,

While shepherds washed their socks by night
All seated round the tub
The angel of the Lord came down
And they began to scrub.

Or

Matthew, Mark,
Luke and John,
You take the wheelbar'
An' I'll dodge on.

For all that, at heart, we were all believers, and monarchists to boot.

The Commission of Government was now well aware, thanks especially to the untiring travels of Commissioner John Hope Simpson and his wife Quita, of the shocking levels of malnutrition, poverty and disease which plagued parts of rural Newfoundland and Labrador. To enhance the existing system of able-bodied relief – a pitiful $1.50 a month per person, later $2.00, and $12.50 a quarter for elderly destitutes – they built cottage hospitals in larger centres and promoted regular TB and immunization clinics. But they knew that in order to make real progress, children's diets must be improved as well. They decided to supplement our diet with cod liver oil and powdered milk.

One fall, the S.S. *Glencoe* brought several mysterious crates. They came ashore in Grandpa's motor boat and were delivered to, of all places, the school. Inside were half-pint bottles of cod liver oil and stout cardboard tubs of pale brown powder. The screw-top bottles were royal blue and flask-shaped, much like the ones men swigged from during dances. They were labelled "Refined Cod Liver Oil; Munn & Company, Harbour Grace." The tubs were metal-rimmed and labelled simply "Cocomalt." We each got a blue bottle to take home: the tubs stayed in the school.

Teacher said, "Keep the bottle in a cool place and take a teaspoon with every meal and you won't get rickets."

"What's rickets?" I said.

"A disease that softens your bones and bends your back out of shape. The cod oil will help your teeth, too." I had my doubts. In Fogo, on a stagehead once, I'd sniffed a barrel brimming with a rancid gurry of limp grey cod livers oozing oil in the hot sun. They smelled bad and looked worse.

At recess I unscrewed the cap and took a whiff. Perhaps it wouldn't poison me. I took a sip – it tasted almost sweet. To show how tough I was, I took a swig. By the time I got home my bottle was one third gone. The next day I cadged the bottles of those who refused to drink it. What I didn't drink I slathered on my leather logan tops. Stray dogs licked it off and cats trailed me, but it kept my feet dry.

Someone said, "Careychicks will come if you pours cod oil on the water on a stormy day." One day at recess when the wind was in easterly, we tried it. Within minutes the little white-rumped storm petrels were fluttering over the slicks, dipping and darting, skimming the oil off the surface.

Some of us started throwing rocks at them. We never hit any. Rearing back to heave one last rock as the bell rang, I slammed my hand against a boulder behind me, mashing my knuckles. For the rest of that week I had to write left-handed. Served me right.

Compared to cod oil, Cocomalt, a blend of cocoa, sugar and milk powder, was an instant success. We loved its look, its smell, its taste. Before recess each afternoon Teacher would start a pot of it on the stove. After recess it was poured, steaming hot, lumber camp style, into our waiting mugs. Then we sat around sipping like church ladies. For the few well-fed ones among us, it was merely a diversion. For the many who came to school without a bite of breakfast it was a godsend.

To spread the word, the Commission sent each school a printed jingle which someone, perhaps the kindly Quita Hope Simpson, had composed. Sung to the tune of "Jingle Bells" – a brilliant marketing ploy – the chorus went:

> Cocomalt, Cocomalt,
> That's what we all say;
> Every boy and girl should drink
> A glass or more each day!

There were several verses in that vein. As the teacher kept time with a spoon, we would belt them out as part of the ritual.

When my family moved to St. John's the following spring, I missed the ritual as much as the hot drink. Surely St. John's had children needing

Cocomalt? Certainly some of my pale, gap-toothed schoolmates at Springdale Street School did. Yet I never saw a drop.

But outside the city, in Gander Bay and all around the island, we children had something to sing about. We may have lost a country, but we wouldn't lose our teeth. Our pretty girls might be wearing petticoats sewn from bleached Robin Hood flour bags – the slogan said, "Fit for a prince," which made the big boys snicker – but from now on, thanks to their daily dose of calcium and iron, they need never hide their smiles behind their hands again.

For me the calcium came too late. My addiction to sweets, plus our lack of toothbrushes, was catching up with me. I suffered agonies of toothache. So did many of my classmates, but theirs were more legitimate. They couldn't afford candy.

And they could get relief, or said they could, by having the toothache "charmed" away. "What did the charmer do to 'e?" I asked a girl believer.

"Can't tell 'e. She tol' me not to tell, for the toothache would come back."

"No 'twon't. I'll give 'e 'alf a stick o' chewin' gum…" But she wouldn't. I had better luck with a boy: "The charmer said for me to go in the woods and find a young dogberry or rowan tree and slit the rind. The I 'ad to pluck a 'air off my 'ed an' shove it under the rind, lay my 'and on the tree and say: 'This I bequeath to the rowan tree. In the name of the Father, and of the Son and of the Holy Ghost. Amen.'"

"Did it work?"

"For a while…"

"'Tis all foolishness," snorted my mother. "Stick this clove between your teeth and make sure you don't swallow it." Clove or no, I went on suffering. The only relief was to hold my mouth open over the hot stove. I finally asked Calvin to help me yank out the rottenest molar by tying it to the doorknob. You braced yourself and slammed the door. It didn't work. When the hospital boat *Bonnie Nell* came, the student doctor pulling teeth told me I'd have none by the time I was twenty at the rate I was going. He pulled seven molars in two days and, amazingly, I felt much better.

Toothaches were the least of Mom's health worries. Her great fear was tuberculosis, and "school is a fine place to catch it." She said TB rotted people's lungs, their bones, even their brains. Hardest hit were the old, the poor and the uneducated. Living as they did in close-packed, extended families with poor hygiene and poorer food, they didn't stand a chance. She herself would catch it in her forties – though it wouldn't flare up for two decades. As local post-mistress it was likely she who pinned up the picture of a winsome baby crawling on the floor saying, "For my sake, don't spit!" If it looked out of place among the war posters – "The Axis Has Ears!" "Buy War Bonds!" – she didn't care. TB, to her, was deadlier than Hitler.

That's why she forbade Calvin and me to drink cow's milk. This was a hard sentence, because Grandpa Saunders had a Holstein cow that gave lots of it, and thick cream too. But in those days rural cattle were rarely tested for TB. Goat's milk, however, was thought (incorrectly) to be safe. Mom had been raised on goat's milk in Fogo, so she bought a nanny and bred her and made us drink it too. It must have helped my teeth; but candy won out in the end.

Erysipelas, a streptococcal skin infection, was endemic in certain poorer families. "My son," she'd say, "never touch anyone's face or scalp that has reddish blotches, or wear their mitts or caps!"

All this medical and motherly advice I took in stride, knowing it was for my own good. But one year she went too far. She deprived me of a great boon. Some kind soul had organised a circulating library for people unable to access the new regional libraries being built. It wasn't much, just a box or two of books each month, but they were books which students could freely borrow. For some, the books would be the only ones, except for the family bible and maybe *Pilgrim's Progress*, they had ever known.

"Never mind," said Mom, shaking her head for emphasis. "Don't either of you bring home those books! What will they think of next? You never know who's been reading them, breathing on them. It might be someone with TB, coughing their lungs out! Haven't we got enough ways to catch TB?"

So I watched the treasure chest being opened, watched my friends sign books out, and came home empty-handed. Every month the same disappointment, the same chagrin. I never even knew what books there were. When the teacher asked why we never took any home, I shrugged and turned away.

Decades later, an outport-born friend told me more about the library. His school got the books too; but his parents – whom he called "literate but not literary" – had no medical qualms. "I'd rush to get my hands on a few good ones before the other lads did," he said. "In this way I got *Kidnapped* and *Treasure Island*, as well as *Lost Endeavour*. *The Hardy Boys* stories were always in the boxes. I devoured all of them."

Good for him.

City Sojourn: Bennett Avenue

I was halfway through Grade 4 when my world capsized. Mom got sick. Not suddenly, as with a heart attack, but gradually, with blood in the urine and cramps in the belly. The symptoms pointed to some sort of tumour. In 1940, Dr. John Olds of Twillingate had treated her for stomach ulcers. Now her fear was uterine cancer. She went back to him.

Dr. Olds diagnosed an ovarian cyst. But he told her that without exploratory surgery – a laparotomy – he couldn't be sure. "Either way, Winnie, you may need a hysterectomy," was how he put it. He could do it right away, he said, or she could have it done in St. John's later. She opted for St. John's. While she admired Olds' surgical skill, she'd heard he was "knife-happy."

In fairness, this perception had more to do with geography than choice. Most of his patients lived remote from Twillingate, in Notre Dame Bay outports cut off by ice and stormy seas for half the year. If, while operating, he spotted a potential problem, say an inflamed appendix, he would fix it then and there, rather than have the patient go home and die a few months later. And if he saw something else wrong, he'd fix that too.

It was such complications that worried Mom. She often said that after my birth she had "never been herself," and blamed the midwife. She decided she would have the surgery in the spring. Beatty and her husband George were living in the city now and could help us find a place to stay. She wired Dr. Olds her decision; he referred her to a Dr. Murphy.

My parents' plan was to go in April, during the Easter break. They would enrol Calvin and me at Saint Michael's Collegiate on Bennett Avenue, he in Grade 11, I in Grade 4, and find a furnished apartment within easy walking distance of the school. Dad would take us to Glenwood and come to St. John's with us, stay for a week or so after the operation, then travel to Corner Brook on the island's west coast to train for his new job as a roving inspector with the Newfoundland Fisheries Board. Then he'd spend the rest of the summer guiding on the River.

I was distressed at all this change. My mother assured me we weren't moving for good. "Only 'till I'm better, my son." I didn't believe her. I knew how she fretted about living in the bay, so far from medical care. She had seen so much illness due to isolation. She had a litany of such woes. The early 1900s diphtheria epidemic, for example.

"What's diph – ther – ia?" I asked, stumbling over the strange word the first time she spoke of it.

"'Tis a disease that hardens the roof of a person's mouth until they can't swallow," she said. She had lost a girlhood friend to it. Her description of the end made me shudder. She still remembered a 1920s outbreak of typhoid fever in Gander Bay, soon after she'd arrived. It was caused by germs in drinking water, she said. "Twillingate offered free vaccinations…"

"What's vac – cin…?"

"…but Main Point wouldn't let the doctor give anyone the needle to prevent it." She said that when I was born, Notre Dame Bay still had remote cases of beriberi, a paralysis caused solely by lack of Vitamin B1. This was two years after the Commission of Government all but eliminated it by adding whole wheat flour to welfare rations. "'Dole bread,' they called the loaves we baked from the brown flour. Wouldn't touch it! Too proud! Fed it to the hens!"

Naturally, she was one of the first in Gander Bay to boil summer drinking water. She boiled it against typhoid in the twenties, against "summer complaint" or dysentery in the thirties and forties and – just in case – against polio in the 1950s. I hated the flat metallic taste and said so. "Well," she'd reply as she set another kettleful to cool, "you'll just have to put up with it. Clarkes Brook water isn't fit to drink summertime. Why, they lets the sheep and horses wade in it, poop in it! I guarantee that in New York, even in St. John's, 'twould never be allowed! Scandalous!" She would extol Fogo drinking water, how it came up cold from deep rocky wells, pure and clean.

She could have been a sanitary engineer.

We came to St. John's in early April 1946. The trip upriver, my first since I went to Gander Lake at age four or five, was so cold we bundled up in everything we had and huddled under a tarpaulin to keep dry. I yearned to study this mysterious River which so often bore my father away but the weather forbade it. Yet Dad clearly liked being out in it. Any weather his beloved River served up was all right with him.

I learned some names on that trip, names of places which, until then, I'd only heard in stories told around the kitchen stove: The Works, Summer Houses, Bread and Cheese Steady (where Uncle Stan lunched sitting on a boulder), First and Second Rattle, First Pond. I asked Calvin where they were and he told me.

Going up Second Pond under a leaden sky, I moved to the bow to watch hill after hill of leafless birch and dark evergreens glide past, each perfectly mirrored in the water. Far ahead I saw for a moment the blue dorsal fin of Mount Peyton. In the loud rattles, amid the tumult of contending waters, I gazed on huge grey boulders smeared with the paint of canoes that came too close. We never bumped one. We passed brook after brook, now to the east, now to the west, all feeding their tithe of water into the braided, many-islanded Gander.

At last we reached the fourth and final pond, navigated Bridge's Angle and battled through the seething lops of Little and Big Chutes. A while later, passing Salmon Brook, as raindrops again pocked the water, I saw Glenwood's spidery railroad trestle against the lowering sky. The rain wouldn't matter now; we were nearly there.

After supper at the home of Dad's longtime Mi'kmaq friends Jim and Ellen John, we headed for the train station. Of the night ride to St. John's I remember little. The gentle swaying of the cars, the muffled one-two, one-two clacking of the wheels that became a dull roar whenever the train crossed a bridge or someone opened a door, soon lulled me to sleep. Sleeping, I seemed to hear the whistle's organ note – so like the *Glencoe's* – and a harmonica keening somewhere. I definitely smelled orange peel and stale socks and coal smoke. Even the taxi ride uptown from the Waterford Station is lost to memory.

Under Newfoundland's denominational educational system, Anglicans like us were supposed to find an Anglican school. St. Michael's and All Angels Collegiate was such a school. Not yet ten years old, bright and airy, with playing fields out back, it offered Grades 1 through 11. Had we stayed in its vicinity I would have been better off.

No matter; I didn't like it. There was nothing familiar about it: no salt water or black spruce, no picket fence or landwash, no big brother in the same room. Coming to it so late in the academic year, unable to speak good English even, I felt disoriented. This would lead to my first and only act of urban terrorism.

One day soon after my coming, Teacher conducted an oral quiz. It was about someone called Jacques Cartier and his doings around a river named the Saint Lawrence in 1535. It was the same great stream that Newfoundland island swam in but I'd never heard of it, or of him. Oral quizzes were new to me too.

But wishing to impress her, I did a foolish thing. Several times, to hide the mystery explorer's true name, she said "Mr. Blank." So when she asked us to identify this Frenchman, my hand shot up. How could the others have missed it? "Yes?" she said, as if pleased to hear from the newcomer so soon.

"Mr. Blank!" I blurted out. The whole class tittered. The teacher even smiled. My ears burned with shame. So smart in Gander Bay, so dumb in St. John's.

A thirst for revenge took hold of me. The next day was Saturday. In our landlord's garage I'd noticed a can of roofing tar. Early next morning while the house was asleep, I scooped some tar into an empty tin with a stick and ambled up the hill to the school. Seeing no one, I tried the main door. It was locked. Good. I smeared a little on the inside of its brass door handle.

The first person to open it – let it be the Grade 4 teacher, I thought, or better yet the principal – was in for a surprise. Revenge was sweet. It quenched my anger at the teacher, at the school, at the city, at my parents for uprooting me.

Then shame and panic overwhelmed me. What if some innocent teacher, or a student, or the janitor – or my brother! – grabbed the handle first?

But there was no undoing my deed, so I hid the incriminating tin and stick in some bushes and fled home as if nothing had happened. Normally this wouldn't have fooled my mother or brother, but things were not normal, and Dad had already left for the island's west coast to train for his new duties as a government inspector.

Monday morning found me still jittery. Part of me wanted to confess to Teacher, to be caught and punished. Another part said no. The day passed without incident. The spring term was winding down and no one had time to investigate. In the following weeks my grades improved. Some students befriended me. My anger evaporated. So I never confessed. Until now.

For a child, the first dislocation is the worst. A cold fog seemed to roll across the landmarks of my mornings, noons and nights, obliterating playmates, grandparents, uncles and aunts, our foxy house, my dog Sprig, my school, my church. Gone was my cove for wading, my brook for trouting, my landwash for beachcombing, my River for dreaming.

Overnight I went from a place where the fastest wheeled vehicle was Silas Fancy's horse-drawn sawdust cart to a city whizzing with cars and trucks and busses. I went from lamp-lit nights to electric street lights, from a village where we lugged water in buckets to a place where running water and flush toilets were commonplace. In short, from the nineteenth century to the twentieth.

In Clarkes Head I knew and was known, had a history, fitted in. Here I was an eleven-year-old nobody, a misfit with a worm of worry in my gut. It was true the pavements were pleasant underfoot; but if you spied a bird there was nothing at hand to sling at it. The trees looked stunted and begrimed. The houses were jammed together, the yards miniscule. The hazy sky was cluttered with telephone poles and a cat's cradle of wires. You couldn't cross a street without looking left and right and left again to avoid being run down.

One thing for sure: had they consulted me I never would have come. And yet…and yet, my spirits revived. I took a deep breath, looked around. The city was no Eden but neither was Clarkes Head. I found a park not five minutes from our apartment, a little playground with metal swings and slides. Down the street was a movie theatre. Over the hill behind the school there seemed to be a scrap of woods. Possibilities.

My mother was less sanguine. A sword hung over her. I racked my brain for ways to remove it. Dad would be gone all summer. Calvin, cramming for final exams, was too busy to be much company. I too would be at school every weekday until late June.

"I'll come straight home from school every day."

"That's good, my son," she sighed.

Thank God we had Aunt Beatty less than fifteen minutes' walk away.

The day came when Dr. Murphy's secretary called to confirm her surgery date. It was in early May at St. Clare's Mercy Hospital. I know because I made her a Mother's Day card and brought it to her bedside.

Aunt Beatty may have helped me make it, for she had taken me to stay at her apartment during Mom's time in hospital. Uncle George was away with something that she called the "Merchant Marine." They had no car, but the place was close enough for me to walk to school. St. Clare's was not too far away either.

At Aunt Beatty's, I sleep well for the first time in weeks. I wake to the smell of toast. My aunt is humming to a tune on the radio. I yawn and pad to the bathroom, then into the sunny kitchen. A geranium glows red on the windowsill. "And how did we sleep?" she asks, pecking me on the cheek. Her brown hair is in bangs and she is wearing a flowered housecoat.

"Like a baby," I say, imitating my father's expression.

"And what would you like for breakfast? Orange juice? Toast? A boiled egg?"

We breakfast together. I like the bemused way she regards me through long lashes. She has known me since my toddler years. She is young and optimistic and makes me feel happy. Perhaps my coming makes her happy too, especially with Uncle George at sea.

I must have been in school when the taxi took Mom to the hospital. Aunt Beatty went with her. Sitting in class, I tried to imagine what it would be like to have your belly cut open and something taken out and then be sewed up again. How did they stop the blood? The time I'd cut my scalp on the Bridgewall stove it bled a lot. Would Dr. Murphy use a sewing machine to close the cut?

That evening when Aunt Beatty and Calvin and I visited her, she was weak but smiling. "A relief to have it over with," she said. "And no cancer. But you know what my greatest fear was? That I'd babble nonsense comin' out of ether." I had no idea what she meant. "People do, you know. They curse like sailors and tell family secrets and make total fools of theirselves!" This sounded more like my mother. She was going to be all right. I gave her my card. It said: "The Ninth of May is Mother's Day. Love, Gary."

And in the three months that followed, she did make good progress. A week or so after the operation she was taking short walks with Beatty or our landlady, Mrs. Andrews. They'd walk south on Bennett to the playground, rest on one of the benches and trudge back. Weekends I'd take my turn with her.

In late August she suffered a setback of some kind. No one would tell me what it was or even talk about it. In fact, it would be some years before Aunt Beatty explained. "She scared me half to death," was how she put it. "I shall never forget it. I had nightmares for a long time. I roused Calvin up and we both stared at your mother in her agony, neither of us knowing what to do. But we did remove her pillow and try to get something between her teeth. I then called Dr. Murphy, and he said that when she became stable and strong enough, to give her tea. When she woke she knew something was very wrong."

When Dr Murphy told my mother she had suffered an epileptic seizure, she was sure he was mistaken. Nothing like it had ever happened to her before, she said. Her family had no history of the disease. He assured her the symptoms were classic grand mal epilepsy. She wept. She was forty-one, five years younger than her mother had been when she died of a brain tumour and stroke. Perhaps that crossed her mind. To have escaped TB all those years, only to fall prey to this! And the worst of it was, people would pity her, shun her, talk behind her back. She'd be someone who "took the fits."

In years to come, back home in Gander Bay, I would understand my aunt's horror. By then my brother was away working. When a seizure came, which they did every few months, my father, strong as he was, would rouse me to help. A grand mal is a fearsome sight. Someone you love is foaming at the mouth like a mad dog. They moan in distress, gnash their teeth, bite their tongue. All I had to do was wait for him to still her threshing body, then insert a wooden rod between her teeth to protect her tongue. Yet this simple act left me exhausted. How my father felt I could only imagine. He said very little. The only good thing about it was that her seizures never came by day or in public, and that she could never recall them. The only clues were a splitting headache and great weariness.

For decades she would suffer so. Any unusual stress: bad news, a move, a quarrel – seemed to be triggers. So did stormy weather, low atmospheric pressure. For instance she suffered one while I was visiting them in Gander on the night of February 15, 1982, during the blizzard that sank the *Ocean Ranger* oil rig on the Grand Banks.

Although she never had daytime seizures, her illness made her reluctant to stay anywhere overnight, even with friends or relatives. One embarrassing episode was all it took to convince her not to. In some ways the few close friends and relatives who knew were quicker to accept her illness than she was. The nearest she ever came to acceptance was to say, cradling her head in a cold cloth on a morning after, "I must have had another seizure." It was a family secret.

My mother never ceased looking for a cure. She perused the medical advice columns in newspapers and magazines. She got Dad to quiz his many doctor anglers, including gynaecologist Richard TeLinde, physician to the wife of the then Shah of Persia. I think she would have tried any promising medication.

All they had to offer was speculation on possible causes. Because her first attack had come soon after the hysterectomy, and because late onset epilepsy was often linked to brain damage, some suggested oxygen deficiency under ether. Or perhaps respiratory problems – she did have dormant TB – had compromised the anaesthetic. The seizures would continue into the late 1950s, when one of Dad's clients found and prescribed an effective medication.

But all that was future. The immediate problem was depression. "I don't know who cried more," Calvin told me years later, "our mother or the landlady. They used to take turns consoling each other." What else could they do? The medical profession had little but aspirin to offer for melancholia, let alone full-blown post-operative depression. She was virtually on her own.

Poor woman, she had grown up surrounded by medical woes. Illness was an enemy crouched at her door. No wonder it was her favourite topic. As a young woman she had lost, in the space of two years, her baby sister Alma and her five-year-old sister Lydia – Lydia who shared the same birth date as Mom, April 1st. In 1927, working as a telegrapher in New York City, Mom got the news saying her bedridden mother had died.

Little wonder she railed at disease. She had me so frightened of library books that not once during our 14 months in the city would I borrow one. She even lectured Calvin and me on the perils of public toilets, showing us how to lay a triangle of toilet paper down before sitting.

So here she was, marooned in the city with her unspeakable illness, Dad still away and only poor Mrs. Andrews to console her. So depressed was she that in June, when Calvin showed her his report card, proud that he'd passed Grade 11 with good marks, she scarcely noticed.

However, Aunt Beatty always managed to cheer her, and us. We basked in her sunny disposition. Having seen her sister through the operation, she visited often and did her best to soothe our fears. "Your mom and I were very close," she would tell me in her eighties. "She was like a mother to me. I loved her dearly."

Late in August, Mom announced we wouldn't be going back to the bay after all. Calvin, unable to find a job all summer, had decided to stay in town and take a Grade 11 business course offered by Prince of Wales College. He felt sure they would accept his St. Michael's diploma. But he would have to board with us, and Bennett would be too long a walk in winter. No doubt Mom's illness was also a factor in her decision.

So it was goodbye to Bennett, but not to St. John's. By now I didn't mind. I'd grown to like the traffic, the level sidewalks, the air of excitement, even the scent of vehicle exhaust; it reminded me of outboard motors. Because our apartment had been furnished there was little to pack. By now, Dad had returned to Glenwood to spend the summer guiding anglers for the caterers Murphy & Steel. There would be no need for him to come all the way to St. John's just to help us move a few blocks across town.

Still, I wished he would.

Then he could have taken us to another movie at the Cornwall Theatre down the street, as he had done last May. The three of us had sauntered there in the warm spring twilight; Calvin was studying for final exams. I was excited to be with my parents again. I hadn't seen my dad looking so handsome for a long time. The last time I'd seen him he was wearing his habitual mackinaw shirt, a trainman's peaked cap and rolled-down long rubbers. Now he wore his Dick Tracy hat (but it wasn't yellow), a dark tweed sports jacket, sharply creased pants and shiny shoes. Mom wore a little feathered hat, new pumps, and a bright print dress – "dark colours make me look so old" – under her raglan. They made a handsome couple. And I their young son walking between.

Movies back home were a mixed blessing. Most were shown in the Orange Hall, a chilly barn with hard wooden benches and windows blacked out with sheets and blankets. The gasoline generator made so much racket outside, it drowned out all but the loudest parts. The film always broke two or three times and had to be respliced. Yet we paid our twenty cents and thought ourselves lucky – didn't know any better.

Standing in line, waiting for Dad to buy the tickets, I tried to imagine the enchantment to come. Walking down the sloping floor to take our seats in the dark interior, munching popcorn while waiting for the lights to dim and the curtains to open, I could scarcely breathe.

The lights dimmed, the curtains parted, the vast snowy screen filled with images and sound. I saw the movie, yet what it was about, who played the lead and how the story ended, I forgot almost immediately. Real life eclipsed all details. But I did remember the velvet drapes, how they mysteriously opened and closed on their own, sighing like surf on a beach.

When we emerged ninety minutes later, it seemed years had passed. The sun had set. Street lamps sent violet shadows across the sidewalks. LeMarchant Road was a river of winking white and ruby car lights weaving through the dusk.

Back on Bennett Avenue for my last night there, I dreamed of that movie, but also of rubber whispering on asphalt, of the heady scent of gasoline, of velvet curtains opening on new horizons. In three short months I'd become almost a townie.

ANIMALS TAME

For a family with no pets and no farm, we had our share of domestic livestock. A parade of cats, hens, dogs, goats and horses yowled, clucked, barked, bleated and whinnied through my young life, watched over by a mythic eagle named Jack.

The cats – except for Calvin's kitten that ran afoul of my father a fortnight before I was born – were more often heard (and smelled) than seen. They weren't pets, but strays that sometimes made noisy love under our house, nuisances that had to be expelled and kept expelled so Mom could sleep. The other animals were both seen and heard, and, except for the horses, belonged to us and we to them. But none of them were pets. Pets were for the well-to-do and hardly anyone kept them. Tame animals should "earn their keep," everyone said.

Our hens certainly did. Of our few livestock they were the most industrious. They also gave the place a look of peace and good government as they gravely foraged, dust-bathed, or just sunned themselves in the coop door waiting for winter to end. For all their industry they were very much in the present, always with one eye peeled for the soaring hawk, the roaming cur.

Where Mom got them I don't know, likely Fogo. We never called them "chickens." That was too close to "chicks," our name for baby hens, as in "neither chick nor child." Our flock was mostly Rhode Island Reds (what was a Rhode, I wondered?) and grey Barred Rocks (another puzzle), with a scattered White Leghorn meat bird. The Reds were the handsomest, especially the rooster with his scarlet comb and wattles, his electric green neck hackles, his gun-metal-blue tail feathers. The Barred Rocks looked plain, but only at a distance. Up close their feathers revealed surprisingly delicate ripplings of black and white like clouds in a mackerel sky.

Hens never scared me, even as a toddler. In Fogo, if Aunt Fanny needed an egg right away, she'd say, "I hear a hen squawking; she's after laying an egg, God bless 'er. Go out now, Gary, put your hand under her and take the egg."

"Will she peck?"

"She might, but if she do 'twon't 'urt, I'm sure." So I went and took the egg, hot from the factory. As I did so, my fingers touched something else, something too smooth to be an egg. I fetched it in too. Aunt Fanny took the real egg, noticed the other thing and said, "Oh, that's a china egg."

"From…China?"

"No dear, it's porcelain…like glass."

"What's it doin' there?"

"It helps a broody hen start layin'. If I sees the rooster treadin' 'er and I wants some chicks, I puts the glass egg in a dark corner nest and pretty soon she's layin' an egg a day, squawkin' away."

"What do 'tread' mean?"

"Thank you for the egg. Run along now. And here, put the glass egg back."

Though our hens earned their keep, their laying season was only five months at best. As the autumn days shortened and cooled, the eggs grew scarcer and scarcer until there were none. A laying hen needs at least fourteen hours of light a day. By September the whole dozen of them scarcely laid enough for breakfast. By November the flock was officially on welfare.

We could have lengthened their day by hanging a lighted lantern in the coop, but the risk of fire and the cost of kerosene forbade it. Come winter, the flock retired indoors except for warm days when Mom opened the door to air out the coop. No longer able to forage (in summer they essentially fed themselves) the flock now ate a pound or two of scratch feed a day. For that reason, and because older hens were poor layers anyhow, the flock was culled each fall. No sense feeding them all winter for nothing.

We youngsters got to watch the executions. Even to take part. Often it was we who caught the unfortunate fowl and brought it to the bloody block. We knew culling was a serious business; yet we found it hard not to smile at old biddies sprinting headless round the yard, squirting blood until they keeled over. They had to be bled anyway. Mom seldom took part; she'd rather do the plucking. The culling rarely took more than a couple at a time. Venison you could freeze and pork you could smoke, but poultry wouldn't keep. Some birds had already been eaten, mostly by guests, over the summer.

Mom's hens loved her. They knew her voice. She had only to appear on the bridge, tap a plate with a fork and call, "Here, coopie, coopie," and they'd come half-running, half-flying to her feet. One of them used to fly the whole thirty yards.

That would never happen in Fogo. Fogo hens wore "yokes." Fogo housewives had vegetables and strawberries to protect. In Gander Bay, with land to burn, we penned them in. To keep them in, you spread old netting over the pen. Or you clipped a wing on one side so they couldn't fly out. Our main crop was grass, which they were welcome to, plus all the insects and worms they could find. Truly free range. Oddly, they never bothered with the landwash. Their ancestors were jungle fowl, Calvin said, so perhaps that was why.

The Fogo hen yoke wasn't a true yoke like *The Family Herald* oxen wore. It was a ten-inch stick tied crossways under the wings. It made them look odd, like people with both arms stuck in their sleeves from dressing too fast. But it protected the town's precious garden plots. A yoked hen could neither squeeze through the palings nor fly over them. If she tried to sneak through, the stick brought her up short. It was laughable to watch a bird take aim, sprint like mad – and tumble backwards in a cloud of feathers. The smarter ones learned fast; some never did.

Fogo hens could swim. I saw it with my own eyes. One evening some boys on a nearby wharf flung one in. Suddenly in deep waters, she quickly got her bearings and struck out for shore. It was slow going without webbed feet, but by and by she reached the nearest cliff, scrambled out, shook herself like a wet dog and scampered home. Tales of adventure in the old coop that night!

While hens gave a homestead the look of domesticity, goats did the opposite. Goats were trouble on four legs. Intelligent and resourceful, bred from Middle Eastern mountaineers, they ran like the wind and scorned fences. As they said in Appalachia, "If it won't hold water, it won't hold goats." Keeping them *in* was never our wish; we needed to keep them out. Outside, they could browse to their hearts' delight on dandelions, goldwithy, willow, wild roses, alders, tree bark, kelp (they loved the salt) – anything remotely nourishing.

My mother would have loved to have a garden when I was small, but Dad hated digging, said it hurt his back. He'd rather buy our vegetables. One year he did put in a crop of potatoes and turnips for her. With the ground already fenced, he foresaw no goat problems. But our nannies surveyed the fence with their golden eyes, noticed a boulder next to it, studied it, hopped up, gauged the fence's height and launched themselves over. By the time Mom spotted them they had beaten down the potatoes and devoured most of the greens. She shooed them out the gate but they were soon back. To save the remainder, my father added three feet to the weak salient. This kept them out; but their milk tasted turnipy for a week.

As a teen, it was Calvin's task to catch them for milking. "The white one was easy," he said, "but the grey one always ran away. You had to corner her in the angle between the fences. One time, trying to grab her, I bent my left ring finger back so far the joint snapped."

It was easier when their udders were full. Then they would bleat at the gate and, once in, trip-trap onto the bridge like the Billy Goats Gruff to wait their turn for milking.

Mom relished milking. Besides the health benefits, it was a link to her girlhood. In return for a crust of bread each, they gave her no trouble. When a shower of black buttons rattled across the floor she'd laugh and say, "Goat poop hardly smells at all, and it's so easy to sweep up."

Calvin would roll his eyes: "Those goats can do no wrong."

Her normal yield was two or three quarts. After scalding it in a pan on the stove for twenty minutes to pasteurize it, she'd save the wrinkled skin of cream for dessert topping. One less tin of "Nestlé's Pure Thick Cream" to buy. She never got enough cream to make cheese.

One fall the Toggenburg got in the family way. Somewhere Mom must have found her a suitable mate – or a suitable mate had found her. Next May she delivered two kids, a male and a female, both healthy, both pure white. By June they were exploring outside the barn door. By July they were frisking about the yard. They and I became close friends.

One day I hoisted them onto the low roof of our root cellar to see what they would do. They pranced over the black tarred surface with obvious delight. Then, since the eave was barely two feet above ground, I trained them to use my back for a ramp. All I had to do was bend over and call. They came running, one behind the other, sprang onto my back, and, one-two-buckle-my-shoe, vaulted onto the roof. This became a game. "At last," they seemed to be saying, "a decent hill!"

No harm in that – while they were small. All our roofs were tarred every year or two anyway, which built a thick, pliable layer. But in time their sharp little hooves left dents that would lead to leaks that could rot the roof and spoil our vegetables if not fixed.

So I devised other games. The kids' agility was amazing. Any surface big enough to bunch their hooves on, even six square inches on a pointy rock, was enough to balance on. The male would spring from one such perch to another, daring his sister to follow. In rocky Fogo I'd seen adult goats spring from ledges twenty feet up without mishap.

The game they both liked best was butting. It started when their horns were barely three inches long. Anything with some give to it – never a rock or a building or a tree – became a natural target. My feet, for instance. If I lay on my back, bent my knees and waggled my boots, they would sniff and nibble and try me with glancing blows. If I shoved, they'd pause to consider, then shove back.

A week later they started charging at me. If I parried the blow with equal force, they staggered and shook their horns with delight. "Hey, this guy's more fun than our mother!" From there they soon mastered the full-bored charge from a running start.

Whump!

By now Billy's horns were visibly thicker and longer than his sister's. Was my game helping them grow? And his body was bulking up. At the outset he could hardly budge me. Now it was all I could do to keep from being flipped. When I tried to discourage him with a solid hit, he'd eye me with a look that said, "So, you want to play rough?" Before long he was bowling me over. I had created a monster. And he was scarcely half-grown.

By September Billy's stocky horns curved over his ears and back like an impala's. By next spring they were sixteen inches long and jutted over his brow in a formidable ridge of corrugated keratin. If I grasped a horn in each hand to throw him it was all I could do to keep my footing. Had my body not been bulking up as well, he would have shaken me like a rag doll. At heart he was just a peaceful soul, but trouble loomed.

It came with his first rut. Sexual maturity changed his personality. He took to perfuming himself with urine. First he'd lower his head and extrude his long thin pink wet penis. Then, as my friends and I stared in mingled revulsion and admiration, he'd close his eyes and spray his face and forelegs, all the while shaking his head for better coverage.

By now we youngsters were no strangers to animal genitalia. We had watched a stallion's black rubbery thing telescope down and down to an unbelievable length and then retract itself. We had seen a bull mating. But Billy took the prize for outright, stinking, animal maleness. Soon, his pale yellow foreparts reeked like a city urinal. No doe within three miles downwind could possibly be unaware of him. Unfortunately, the only eligible females were his sister and his mother. His sister would have none of it. His mother was still lactating. That fall he took to wandering. Often he'd stay away for days. Then, just when we'd given him up for lost, he'd reappear, lonely as a unicorn, to slouch about the roads day and night.

I missed my old wrestling buddy. Would he ever be himself again? Yet part of me didn't want him back. It was too risky. At heart he was a gentle enough guy and with me he was still polite because he knew me and because I never hesitated to knuckle him if he got too surly.

When he started to shake his horns at passersby, we advised the neighbours to be careful. "He'll have to go, you know," my father said one day. "You've trained him not to respect people. You didn't know any better; but now he's dangerous. With those horns he could knock a child unconscious, or cripple an old person."

Late that fall, on a day when we were at school and before the ground froze, my father reluctantly took his rifle and a shovel, put a rope on Billy, led him to the woods and made away with him. It was too bad. That goat had good Saanen bloodlines, might have sired many fine milch goats. I couldn't blame my father. And I couldn't blame Billy. The fault was entirely mine.

Our sled dogs, though they had summers off, earned their keep too. "To work like a dog" was a standard expression among Newfoundlanders and Labradorians. When I was small, my father generally kept three to pull his winter komatik. All three were mongrels; nobody wanted a purebred. Mongrels had more stamina and smarts. The giant Newfoundland dog was an exception; but it was bred for water rescue and hauling firewood and fish, not for long-distance running.

Though our dogs were friendly and obedient, Dad kept them strictly chained all summer. Chained, because they'd soon chew through a rope. He knew that if let run free, the gentlest dogs will form packs and go on to kill sheep and hens. He also never let them in the house. Few people did in those days. The modern notion of letting a dog sleep on your bed would have scandalized them. Theirs were working dogs, not pets, and to treat them otherwise was to compromise their training and to confuse them.

It was different on the trail. More than once my trapper father, bedding down in a wigwam or tent before he owned a sleeping bag, would place a dog behind and before him to keep from freezing. And it was different with our goats. We milked them indoors for sanitary reasons. Such exceptions proved the rule.

It didn't mean that Calvin and I couldn't play with our dogs. We did so when we fed or watered them. That was how I became so close to Sprig, Dad's youngest on the team. A long-haired black-and-white retriever-spaniel hybrid, he was the nearest thing to a childhood pet I ever had. My brother in his time had known others, Gelert and Spot and Dad's faithful lead dog Jack. Jack had a sad ending. Retired and going blind, one day he was racing to greet his returning master and impaled himself on a fence rail and died at Dad's feet. All of our dogs knew, long before we did, when he was coming home.

Sprig and I became friends after I was promoted to spearing flatfish – young flounders – for the dogs' meals. Flounder was standard summer dog food in Gander Bay, just as table scraps, rabbit meat and dried caplin were winter staples. It was no trouble to launch a boat and stab a dozen with a hay prong, or to catch them off the wharf by gently lowering a baited net made of sacking. But you had to scald them before the dogs would touch them. After his meal I'd unhook Sprig and romp with him for a spell. It wasn't much exercise and it wasn't fair to his mates; but I didn't dare unchain them all.

When we left for St. John's in the spring of 1946, I went to say "so long" to him. It was awkward because my father, unsure if he'd ever trap again, had given the team away. Sprig went to his cousin Stanley Gillingham up the road. Saying goodbye in someone else's yard felt like a double betrayal. Sprig wagged his tail uncertainly. When I left he followed until his chain brought him up short.

The horse was another hard-working domestic. Some, like the Morgans and Clydesdales brought in from PEI to work the lumberwoods, were as big as bull moose and ate accordingly. Most were half that size, tough little Newfoundland horses in piebald colours. Like sled dogs, they had their summers off – except they could roam free. Their owners believed the savings in hay were worth the small risk of loss.

So all summer, in groups of half a dozen or so, these horses roamed the brook valleys, marshes and pond shores, cropping whatever grass they could find, whipping their tails against the flies, seeking open spaces for that reason. Come fall most of them would remember their cozy stalls and tasty oats and wander home. The rest were rounded up, a tedious task. Sometimes the searches would find one belly-deep in a marsh, half dead from thirst and hunger but otherwise all right. A teamster joked that the quickest way out was a hot potato under the animal's tail. Those alive and whole were rescued. Crippled horses, a rare thing in summer, were shot or poll-axed and left for the crows and the jays.

Our family never owned a horse. I never got to know them the way my cousin Frank did. By age ten he could harness King by himself, a feat I envied. Truth to tell, horses made me nervous, especially big ones. All except one dappled grey mare who did a beautiful thing for me. One winter afternoon, as she was leaving the mill with a sled-load of slabwood, she found her way blocked by my new Rocket Racer sled that I'd gotten for Christmas. I had thoughtlessly left it there while watching Uncle Harold make something in the forge.

When I came back out, here was this huge horse bearing down on my prize sled. The teamster couldn't see it and I cried out, "Please don't step on my sleigh!"

As if she understood me, the bay horse stopped, lowered her head, took the coaster in her teeth, lifted it high and set it aside. My heart was fit to burst. After that, I sometimes screwed up my courage and gave her a candy. It was the best treat I could think of. Her name was Gray.

I saw a workhorse shot once. She had broken her leg and couldn't work and the owner asked Dad to put her down. He chose my father because he was an excellent shot and the man knew she wouldn't suffer. We youngsters weren't supposed to see such executions. However, this one took place on Grandpa's beach at low tide – for a reason – and we got wind of it. Dad must have thought we were at school, but on our way there we sneaked down to watch.

The horse was standing half in the water. I saw my father take aim. Heard the rifle's *crack!* Saw the red hole appear between her eyes. Saw her legs buckle like rubber. Heard the splash. Then, before anyone noticed, we hurried off.

When the tide rose my father roped her floating body to his canoe and towed her to some island far down the bay for the cormorants and gulls to feast on.

Jack the eagle was a bit before my time. Dad had taken him from a nest in 1931 and brought him home to raise, whether on a dare or from curiosity I don't know. In those days birds of prey were shot on sight. Hawk or owl, it was all the same. Full-grown eagles were thought to carry off lambs and snatch babies. Jack was nearly full grown.

Perhaps my father merely wanted to debunk old wives' tales. Perhaps he thought: I've hand-fed this bird from a nestling, I've trained it to snatch a flatfish out of the air, day after day I've watched him soar away and come back to roost on Pop's barn roof, what danger could he be? Perhaps my father was looking forward to the day, a year or two hence, when his protégé would develop the snowy head and tail of the mature bald eagle.

It was not to be.

On a hot day soon after Mom and Dad came back from Away, while they were still living with his parents because the foxy house was being renovated, Mom dressed my brother, aged four, in short pants, halter and sun hat and let him out to play. Dad was somewhere working.

Jack, on his usual perch, eyed the interloper. No sooner was my mother in the house but she was running back out again. Jack must have spread his wings and dropped to the ground by the child. Calvin, feeling the gust against his legs, would have turned to look and seen a yellow-beaked raptor beside him, tall as himself, folding its yard-wide wings, regarding him with fierce golden eyes. A child's natural instinct is to touch. Perhaps he did, but the look in Jack's eyes made him start for the house. The eagle, walking and hopping, came after him. Calvin shrieked and ran faster. It was at that moment my mother heard the screams and came running. Through the screen door she saw, like a scene from some horror movie, her little Calvin, red-faced and terrified, trying to reach the latch. Jack was only a jump away when she swung wide the screen door, snatched up the child and slammed the inner door in his face. By nightfall Jack was no more.

BERRY-PICKIN'

When I was small, every grownup Newfoundlander who wasn't blind or halt went berry-picking, serious berry-picking, at least once a year. Like haying and potato-digging, it was a harvest, part of a complex survival strategy, and children were expected to pitch in.

They started you off with an "emper" or cup which you emptied into your parents' bucket. Then they gave you a covered one-pound lard pail. By age eight you were a veteran. Yet it wasn't all work. Like so many aspects of outport life, berry-picking was treated as a family outing, a chance to escape the fish flake, washtub and woodpile.

Before tackling the big three – bakeapples, blueberries and partridge-berries – children practised on nine or ten lesser berries: crackerberry (too mealy), crowberry (too medicinal), dewberries (too scarce) red and white currants (sour), mishberries (too small), chuckly pear (seedy), dogberries (bitter), teaberries (strange) and wild cherries (stony).

Of these minor fruits I liked teaberries best. Botanists called them

Gaultheria hispidula, a hairy little member of the heath family, a cousin to the partridgeberry, blueberry and bog cranberry. We called it "man-yan tea." It trailed over mossy carpets under evergreen woods; its egg-shaped, whitish berries were underneath. They looked unripe but tasted sweetly wintergreen, like the bottled oil we sometimes used for toothache.

Wondering why no one bothered with teaberries, I picked a cupful – it took forever – and patiently jammed the tiny fruit. The jam came out gluey white and tasted more medicinal than sweet. Adding sugar didn't help. I should have ignored the berries and steeped the leaves.

The only berries we actually shunned were baneberries – white and red – and "blue beads," also called yellow bead lily. All three are mildly poisonous. Six baneberries would craze you with cramps and vomiting. A handful of lovely blue beads could blister you for a week.

But you couldn't go by taste alone. My first taste of squashberry was a shock. Dad had picked a pailful at Bellmans Brook on his way downriver one August. "Try some," he said, casually mouthing a handful of the translucent, white-seeded berries. I tasted one – and made a wry face. "Some sour, eh? But my son, wait till you tastes the jelly! On toast…oh my!" Another tart and rare fruit he sometimes brought home was cranberries. Not the mountain type we called partridgeberry, but the big fat red and speckled yellow globes that grew on wet bogs far up the Northwest Gander in caribou country.

Every berry had its season: July for raspberries, July-August for bakeapples, August-September for blueberries, September-October for partridgeberries.

The place to look for raspberries, or brambles as Grandma called them, was in the woods around old cutovers. Small children seldom picked them; the prickles tormented them and they might get lost in the tall bushes. But once we reached age ten or so we might pick alone.

My first time picking alone was on Fogo Island. I'd gone in over the hills trouting with my older cousins Phyllis and Greta Hart. Our trail skirted the old Anglican cemetery and the girls wanted to investigate. We laid our trout poles against the fence and tried the rusty iron gate until it screeched open.

While Greta and Phyllis were hunting headstones, I discovered tons of raspberries so ripe they were falling off the canes. Since I had no emper, I began to stuff my mouth. Some time later I heard Phyllis call my name from outside the fence. "Where are you to?"

"In 'ere, pickin' raspberries! There's t'ousands!"

Suddenly Phyllis's freckled face loomed above the canes. "No, no, my son," she cried. "We's not supposed to pick berries in the *graveyard!*" She started wrestling me toward the gate.

"Why not?" I yelled, dragging my heels.

"'Cause there's dead people down there!"

Back at Aunt Fanny's she told on me. "Aunt Winnie, Gary was pickin' berries in the cemetery." I was in trouble.

Before Mom could answer, my aunt asked, "Didn't you notice all the humps and hollows?" Come to think of it, I had. "Those are graves!" she said.

"But I never walked on none," I said.

"Well, perhaps you never, but 'tis wrong all the same!"

My mother didn't always back her sister but that time she did. Of course she took a medical approach. "Those berries could make you sick. For all you know their roots reach clear down into them coffins."

"Then how come they tastes so good?" I said.

Uncle Jabe, smoking as usual on the couch by the window, studied his cigarette and winked at me through the blue haze. "Fanny," he said mildly, "you and me both knows the people in that cemetery. In their day they loved pickin' raspberries. I 'lows they was glad of Gary's company. Stuck off up there, nar visitor for months on end…"

It was no use. I had violated the dead. I felt outcast.

Our two best bakeapple picking places in the bay were Gander Bay Island and up to The Gut. The first was a two to three hours' steam out the bay, the second was on our doorstep. From afar the island looked like a battleship moored off. Up close it was a wild, high-cliffed place of windblown spruce and rolling peat bogs. Some years the bogs were golden with berries. Other years, if a late June frost nipped the flowers, there was nothing but leaves.

That was how it was the time we went with Uncle Harold and Aunt Kathleen. "A waste of gas," he said, after scouring the island in vain. But the sun was shining, the sky was blue, the black flies and nippers were gone. So we boiled salt beef and turnip greens and new potatoes and made a picnic of it.

Up to The Gut we generally fared better. The first time we went, I couldn't have been much over six. On the muddy trail up from the beach I kept falling on sharp rocks and getting tangled up in the alders. This slowed my family down and annoyed my parents because other families might grab the best spots.

There was room for all. People spread out until the high, dun-coloured bog was dotted with slow-moving groups wandering under the silvery sky, their voices blending with the cries of shore birds. Dad picked a leaf to show me what to look for. It was dark reddish green and crinkly and grew tight to the moss. "Find a patch of that and you'll soon see berries," he said. Pick the yellow and pink ones," he cautioned, "not the white ones. The pink ones we can ripen back 'ome."

I found a patch not far away, hunkered down, but soon moved on, looking for a place without nippers biting my ears and neck. Tramping over the spiky hummocks and quaggy hollows made me sweaty and thirsty, so I went for the ripe ones and ate them. Unlike raspberries, they were right juicy and burst in my mouth in little explosions of flavour. It was my first taste of cloudberry. Like baked apples without the cinnamon, I decided.

Blueberries were more dependable. A person could find ripe blueberries somewhere most years. Even the country around Gander Lake had good patches if you knew where to look. One fall, Dad brought home a shirtful.

"You picked them in your shirt?" said Mom, incredulous.

"'Twas all I had," he said, avoiding her eyes. The truth was, he'd been hunting caribou, got hungry and chanced upon a nice patch in open country. And while he was picking, he heard a gruff "Woof!" Cautiously parting the bushes, he saw a black bear with a half-grown cub. She was already on her hind legs sniffing the air – a bad sign. If she got his wind she might charge. He could not outrun her. There was nothing to do but shoot.

He stood up, aimed for the heart and fired.

As she collapsed, quarts of blueberries gushed from her mouth onto the moss. Too good to waste, he thought. Knotting his plaid shirt into a sack, he scooped them up hand over hand. He rinsed them in the river, donned a sweater from his pack and returned to camp. The last he saw of the cub, it was bounding over the barrens. You'll be okay, he thought to himself.

Mom bought his story and made the berries into pies and jam and no one was the worse for it. By the time she got the rights of it, we were heading for Charles Cove again to pick blueberries the proper way. That year its rocky ridges were fair blue with them, as if the sky had fallen.

Charles Cove was only a mile beyond Victoria Cove by boat. Whole families converged there briefly each September: babies, toddlers, grandparents and all. Like the ancient Israelites, they pitched their tents and fanned out for manna. There was some urgency to it. The blueberry season was short, a few weeks at most, less if frost struck early. A light frost sweetened the flavour but a hard one blackened the crop, making the fruit tasteless and watery.

Picking blueberries was easy enough for me. There were several types of plant, some taller, some shorter; but we made no distinction, ignoring only the tiny *hurts*, the ones our English ancestors called whortleberry. The sound of plump berries drumming on our bucket bottoms was like the music of nature's largesse. It was assurance of winter food, of jam and pies and maybe even wine.

My problem was distractions. We were scarcely six miles from home, yet already I yearned to explore. Here was this new landwash: who could say what one might find? Girl pickers ignored distractions. They seemed to rejoice in this grownup activity. Unlike us, they never strayed from patch to patch, never ate berries while picking. Unnatural. Even the youngest filled their lard pails faster than I. Time and again they came beaming back to pour their offerings, leaves and twigs and all, into their parents' pails. Their industry shamed us.

None the less, first chance we got, my boy cousins and I begged off. Roaming the wide sandy autumn beaches, we skipped rocks, dabbled in tidal pools, dug clams with sticks. We'd never seen sandpipers so plentiful and so tame. The tiny long-billed shorebirds were migrating, said Dad, gorging on the worms and amphipods they found by probing the soft silt. That explained why they all but ignored us. When we chased them they ran as if on tiny wheels, straight ahead, heads level. Only if we got too close would they fly, and then not far. They lifted off with rapid concave wing-beats as if still running, a seamless locomotion.

We mimicked shorebird calls. The auntsareys, large sandpipers with bright yellow legs and feet, were the loudest. The one Calvin called curlew, paler with an upturned beak, had a sad cry like its name. And there was a

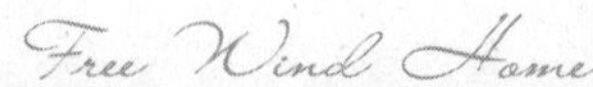

brownish bird called a willet that fed on bog berries. All were heading south, said Dad, as fat as they could be. So he and others always brought their shotguns along. One day Calvin shot an auntsarey and proudly brought it into camp for supper. It was tougher than duck but just as tasty. It was a treat after a hard day's tramp lugging heavy pails.

That year it only rained once the whole week. Soon every tent had several full pails parked in the shade. Toward the end we had so many Dad had to wrap several gallons in an old tablecloth Mom had brought. The harvest assured, people relaxed and mingled. Campfires twinkled in the starlit dusk; accordion music trembled on the frosty air. Old quarrels were mended and, as moonshine made the rounds, new ones incited. Trysts were contrived, pranks were played, lusts were consummated.

A big advantage of the partridgeberry was that it kept for months without being jammed. While other berries fermented and spoiled if not soon bottled, the tart partridgeberries would stay fresh all winter in just a keg of cold water. A great advantage before we had fridges and freezers.

Another advantage was the high Vitamin C content. Dr. Olds urged it on patients as a defence against colds and scurvy. Naturally my mother swore by it too. The jam took a lot of sugar, which some could ill afford. But for those who could, it was worth it.

Gander Bay was partridgeberry poor. Our climate was too tame. This plant needed wild winds and salt air and gull shit to prosper. Exposed headlands and barrens were its natural habitat. Charles Cove was suitable, Farewell Head and Indian Islands better, and Fogo was the best. Yet I don't recall ever picking there. I suspect we relied on Uncle Tom or Aunt Fanny to supply us in return for rabbits or the like.

Partridgeberry pickers sometimes paused to glean a few cups of a fruit they called "blackberry," which purists call crowberry. They picked it not to eat raw, nor to jam – though juicy, it tasted bland and metallic – but to substitute for raisins ("figs") in figgy duff or pudding. My mother, always on the lookout for natural iron sources because she suffered from pernicious anaemia, added them to her health food list. She knew they were rich in the mineral because, in the delicate phraseology of a columnist she had read, they "darkened one's stool." I could vouch for that. "Tasteless or no," she'd say, "'tis better than that awful blackstrap molasses!"

In the summer of 1947, Frank and I heard that Salt Island was overrun with gooseberries, not the small wild kind but the fat stripy garden type that bursts in your mouth. And because the island was only half a mile away, and boasted Gander Bay's oldest house plus a pioneer cemetery rumoured to hold a headless corpse, we decided to go there.

Gooseberries and history in one expedition.

Borrowing a canoe without permission early one windless afternoon, we took our pails and poled and paddled across. Our plan was to explore the house and cemetery, pick a ton of berries – outside the graveyard if possible – and be back before supper.

The tottering saltbox house was disappointing, though we found, underneath its peeling layers of wallpaper, some newspapers dating to the early 1800s. The graveyard wasn't much either, just a few stones smothered in hay. We decided to skip the history and just hunt gooseberries. It took us an hour to find a few bushes near the landwash. Some of the berries were big as marbles, tart and delicious. After eating all we wanted – no point in taking them home and having to explain where we got them – we explored some more.

This time we paid more heed to the gravestones. Two or three were large and smooth and finely graven. Our great-great-great grandfather Robert Gillingham was there, as well as his wife Frances and their son Robert Junior. William Hodder, a salmon fishing partner, was there too. And we found the headless man's stone.

That put us in mind of Grandma's story, how in the late 1700s, a time of relative peace between natives and whites here, some of Robert Sr.'s men were dipping salmon from their weir at tidewater when a canoe-load of Beothuk braves attacked. The fishermen, having for once left their muskets ashore, were soon overpowered. One of them was beheaded. The warriors paddled away holding their dripping trophy aloft, whooping.

After reading the inscription we found some excuse to leave.

Our expedition having gone faster than planned, we decided to visit Little Salt Island. A few hundred yards to the south, it was where some Clarkes Head people had taken refuge during the 1912 forest fire. Perhaps they'd left something valuable behind. Ten minutes later we beached the canoe. After we hauled the heavy boat up as far as we could, I laid the painter on a flat rock and rolled a heavy stone on top, but I forgot to knot the rope's end.

This exploration went even faster: tiny meadow, cliffy outcrop, landwash, tidal pools – that was it. And there were no gooseberries. All we found was mouse burrows. After probing with sticks and killing a couple of mice, we flopped on our backs on a dry hummock to rest.

Under the westering sun, the windless estuary was a field of burnished brass. Shading our eyes against the glare, we gazed at distant Point Head, at the wharf with our cove behind it, at the mill, at our homes and all the other houses strung like children's coloured blocks along the landwash. Starting with the mill, we identified the church, the school, Horwood Lumber Company's barn and store, Tibbys Point and, low on the northeast horizon, faint and blue, Gander Bay Island. We felt like explorers, or pirates resting from a raid. We had this island to ourselves. Treasure Island with no treasure.

The warmth made us drowsy and we dozed. Upon waking, we found the sun much lower and redder. Sitting up we saw the tide had risen. We stretched and rubbed our eyes and told each other it was time to go. We walked round to the boat. Where *was* our boat? Someone had taken our boat! But no, the rock I'd laid the rope on was still there – half under water. The rising water must have lifted the canoe and tugged it free.

We gazed wildly about. "Our boat is drove away…" we wailed to no one, "drifted clear out to Fogo Island for all we knows!" We sat down and clasped our heads and tried to think. Where could it be?

At length Frank said, "There she is!"

"Where?" I said, blinking back tears.

"Over there, my son…there agin' Harris Point." Now I saw it too, a flake of white lodged side-on by the shore. That was something. But we were still marooned. Too far from shore for anyone to hear us sing out. Perhaps too far for anyone to see us either. No grub or drinking water, no matches to light a signal fire. Worst of all, no one knew where we were to. We'd told no one our plans. We had been willful and stupid.

We shouted anyway. It made us feel better. We waved our arms, pulled off our shirts and waved them too, ran haphazardly about. After a while we put our shirts back on and sat down again, exhausted and disconsolate. Wrapping our arms around our knees, we stared at the distant canoe, so near and yet so far.

A breeze came cats-pawing in, fanning our hair, raising goose pimples on our bare arms. As if on cue, we turned our heads and gazed at our warm homes across the water, Frank at his grey one under the great fan-shaped Balm o' Gilead tree, me at my foxy one half hidden behind his father's mill. Never had they seemed so beautiful.

Then, turning back to the near shore, we saw a movement. It was low in the water, hard to make out at first. Yes, it was a boat, a rowboat, inching toward us! Slowly, rhythmically, we could see its twin oars lift, flash wetly in the sun and dip, flash and dip.

Our spirits revived. Then an awful thought intervened. What if our rescuers were Alex and Arthur Hodder, the two ancient bachelor brothers – we didn't know they were married men with children – who owned Salt Island, who were said to fall into violent rages if anyone trespassed on their land? What if they had seen us picking berries there, or worse, poking through the family cemetery? Might they horse-whip us? Leave us to die? Tell our parents?

The boat drew closer. It had a single rower, not two. Still, he might be one of the brothers. He certainly looked old. As the boat neared, we saw he wasn't ancient after all; it was just his long drooping mustache and slouch hat made him appear so. That must be why Grandma always called the brothers "The Mountaineers."

Our rescuing mountaineer shipped his oars and let the punt coast ashore. With his forehead in shadow and his whiskers highlighted by the raking orange light, suddenly he looked scarecrowish and sinister. Under the hat brim his keen eyes scrutinized our faces. He spat a brown streak of tobacco juice overboard and adjusted the quid in his cheek.

"Be 'e 'arold Saunders' b'ys?" His manner was gruff but not severe.

"This is Harold's son Frank and I'm Brett's," I stammered.

"I seed a canoe drove ashore," he said, jerking his head toward Harris Point, "and then I spotted 'e wi' the spyglass. Hard to see, lookin' inter the sun. Anyhow, clamber aboard. Yer folks'll be worriet."

Relief, joy, gratitude, contrition swept over us as Mr. Hodder wheeled the punt around, unshipped his oars and took us to our lost canoe. Once there, we thanked Alex or Arthur – he never said which one he was – and made for home. We got there in time for supper, dead on our feet but no questions asked.

Watching Work: Indoors

"They were trained and taught for their own little world, and what could be better?"

– KNUT HAMSUN, *Growth of the Soil*

My mother is sewing. I can hear her Singer singing downstairs. Its sound draws me like a magnet. Everything about the process – the nimble leap and tuck of her fingers on the fabric, the twinkling needle, the thread reeling off the spool – fascinates me. To me her Singer is an intricate toy she plays with, a toy which not only makes purposeful whirs and clicks and has many moving parts and secret compartments, but which magically creates things to wear: an apron, a blouse, a wedding dress.

Now her right hand disengages the small rubber-tired drive wheel, rotates the flywheel to raise the needle. She unclamps the fabric, reorients it, re-clamps it and resumes her sewing. This machine isn't a treadle model like Grandma Saunders' more expensive one. Instead it is hand-driven by a knob on the flywheel. That wheel engages a rubber-tired smaller wheel, which activates the internal machinery which drives the needle that makes the sounds I love.

This power to create, to transform unlikely stuff into things useful and even lovely, is one of the things I admire about my parents, about grownups in general. They turn a bolt of raw cloth into a beautiful dress. They turn soggy batter into delicious cakes, bits of lumber into a graceful *komatik*, a slab of slimy caribou hide into delicate snowshoe webbing. How they can see the finished article in the raw material, I cannot imagine.

For now, I content myself with watching and learning.

I especially like watching her sew because it makes her so happy. Not when a needle snaps, of course. "Oh!" she says, and reels off some all-purpose curse like "Helldamnshit!" (Like my father, she's never learned to swear properly. The most he ever says is "Hell's flames!") Or when she complains that the machine is too slow: "Oh!" she mutters, "A body needs three hands to run this thing!" But such tempests soon pass. And, being ambidextrous, when one hand tires of spinning the flywheel she can switch, so that the machine, antiquated that it may be, is still much faster than hand sewing.

When things go well, which they usually do, the worry lines around her eyes and forehead soften. It is the same soft look that comes with playing the organ. Then her dark brown eyes become focused and intent, her face relaxed.

One day, watching her sew, I asked on a whim if I could have her Singer when she died. She paused in mid-stitch, looked into my eyes and said, "Yes, my son, you can." But, as with so many things, I never followed up on the request.

The Singer's relative speed may be why local women bring her things to sew. But I think she is also a good seamstress. Anyhow, they arrive with yards of fabric and spread it on the couch and consult in quiet tones and drink tea and laugh. And when the garment is finished, they praise her and this makes her happiest of all. As it does me.

Almost as admirable in my eyes was the grownup power to fix things. My father was forever mending something: a broken plate, a split axe handle, a plugged carburetor, a leaky boat, a leaky kettle. Not that he was especially handy or that he loved tinkering – it just had to be done.

"I hear that kettle sputtering again," Mom would say.

"I'll take a look." He'd empty the kettle, remove the lid and hold the bottom to the light. "Winnie, you're right," he'd say, "there's a pinhole." I was hoping for a bigger hole, which would mean soldering, which would mean seeing the blowtorch's fierce jet of orange flame. The roar and flame scared me but he tamed it to a slender ice-blue cone with a twist of the knob. "Blue is your hottest flame," he'd explain.

That particular leak was too small for soldering. All he did was rummage in his toolbox for a Mendit, a store-bought gimmick that "fixes small holes in a jiffy." In five minutes he was tightening the tiny nut.

"Good as new," he said, grinning with satisfaction.

One time he fixed Mom's pedal organ. It was after our St. John's sojourn. She'd tried to play it and found several keys had gone mute. At first they thought it was dampness, but on removing the back panel Dad discovered mice had chewed off some wooden rods that worked the reeds. The rods, each a slightly different length, must be replaced – but what with? No one sold wooden dowels back then. A pencil was too thick, a twig too crooked.

"I know! A sucker stick! We needs some lollipops!" Removing the candies, he cut each rod to the proper length, replaced the damaged ones and let the glue set overnight. In the morning Mom had her music back. And I had a handful of stickless suckers.

Watching all this making and mending began long before we started school. In a sense it was our pre-school. Whatever else it did, it made us good observers. We learned to pay attention, to *attend.* Boys watched horses being shod, steamer freight being block-and-tackled from scow to wharf, gasoline being pumped, potatoes being dug, ice blocks being sawn from winter ponds and stowed in icehouses, trees being felled, dogs and horses being harnessed, goats being milked, parcels being wrapped, shoes being soled, hair being cut, toilets being dug out and limed, hens being beheaded, salmon being gutted, eiders being plucked, foxes being pelted, glass being cut.

By age sixteen a boy needed to know how to do many things: helve and hone an axe, saw and split wood, catch and cure salmon and cod, snare a rabbit and shoot a turr; how to pole and paddle a riverboat – to build one if need be – how to scythe hay, tar a roof, shoe a horse, get rid of a troublesome hornet's nest, build a winter tilt, manage a dog team, trail and trap various furbearers, stalk and kill and paunch a caribou.

Girls, by the same accident of gender, watched and learned a different repertoire of tasks: cooking and baking, cleaning, carding and spinning wool, knitting "garnseys" and finger mitts, hooking rugs and mats, ironing, mending. How to pull a splinter or a tooth, make a bread poultice, tend a baby or a sibling, turn a bedridden grandparent. How, God forbid, to wash and dress a corpse.

A world of work and worry awaited us, but we wore the knowledge lightly. We knew the meaning of "Go to the ant, thou sluggard," but didn't take it too seriously. We knew what the Little Red Hen in the nursery story meant when she refused bread to those who were too lazy to help her bake it when she asked. Those who were able to work and didn't should not expect to eat. We also knew that for a while we were exempt. Our elders' motto was, "Let the youngsters play – they'll be slavin' soon enough. All in God's good time."

That was why they hid their worst sorrows from us. We imagined them to be enjoying themselves, as indeed they sometimes were. We saw their work as a kind of adult play. And the wisest of them saw our childsplay as a kind of work.

Not that we lacked chores. Watch anything too long and you'd hear:

"Enough gawkin' now; haven't you got sums to do?"

"Go 'elp your brother fill the woodbox."

"Go check the henhouse; I needs two eggs for a cake."

My favourite chore was running errands. One day I was sent to buy a smoked salmon, something new for me. Only two or three local men knew this art, one of whom was Levi Harbin who lived down the shore. After a long walk I rapped to his door. An older man wearing bib overalls answered. I stated my errand. He nodded for me to follow. His clothing smelled nicely of smoke and oil. His smokehouse was a makeshift wigwam near the landwash, wreathed in blue haze like a Viewmaster volcano. He lifted the sail-canvas flap and motioned me inside.

Everything was in shades of brown, like an old photograph. A fire of alder wood and turf smouldered in the middle but gave no light. The only light came from a smoke hole overhead. As my eyes adjusted, I could see the sloping walls were hung with salmon triangles of various sizes and various colours depending on their stage of cure, all glistening with oil. Each was split down the back, not the belly, and each hung head-up and flat in a lightweight wooden frame like a wire toaster for easy turning.

Crucified salmon oozing sweet oil.

Mr. Harbin was already turning his precious fish. He told me that a salmon cured unequally, or taken from the frame too soon, would fall apart in his hands. "How long do it take?" I asked. Up to two weeks, he said. Then, selecting one the colour of shoe leather, he removed the rack and cut me a piece to chew while he wrapped my purchase in brown paper. It tasted smoky sweet, raw yet cooked. Walking home, I had great trouble not to eat the rest.

Another time, Dad sent me to buy a woods kettle, what some called a *quick*, from tin-smith Reuben LeDrew of Wings Point. Expecting to pay for my purchase and go, I watched in wonder as Mr. LeDrew laid out odd-shaped pieces of tin on his work bench: a big circle, a small circle and two or three other pieces, Using a wheeled crimper and a soldering iron, he deftly assembled the puzzle. The pieces became bottom, sides, spout, lid and handle. In fifteen minutes I proudly walked home with a bright new kettle.

In Fogo as a young boy I watched wooden barrels being made. The cooper was Mom's younger brother Tom. Uncle Tom had taken over his father's shop when Grandpa Layman retired in the 1940s. Though six years younger than she, he was already stooped from years of bending. Yet he worked with the steadfast purpose of a surgeon.

I recall his stacking flat fir staves outside – or was it inside? – a heavy metal frame, then winching them bar-tight with a coil of stout rope until the wood groaned, then making a little fire inside the staves to steam them into shape. Before the smoke found its slow way up the flume my eyes were watering. Uncle Tom had a permanent squint.

He loved coopering though. He'd learned it from my grandfather Henry (some called him Harry Sr.), who had learned it from his father Thomas William, who had learned it from *his* father in the south of England.

Not every Layman male loved coopering. Uncle Tom's brother Harry, two years younger, hated everything about it: the choking smoke, the back-breaking labour, the temperature extremes. He said the cooper shop could go from tropic heat when barrels were being fired to arctic cold when icy stock was brought inside to thaw. The splintery wood tore his mitts and froze his fingers.

So, as soon as he could, Uncle Harry fled the cooper shop to take up a more delicate and dexterous trade, my mother's trade, telegraphy. He apprenticed himself to Fogo's Postmaster Bannister, who taught him Morse and International code and helped him get his government certification. Yet decades later he could still recite the cooper's terminology and tools: butt, firkin, barrel, keg, croze, brace, bevel, cresset, bun.

Fogo's star blacksmith was Lemuel Anthony. The moment Phyllis' younger brother Aubrey mentioned the smithy, I hankered to go. "Lem's door is always open summertime," said Aub, who took me there. Inside we found a place of lurid light and hellish clanking. The very air smelled of fire. Mr. Anthony stood there in a leather apron the colour of iron, his eyes shaded by round goggles. One upraised callused hand held a sledge hammer, the other grasped a pair of tongs holding a white-hot iron rod against the waist-high anvil. Down came the hammer, once, twice, three times. He was doing something with an iron ring in the end of a shank – but what? As the pounded metal faded from white-hot to carrot-red, he flipped it and delivered three more quick blows. Then he plunged the other end, the cooler end, into the live coals.

Only then did he turn toward us, raise his goggles and nod a greeting. "Stand back now, lads; we don't want any sparks in your hair!" As he went to work on the shaft's other end, I saw that he was making a grapnel, a small anchor. It was intricate work. One moment he was heating five thin rods, then he was beveling their ends, then he was pounding the other ends into gracefully curved hooks; finally he was fastening the reheated hooks to the reheated shaft and securing them with a sliding iron collar.

I saw that he was always working against the metal's cooling, its hardening. Against time. And he had to keep his fire hot. Every so often, he'd reach over and pump the bellows to brighten the coals with fresh air. When he finally quenched the grapnel in the tub of water by the door, its sudden "*Pfftt!*" made me jump. It made me jump in Uncle Harold's forge too.

I never did see Lem's shop in other seasons. But my mother-to-be and her siblings did. Every student at St. Andrew's School in Riverhead did. The school stood west of the smithy, just beyond the Canal. Going and coming, they trudged by it from September to June, They saw Lemuel make all sorts of things: boat hooks, bobsled runners, gate bolts, latches, and, most amazing of all, horseshoes complete with nail holes and pointed *starts* to keep a pony from falling on the ice. They would even have seen him shoe the horse, hoof in hand, while its owner waited.

Children went to Lem's as much for the banter as the fireworks. The man was well-travelled and well-read. Before succeeding his blacksmith father Abe in 1932, he'd lived and worked in New York for nine years. He knew his scripture too. For years he'd been lay reader in the local United Church. And when he felt they needed it, Lem preached to the children too.

"Run along now," he said to Aub and me, "your mothers will be wonderin' where you be." We thanked him and skedaddled.

Like most older boys, I had watched enough housework to know how it was done – and would have been content to leave it at that. My often ailing mother had other ideas. Saturday mornings regularly found me mopping floors. Calvin had been luckier. In his time she generally had a servant girl. Not that I minded much. It was more the embarrassment of having my friends see me at it, the frustration of planning an expedition and having them leave without me, snickering about "girls' work." Girls' work it may have been; but I found it damned hard on my back and harder on my knees.

Monday was wash day, a day of steamy windows and the lemony smell of Sunlight soap. For some reason, perhaps because with Calvin away working and because I now fetched all the water, I was spared the scrubbing board. Washday took gallons of hot water. So this nimble-fingered telegrapher and organist scrubbed her knuckles raw, grinding dirty socks on the corrugated glass board, wringing heavy woollens and towels until her slender wrists were aflame, filling the clothesline with fathoms of wash. She might as well have been making fish in Fogo. "How does Kathleen do it at all, at all?" she marvelled. "Kathleen has five times my wash to do. But then she has Susie and the twins to help…"

Even so, my only Monday input was to lug extra heavy hampers to the clothesline and back. It wasn't all toilsome for me. Sometimes in bitter weather I brought the clothing in off the line stiff as boards. We'd stack it round the stove to thaw – a weird tableau. In fifteen minutes we'd come back to find the garments dancing – or something. In the sudden heat they had relaxed, nodding to each other, caressing each other, bending in slow motion as if dancing a minuet or collapsing over a terrific joke. But washday was no joke for a woman.

Cooking I admired as a toddler. It was messy and it smelled nice. I liked the runny eggs, the coils of molasses and butter and flour, the clots of bubbling, yeasty barm oozing into bread dough. I savoured the fragrances of cinnamon and ginger and pestered Mom to let me into their alluring chemistry.

She seldom would. I don't know why. She would let me lick the spoons or clean the bowl; that was all. No, she was too busy. No, she couldn't afford to waste costly ingredients. It was true I was unreliable, easily distracted. Perhaps she thought cooking too girlish, that Dad would disapprove. Maybe she simply enjoyed it too much to share. Perhaps all of these.

One summer day, frustrated with her refusals, I snitched some matches, snitched an egg from the hen coop, got an empty bean can and headed for a secret spot in back of Grandpa's meadow. Cradling my precious egg, I dodged out our back gate, climbed the stile and crossed the meadow. Soon I had a small fire of alder twigs crackling under my makeshift pot of brook water.

How long did an egg take to cook? I had no idea. Not too long, I thought, or they would miss me and come looking. So there we sat, the egg and I. Gradually a flock of little tiny bubbles gathered on its brown shell. Slowly the bubbles grew. The egg twitched once, twice. By the time the water started to boil, it was fairly dancing and so was I.

It came out tough and rubbery. What odds? Sitting in my dappled hideout eating hard-boiled egg with grubby fingers, I could not have felt prouder had I cooked Muscovy duck with sherry. All it lacked was a pinch of salt.

I often watched my mother trimming and refilling our oil lamps. It was her weekly chore because she did it best. Trimming looked easy enough – a few snips with scissors – yet few could do it well. Snip too much and you wasted good wick; snip too little and your flame came out raggedy. Cut them crooked and your chimneys sooted up. The secret, Mom said, was sharp scissors and a sharp eye. After cleaning the glass globes with a crumpled page of *Family Herald*, she'd refill the basin with kerosene, wipe it clean and set the lamp back on high. Her reward was a perfect flame in a sparkling chimney.

Fixing footwear was a crucial male skill. "My shoes need *tapping* again," Mom would say when Dad got home from his latest river trip. "The soles are thin as paper; I can feel every pebble underfoot." For shoe work he kept on hand a slab of pinkish cowhide bought at the shop. He'd fetch his ball-peen hammer, his sharp cobbler's tacks and his cobbler's *last.* This was a free-standing, upside-down iron ankle slotted to take metal feet of different sizes. He had three: baby, child and adult.

First he'd remove the insole and trace the outline of the shoe on the new leather. Then he'd cut a new piece to fit. Slipping one of her shoes over the adult template, he'd strip off the worn sole and hammer the new one on. Each tack would be carefully pounded flat – he called it *clinting* – against the metal below with precise blows of the hammer's round head. Feeling inside the shoe with practiced fingers, he'd make sure each point was declawed and safe. Then the inner sole was replaced to cover any rough spots.

A little paring around the edges, a little more hammering and the job was complete. "Good as new," he'd say. "Once you walk the stiffness out."

Compared to cobbling, fixing rubber boots was so simple anyone could do it. For waders you bought patches and stuck them on with rubber cement after cleaning and scuffing the leaky part. Worn-out rubber soles were fixed by smearing on a tinned paste and letting it cure overnight. Both operations left a lingering odour of acetone or something, not unpleasant at a distance.

Logans – leather lace-up boots with rubber bottoms – were another cobbling challenge. To punch and thread the holes Dad used an awl, a curved and flattened steel needle with a wooden handle. Afterward he threaded waxed linen or *tacker* through each hole, down and up, up and down, snugging it carefully until the gap was closed. A coat of waterproofing dubbin or mink oil and the logan was again tight.

Good as new.

As a trapper's son I saw a lot of wild furs pass through our home. Put me in a dark closet with pelts of fox, lynx, weasel, otter and muskrat and I could have named them all by feel and touch and smell. Such furs were true wealth in the post-Depression years. Not only that, they freed my proud young father from two unpleasant choices: clerking under his father, or toiling for starvation wages in some remote, bedbug-ridden lumber camp with only Christmas off.

Trapping, he was his own boss. It let him keep his dignity. The fresh air and long treks and plain food made him healthy. "You never catch a cold in the woods," he always said. Besides, it was a family tradition. His Gillingham ancestors had been furriers since the early 1800s if not before. Uncle Stan had taught him the ropes at seventeen. Together they had worked the family traplines until 1924, the spring Stanley drowned. And trapping let him get home at least once a month.

These homecomings were always exciting for me. For one thing, he often brought me a paper bag of spruce frankgum to chew. This made up for the sandpaper roughness of his three-week beard, and the scary way he sometimes tossed me overhead and caught me. For another, he would proudly display his catch, his furs, which he'd prepared in camp during long nights alone.

Well-cured, lustrous pelts were things of beauty to us then, as well as money for groceries. Seeing them, I wanted to be a trapper *and* a fighter pilot. But first I must learn how to pelt the animals.

Each homecoming entailed some skinning. The animals would have been caught the night before or en route and brought back whole and usually frozen. The woodshed being then too cold for such bare-handed work – you didn't wear mitts or even gloves – he had to do them in the house. But Mom wouldn't hear of it downstairs, so he used the attic – my (later) bedroom, in fact.

I used to lie in bed and watch. Sometimes, if the oil lamp was not enough, I held the flashlight for him. Without really trying, I was learning animal anatomy.

For small animals like weasels and muskrats he'd work on his knees; for larger ones he might get down on the floor. The work wasn't messy, for the animals weren't being gutted. Still, he always spread newspapers.

After honing his knife and thumbing the edge – too dull and it wouldn't cut, too sharp and it might slice the precious pelt – he'd begin. His method varied little from species to species. It was something like peeling off a tight wet sock. Holding the animal belly up and starting at the rear, he'd cut from paw to the vent on either side and out along the tail's underside to the tip. Then, with surgical finesse, in tiny strokes, he'd cut and peel, cut and peel, pulling downward all the while, freeing ankles and elbows and belly and head.

Ten or fifteen minutes later, he'd have the inside-out skin entirely off, hanging limp from one hand. And on his knees lay the pearly pink and beautifully muscled body, stiff and naked, remarkably human. Save for the faint effluvia of fox urine or weasel musk, the whole exercise was as bloodless as peeling a turnip.

Compared to that, skinning a rabbit was simple. I could do it by age ten. You hardly needed a knife. A rabbit skin peels away like long underwear. All it takes is a strong arm and a fairly good stomach. There is some blood from the liver, heart and *lights* (as Dad called the lungs); and there is some smell from the intestines, especially if the rabbit isn't fresh-caught.

"Don't worry," Dad grinned, "I guarantee your appetite will come back when Mom bakes this in a pie with pepper and salt and onions and a nice pastry on top." And so it did.

I saved my first two pelts to make mitts out of. They fit fine and were wonderfully soft. However, the untanned hide became brittle and soon fell apart. Yet I understood that Beothuk mothers made baby sleepers from rabbit fur. "Yes, but they first softened the skins by rubbing them with birds' brains," said my father.

One spring he let me skin, stretch and dry a muskrat pelt by myself. And he graded me on the result. We did the stretching on a pair of thin softwood slats laid edge to edge with a long narrow spreader wedge to tighten the hide. After securing the tail end with tacks he made me scrape off every shred of fat with a blunt knife.

After a week's drying and further scraping, I removed the stretcher. There was one nick but he advised me not to sew it; a good fur buyer would spot it and dock me anyway. "Better to have none in the first place." Finally, I reversed the pelt and combed it. He examined my handiwork. First he shook the skin. It rattled like paper. "Nice and dry," he murmured. Then he felt inside for grease, gently smoothed the guard hairs, checked the ear and eye holes.

"Not bad," he said. "Not bad at all. Fifty cents from the Hudson's Bay Company for sure." My dad was a fur buyer; it was one of his sidelines, so he should know.

I rushed downstairs to show my mother. "'Tis nice," she allowed. "Another hundred and we'll have enough for a fur coat." She sighed. "I wish your father wouldn't put ideas in your head. One trapper, one riverman in the family is enough. I wants you to grow up and have a nice clean office job…"

Muskrat meat was good, sweet and not at all musky. Broiled, it tasted like duck. We ate it every spring. It took two or three to make a meal, but after eating salt beef and venison all winter it was a nice change. "Winnie," Dad would say, sucking on a leg bone, "remember 'ow in fancy New York restaurants they called it 'marsh hare'?"

"Yes," she said, "but don't expect me to eat any!"

"More for us," he'd laugh.

Anyone training to go furring had to know how to make and repair his own snowshoes, or *racquets* as we called them, copying the local Mi'kmaq French term, I suppose. Making them took forethought and skill. Forethought, because your frame wood and hide had to be prepared well beforehand. Skill, because everything had to come together properly or they wouldn't be very satisfactory.

Our best snowshoe wood was white birch. It was strong and flexible and easy to steam into shape. Our best filling material was caribou hide. Moose hide was stronger but soaked up water and stretched badly unless coated with alum. Dad always used caribou.

To make the frames, he steamed and softened two sawn-out, six-foot frames in a boiler tube from the abandoned steam mill up the road. This was done by filling the three-inch diameter tube a third full of water, propping the closed end in an open fire, bringing the water to a boil and inserting the wood.

An hour or so later he'd remove the strips, now limp and soggy. He then bent each around a teardrop-shaped pattern outlined in nails on an old door. This was our standard pattern. After fastening the tail ends with copper rivets, which never rust, he mortised thin two-inch-wide birch slats fore and aft to prevent twisting and to hold the harness. Finally, using a gimlet, he drilled holes an inch apart around the entire frame, including the cross-bars. These were for the webbing.

The finished frame lay flat – no upturned toe. That was also standard. I wondered why. In the *Family Herald* they always had upturned toes. "That's for flat country and loose snow," he said. "I used them in northern Ontario, but here, with our heavy snow and icy conditions, a flat toe grips better, especially when climbing." So there.

To prepare the webbing, the first step was tanning – removing the hair. Some soaked the hide for weeks in cold water, then shaved it with a keen knife. Others buried it in fresh manure for a few months. Either way, it was a messy business. My father mostly soaked his. The skin came out deathly white, slimy as a dead fish.

The filling process – he called it lacing – was a three-way dance of hands and fingers from top to bottom and from side to side, like a spider spinning a three-cornered web. When the middle was done he filled the nose and tail with finer webbing made from caribou sinew.

So tedious and painstaking was the process that I always lost interest before he finished, wandering off in mind or body or both. A lapse which I, as a father of snowshoeing children in later years, was to regret.

He admitted it was boring. The best way to learn, he said, was to unlace an old pair. I never even did that, but then I never had to. My mother had no use for any of it and neither did my world. I was apprenticed to the wrong century.

Watching Work: Outdoors

"My son, run down the road and see if Uncle John is in from 'is net. I needs a salmon for supper."

I race to Grandpa's shop to get a clear view. Uncle John has just shoved off to row out to the pound to check his net. He moves with the stiffness of his eighty years, yet wastes no energy. He doesn't even turn his tar-blackened punt around. Instead he rows stern-first, standing amidships, facing where he's going.

Uncle John is actually my father's step-uncle, born to his father William's first wife. I imagine his eyes, squinting into the morning glare under the brim of his old felt hat. His elbows move in wide slow arcs like those of a saddleback gull in leisurely flight. As the boat glides along, he pauses now and then, like a gardener weeding, to pluck a hank of eel-grass or a bit of flotsam from the meshes of the leader, the long net, slung on poles, that serves to lead the salmon into the deadly pound.

I report back to my mother. She presses a large silver coin into my palm. "Mind you don't lose this!" she shouts as I pocket it and go. "'Tis all I've got."

I open the gate and dodge back down the road to my lookout. No need to rush now. I finger the coin as I pass the candy bottle in Grandpa's front window. Fifty cents would buy a lot of pleasure. I feel the disc's rough edge and its raised inscriptions. My brother, who knows almost everything, says the words are Latin for "George VI, by the grace of God, King & Emperor of India." Temptation and responsibility war within me. This must be how King George feels, I think. I remove myself from the temptation.

Watching the punt's slow progress, I try to imagine Uncle John's thoughts. Perhaps he thinks of his father William, who fished salmon here before him. Helping William as a boy and young man, he must have learned much about this handsome silvery fish. How each year those ready to breed left their Labrador and Greenland winter feeding grounds to feel their way by taste and smell back to the very rivers where they had been born five or more years ago. How the sleek Gander River fish, weaving their way south through Notre Dame Bay's filigree of islands, veered toward the Gander's distinctive sweetness until they felt the thrust of its current. How they lunged up the estuary, trimming both shores where the going was easier, eager to reach the first riffles where overnight they could shed the black sea lice that clung and sucked.

Young John would also have learned how his father, divining the best place to intercept the fish on our side, had run his first net out from Point Head where he lived, just as others had from Burnt Point and other juts of land. How the next generation had found their own salmon berths where they could, the best sites, including Salt Island, having been already taken. How the homing fish, sensing the turbulence from John's fence of poles, the whisper of his wall of linnet, had wheeled offshore along the leader in fright, lunging for deeper water and freedom. How the younger salmon, failing to bank away in time, had charged straight through the pound's slit door to die.

No salmon young or old could be blamed for not seeing the old man's cunning meshes. Every spring he steeped them dark brown in a tea made from peeled spruce bark and ripe cones. Other fishers did the same. "Barking the linnet," they called it. "Keeps out rot and makes un 'ard to see." It was a process I relished; it meant a bonfire on the beach. It meant a great black cauldron chained under a timber tripod. It meant men sloshing buckets of brook water, tossing in the fifty-yard net, feeding the fire. It meant hours of

Clarkes Head in late 1940s or early 1950s, showing, left to right: Christ (C of E) Church, my elementary school, Horwood Lumber Company horse barn, HLC store. Pine tree marks site of pioneer Bursey gravesite on Burnt Point (Author's Collection).

Little Harbour, Fogo, with cousin Greta's daughter Bernice and salt cod, 1961 (Author's Collection).

Jabez (Uncle Jabe) and Frances (Aunt Fanny) Hart, 1980s *(Author's Collection).*

Billy was a handsome fellow *(Screened facsimile).*

Little Harbour, Fogo, late 1940s (Author's Collection).

Little Harbour, Fogo, 1980s (Author's Collection).

View from our west gable window: Uncle Harold's and Aunt Kathleen's home, Balm o' Gilead Tree, the cove, Point Head wharf. Salt Island and river mouth beyond, c. 1951 (Author's Collection).

My paternal grandparents Frank and Mary Saunders, c. 1959 (Author's Collection).

Me, at 3, with Dad and Spot and komatik (Author's Collection).

"Gray," me, Mom and Calvin, c. 1940 (Author's Collection).

Dad, at 38, posing in a winter trapline wigwam on the North West Gander (Author's Collection).

Grandpa Saunders in Willy John's prototype Gander Bay boat, c. 1930 (Author's Collection).

My father with salmon angler, Gander River, late 1940s (Author's Collection).

Trouting in Clarkes Brook at high tide (Author's Collection).

The shop from Grandma's garden, early 1950s, with Patsy Saunders, Uncle Aubrey's and Aunt Mamie's eldest daughter (Author's Collection).

The Saunders wharf and scow, 1950 (Author's Collection).

Paternal grandparents' house, Clarkes Head, Gander Bay, c. 1959 *(Author's Collection).*

Uncle Harold's mill, 1950s *(Courtesy Zena Gillingham).*

My Lewisporte school eleven years later (expanded) (Author's Collection).

Fox Moth which had mishap in Clarkes Head (Courtesy Edgar Baird).

Salt Island headstone of William Hodder, fishing partner to my great-great-great grandfather Robert Gillingham Sr., original settler (Author's Collection).

Henry Eldred Layman, my maternal grandfather, is second from the right in this group of Fogo men engaged in the coopering trade. (From A History of Town of Fogo Newfoundland 1728-1992*; Courtesy Patrick Pickett, Ed.).*

My father Brett guiding on his beloved Gander River (Third Pond Bar), August 1949 (Author's Collection).

My late cousin Aubrey Hart at about age 10, when I knew him best (Courtesy Phyllis (Hart) Newell).

Aunt Beatty, Mom's younger sister, and husband George, Christmas 1948 (Courtesy Beatrix (Layman) Brown).

Aunt Kathleen and Uncle Harold Saunders, c. 1955 (Courtesy Dan Brake).

Mom's younger brother Harry, postmaster at St. Brendan's, Bonavista Bay, during WWII, with his first child Winnie, named for my mother (Courtesy Winnie (Layman) Garibay).

Aunt Beatty fly-fishing at Buchans, Newfoundland, 1944 (Courtesy Beatrix (Layman) Brown).

Calvin's river boat at rest near Grandpa's wharf in Clarkes Head, Gander Bay, mid-1980s; now at Canadian Canoe Museum, Peterborough, Ontario (Author's Collection).

poking and turning the linnet with sticks until they were done. It meant onlookers, yarning, a festival of sorts. The whole thing smelled like tea. Uncle John's High Tea.

At such a time no one paid much heed to dogs and youngsters. My friends and I darted about, circled the crackling fire and steaming pot, got in the way. Uncle John and his son Dolf waved us back, reminding us that bark pots could scald careless children to death. To mollify them we'd collect driftwood for the fire until we wore them down.

The punt is over halfway now. Perhaps the old man isn't thinking salmon at all. He's done this for so many times, so many seasons, in all weathers, at all hours ("Time and tide wait for no man.") that he can do it in his sleep. As for me, I feel chilly now the sun has moved around the corner of the shop. Chilly and a little bored. Absently I finger the coin.

"Le's go sit in the sun on that rock and watch," says a voice behind me. It's my friend Everett.

When we're comfortable I say, "Look what I got," and fish out King George. "I got to buy a salmon when 'e comes in." He fingers it a bit too long so I slip it back in my pocket. We go back to watching. We are like two gulls on a rock.

Our salmon fisher seems to be growing taller as he nears the pound. It's because the poles beside him are marching into deeper water. For the last few yards he rests his oars and lets the punt glide. Leaning over the gunnel, he peers intently down. Everett and I trade glances. Does the old man see gleams of silver in his diamond stitches? He should, for this is where the midnight travellers always meet their end. Here they lash their powerful tails in silence as the sharp twine shreds their scarlet gills, clouding the moonlit water with blood, drowning them in agonies of suffocation.

"Look, my son, 'e's reachin' down!" says Everett. And his arm comes up wet and flashing silver. "Now 'e's gonna use the gaff." Two, three, six times Uncle John thrusts deep, each time flipping a salmon in over the gunnel. Minutes later he's rowing ashore, bow-first this time.

For once our tongues are tied. The perfection of his ancient art, the beauty of his stately progress, makes our talk seem cheap. In France this morning, armed nations grapple to the death amid smoking peach and almond orchards. Here in sleepy Clarkes Head, one old man who never smelled a war is bringing in his catch of salmon to feed his family and supply his neighbours.

And it wasn't easy done. It was hard knitting all those fathoms of linnet in his chilly twine loft all last winter. It was hard felling and rinding and sharpening thirty new spruce poles a year ago. It was hard pounding them into the mud with a homemade birch maul while balancing on the punt's thwarts at high tide, filling the cove with wooden echoes. It was hard stringing fifty fathoms of heavy net at low tide with the spring sun beating down.

We rise and scamper down the shore to meet the old salmon fisher. We do so often when school is out. Sometimes he nets two dozen fish on a single tide. Come fall, he might take some to Levi Harbin to smoke for his family, but most of it is either sold fresh or pickled for winter as great-grandfather Robert Sr. and William Hodder used to do over to Salt Island.

Under our admiring gaze, rowing a boat he built before we were born, he comes. Past the nearby brook, past the church, dedicated in 1910, where his children were baptised and where he sits on Sundays and hears the word preached and finds no fault in it. Coming steadily closer, he puts us in mind of Sunday School stories of old Zebedee and his grownup sons James and John, fishing on the Sea of Galilee and soon to become fishers of men.

In simple trust like theirs who heard
Beside the Syrian sea
The gracious calling of the Lord,
Let us, like them, without a word
Rise up and follow thee.

As his keel grates on the beach, we crowd close and crane our necks. Zebedee nods to us, ships his oars and swings a long leg over the side. Salmon scales sparkle on his fingers, on his rubber boots. He lets us help him haul the punt up, deftly looping the painter round a rusty grapnel he keeps on the landwash for that purpose. He hoists several fish out by the gills, slips a short-handled dipnet under them, shoulders the net and goes toiling up the bank and across the road and past his house to the splitting table by Clarkes Brook.

God may provide the fish but Uncle John still has to clean them.

He is already tying his yellow oilskin apron on when we arrive. On the table lies a narrow knife and a grey whetstone hollowed by long use. The table is dark with the dried fish blood. He dips a bucket in the brook and sloshes water across it, scraping as he goes. The first few salmon lie in a wooden half-barrel with rope handles. They're what we call grilse, smallish fish from early in the season, not lunkers like the ones that come in late July. Before going back for more, he turns to us and smiles.

"Now, me zuns, wat can I do fer 'e?" All the Gillingham men are tall; Everett and I are part-Gillingham and already tall for our age. His teeth, yellow from chewing tobacco, are nearly all gone. He speaks with the sing-song dialect of his Dorset ancestors; the dialect of Thomas Hardy. He and his generation say *var* for fir, *athwart* for across, *duckish* for dusk, *doman* for woman, *mish* for marsh, *emmet* for ant. The words are oddly comforting, like news from a far country. But our parents rarely speak them purely any more, and we youngsters even less so. All we retain is the accent, the cadence.

"Mommy sent me to buy a small salmon, sir." I flash my Newfoundland 50-cent piece.

"Oh aye," says he. "I 'lows this five-pounder will do." He slaps it sideways onto the table and proceeds to pick flat black things from its flanks. "Sea lice," he grunts, squashing them into the wood. He takes the knife and whets the blade, two strokes this way, two strokes that. After scaling the fish's flanks, he deftly slits the snow-white belly from vent to gills, slashes the snowy throat. Fish fragrance wafts over us like the smell of fresh-cut grass. He scoops out the guts, flings them into the brook behind. "Fer the eels," he says. "They comes out after dark for the pips."

His dancing knife has already scooped out the air bladder with its curdled dark blood before I notice the thing he so gently lays in my palm. I open my fingers a crack. It is a pale pink pulsing thing no bigger than a bean. It is the salmon's heart, still beating. My own heart leaps. Uncle John chuckles.

Mom's salmon washed and ready, he lifts it by the gills. I give silver coin for silver fish and brace myself against its slippery weight. To drop and soil the fish now would disgrace me. I hesitate for fear of the tiny gill rakers and indicate the tail instead. That is how my father always carries a salmon. The fisherman nods. I place the heart in my left hand for safe-keeping and wrap my middle and index fingers round the small of the tail and clamp my thumb firmly behind. Everett offers to help but I shake my head firmly.

Holding it so, frowning with concentration, I parade up the road, past Grandpa's shop, past the ice-house and wharf, past the meadow and in to our gate, which my friend opens for me. My fingers blaze with pain, my arm is falling off; but I don't care. All I want to do is show my mother the beating heart.

A heart out of a fish out of water is twice doomed. Exactly when its pulsing ceased I do not know. All I know is that when I open my hand, the beautiful thing lies still as a stone. For a short time, maybe an hour, I grieve for it. Then something, perhaps a bird or a butterfly, perhaps the smell of salmon frying, distracts me. But the meaning of Uncle John's strange gift resonates: beauty and sadness are one.

Fogo had a different sort of fishery, a real fishery. Salmon was technically fish, but not *real* fish like cod. Cod was king. In Cod We Trust. And most summers my mother spent a week or ten days in the cod's kingdom visiting kin, and she generally took me with her. I don't recall Calvin's ever coming with us. Perhaps he had outgrown it, or he may have preferred tending counter for Grandpa Saunders.

My favourite time to go was August. It was then that boats from a dozen outharbours – Joe Batts Arm, Tilting, Seldom-Come-By, Locks Cove, Seal Cove, Sergeant's Cove – converged on Fogo, laden with their summer's catch of salt cod, with kegs of cod oil, to sell to Messrs Earle & Sons or to the Newfoundland & Labrador Export Company. Both premises were beehives of activity.

When I wasn't hunting rock crabs or trouting or berry-picking, I haunted both places. Earles' was handy and the Export Company, on the north side, was far; but I preferred the latter. If Mom or Aunt Fanny forbade me and Aub to go alone, I whined until Phyllis or Greta chaperoned us. But after age ten I went by myself, up the long road over the canal and around.

I loved the immense wharves, the dim store smelling of oakum and tar. Fogo had other stores – Mrs. Furze's and Jack Baker's for example – but those were small and ordinary. They never sold cod jiggers, squid jiggers, cast-nets, trawl line, piggins, net needles, cork floats, oakum, splitting knives, rope in all sizes, oilskins, Cape Anns, rubber boots. Not that I needed these things. They were just nice to look at.

Out on the wharves we watched yaffles of fish, armfuls hard as boards, heaved up from boat standing-rooms into waiting arms that rarely missed a throw. On the wharf, cullers and graders were hard at work. We watched hand-bars – four-handled rectangles of wood borne by pairs of men, something foreign to Gander Bay – being trotted into dim, cavernous warehouses that smelled deliciously of new barrels and sun-warmed cod.

Inside, blinking from the glare of sun-bleached planks and brine-dusted fish, for a moment we could see nothing. A risky moment, for you could be run over. Here the handbars were being dumped. Packers were packing and coopers coopering. Weighers with enormous brass scales and various weights were scribbling in great blue ledgers. Shippers with brushes smelling of linseed oil were stencilling words like Oporto and Madeira and Jamaica on barrel heads. Handlers were rolling finished casks into adjoining warehouses for shipment to St. John's and overseas.

One misstep and a boy could end up in Portugal.

I couldn't help but strut a little, knowing that Grandpa Layman or my Uncle Tom had made some of these barrels and casks, that my Uncle Jabe worked over here somewhere too.

If there was one thing I missed in Fogo it was the woods. My Gander Bay was rich in them. One could walk north or west or south for a week and not run out of forest. Clarkes Head had been carved from forest. Half of our living still came from logging in winter and sawing in summer, not to mention the spring log drive. Then there were all the trades like furring, guiding and hunting that owed their existence to trees.

I learned something of all this by swarving about Uncle Harold's log booms and lumber yards, by watching my father cleave firewood and by helping Calvin cut down a tree once (thanks to me, the bucksaw blade broke and cut my chin). But I learned a lot more the winter my father took me, at age six or seven, to Clarkes Pond to cut and haul firewood.

It seemed an immense journey. In fact it was only a mile. We went in March month, the best wood-hauling time. By March the sun had warmed enough to melt the snow on the hauling roads by mid-day, while the nights were still sharp enough to re-freeze it slick as glass. So you had good hauling early and late, which was important with a heavy wood like birch. The easier the hauling the bigger the loads and the fewer the trips. Less hay and oats for the horses, too.

We went by horse and bobsled, my father having borrowed King for the week. I rode beside Dad on the forward bunk, sitting on a brin bag full of soft hay tied to the horn of the forward bobsled. "Hold onto the horn now son," he said. Then he made the kissing chirp which to every workhorse means "Giddup." The sturdy Newfoundland roan, finding himself harnessed to empty bobsleds, fell into an easy trot up the road, his breath steaming the frosty air, his thick mane and short ears bobbing, his shod hooves flinging clods of snow behind. Soon we were past Jim Allen's house and entering the Portage Road.

Though some snow had fallen overnight, the traffic of Horwood Lumber Company loggers, who always left home before daylight, had already smoothed the track. Behind us the rising sun rinsed the feathery evergreens with salmon pink and seemed to keep pace with us. Spears of sunshine slanted down the glades and spangled the blue shadows.

Clarkes Pond was where the best birch grew. A huge grove had sprung up after the forest fire of 1912 raced nearly forty miles before a southwest gale from Salmon Brook near Glenwood to Charles Cove. At age eight Dad had watched it from the safety of Point Head, where his family and others had spent the night praying it would spare their homes. As it happened, the fire trimmed the shore of Clarkes Pond on its way to Victoria Cove, where it took at least two houses, one belonging to a Mr. Reccord, the other a new one Noah Webb had built for his bride-to-be. They had to postpone the wedding. The only reason it halted at Charles Cove was that water won't burn.

On reaching the pond, King broke into a brisk canter. The ice under us was grey-green, rippled with thin drifts of snow. Once across, Dad took the road to a suitable stand; halted, threw a blanket over King, watered him and fed him hay. Then we left the trail and he started felling and limbing trees. Free to roam and stiff from sitting, I rambled over the crusted snow, traced rabbit tracks and collected twigs and birch rind for our lunch fire.

By dinnertime my father had cut the better part of a load. He kindled a small fire with wood from a dead snag and boiled water for tea. Some neighbouring cutter noted our smoke and dodged over. Hunkered around the fire with the men, gnawing on roast caplin and eating jam bread, I felt grown up.

By mid-afternoon our twin bobsleds were piled high and chained tight and we were homeward bound, going downhill for a change. King made good time over the polished snow despite his heavy load. Once on the pond I glanced back to where the westering sun poured liquid gold through a lattice of birch and fir. Against the sun the birches were purple-grey, while their long shadows on the ice were deep blue.

Suddenly the ice boomed. I jumped. King lunged; but the load held him back. In the darkening glades our steel runners wakened raspy echoes when they struck bare gravel. Perched on the load above the swaying bobsleds, nostrils full of warm horse smell, mouth full of fresh spruce gum, I was supremely happy. The morning's landmarks paraded by in reverse, becoming more and more familiar as we went. We passed Big Mish, The Drong, walked the horse down Big Hill, skirted Steady Water, toiled by Jim Allen's. At last we reached our own back gate. I climbed stiffly off to open it – and stumbled because my left foot was asleep. While Dad unloaded the wood and watered and fed King, I clumped into the warm kitchen to tell the marvels of my day.

Though the foxy house had running water of a sort – Dad's rain barrel – we lacked a well. Our ground was too low, too prone to surface runoff. Every other drop we used had to be lugged home in buckets from the brook, some 300 yards away. By custom, fetching water was man's work – though in Fogo, with the fishermen away so much all summer, women often did it.

Being a guide, my father too was often away summertime. So the job fell first to Mom or her maid to fetch water, later to Calvin and finally to me. He recalled being outfitted, at age ten or so, with a small round birch hoop and a pair of one-pound lard pails. My brother's first "turn o' water" – one return trip – was a proud moment; but the task soon turned to drudgery. At roughly a gallon a trip, it took him nearly a dozen turns and half a mile of walking to fill our green barrel.

Two or three years later he had graduated to man-sized, 2.5-gallon buckets and a man-sized hoop. A hoop was important because it steadied the load, eased the strain and kept the water buckets clear of one's legs. A grownup's hoop was actually square: four corner-braced spruce bars. Thus equipped, Calvin could fill the barrel in three to four trips.

My own water duties, thanks to our living so much in town, began at a later age than his. This meant starting off with full-sized gear. I eased into it with half-filled buckets. Not that I was a novice. I had sometimes spelled him off while he helped Grandpa in the shop. One winter, testing one of his bright ideas – "Why not take the barrel to the water?" – he enlisted me as sled dog.

No sooner dreamt than tried. One bitter February evening, we wrestled the empty barrel onto Dad's dogsled and set out. The road was slick, which was fortunate. He pushed and I pulled. We reached the brook in no time. Filling the barrel was also very easy. What a difference this makes, mused my entrepreneurial brother. Why hadn't he thought of it sooner? Come summer we'd do the same with a cart!

We started home in high spirits. Halfway along, we stopped for a spell. The water, still travelling west, slopped out under the lid and instantly froze our runners to the road. Borrowing an axe, we chopped them clear. The same thing happened each time we stopped. We arrived home with scarcely a third of a barrel left, our mitts sodden, our pant legs soaked, our fingers freezing. The only warmth was in our tempers.

Soon after that, we moved to St. John's, where I toted coal, not water. By the time I got back to the bay, Calvin was working in Lewisporte. That summer I faced the green water barrel alone. Oasis of my childhood years, it now became my taskmaster. Once a week, sometimes twice, it threatened to run dry. Many's the fine Saturday outing I sacrificed to it. Yet there was pride of accomplishment in it, and penance for past sins, and the beginnings of adult responsibility. And it *was* building those Tarzan-like deltoids and biceps.

During the war, airplanes played a big part in my life. For a time I wanted to be a fighter pilot. But I never saw a warplane up close until age eight, when my father helped salvage a Hurricane fighter. Even that was only a glimpse of wings and fuselage lashed to two canoes.

With bush planes it was different. They not only flew over, they landed, especially in winter, especially after The War. Wintertime, they landed on the ice on skis and taxied right up to our wharf with mail and parcels. They also sped the sick to hospital; in summer they did the same on pontoons. I even met a bush pilot or two. Naturally I wanted to be one of them.

Sheer magic, that, to see a shining mote against the sun, unreachable, and then to watch it come down to earth. To touch, or at least stand close to, the thing itself in its riveted and cabled reality. To marvel at its struts and vanes and paint-scuffed wings, and its miraculous propeller. To see its godlike pilot, that goggled and leather-jacketed man-of-the-air, climb slowly down, turn and smile and wave and walk about on two legs like the rest of us: a human being after all, and doubtless once a child like me.

Mystery come down to earth.

One such epiphany is etched forever on my brain. Someone had heard the unmistakable drone of an incoming plane. The inevitable knot of spectators had gathered on the ice to watch. After a while we saw it circle and glide down and down, now dark against the pale sky, now bright against the purple hills. We saw the bounce of its skis on the far ice – one, two, three spurts of white – and waited as it charged toward us, chased by its own small blizzard of snow, to halt scant yards away. We saw its invisible propeller materialize from silvery disk to two solid blades, chop-chopping the air, slower and slower, until they halted in a final hiccup. In the sudden silence, we stood gawking like the hicks we were.

Later, the pilot's business done, we watched him take off. This time the blizzard engulfed us, stinging our eyes and cheeks with gasoline-scented ice crystals. I knuckled my eyes so as not to miss the always startling moment of lift-off, the swift diminution of the aircraft into a bird, a mote, a silence.

Alone with ourselves again. You'd think we'd be used to it, having lived in virtual isolation, without railway or highway, for several generations. Yet the bystanders always looked mildly bereft after a bush plane took off. At least we youngsters could act out our feelings and fantasies.

It was sadder still to see an aircraft crippled and earthbound. I saw it happen twice. The 1943 accident involved a Fox Moth biplane, one of two bought by the Commission of Government around 1935 and based in Norris Arm over Botwood way, used for fire patrol, mail delivery and seal-spotting. It was on a school day the accident happened because I recall we were home for dinner when we heard the plane land. I bolted my jam bread and raced outdoors to see it.

The little grey biplane was already parked on the ice next to the wharf. The pilot, Joe Gilmore of Ferry Command, had gone to the shop to see Grandpa. By the time Joe returned a fair crowd had gathered to watch the takeoff.

Before climbing aboard, Joe grabbed one wing and turned the plane to face the southwest breeze. Then, to choke the engine before turning on the ignition, he grasped the prop to give it the customary turn or two. At his touch the engine coughed and came to life. Seconds later the prop was a gleaming blur. Someone had tampered with the ignition; not only tampered but moved the throttle lever. Joe nearly lost his arm.

The Fox Moth was trundling forward with the pilot jogging alongside. Joe tried in vain to open the door. The prop wash kept banging it shut. When he lost his footing and fell, we gasped. But he managed to duck under the tail-wing, leapt up and, running hard, tried again to board. All he managed was to alter the plane's course.

Then we heard him shout, "Mr. Saunders! Watch out!" My grandfather had hurried offshore to what seemed a safe viewpoint well downwind. Now he found himself directly in the plane's path. He turned to run, but Gilmore could see the stout man was losing the race and yelled, "Get down!" As Grandpa flopped on his belly, the biplane's lower wing took the cap off his head.

If the school bell sounded we never heard it. I couldn't have torn myself away if we had. The plane had now reached throttle speed. Lightweight to start with and now pilotless, it seemed about to take off. But the flaps were set for level flight. Joe watched helplessly as it sped away. Perhaps the poor man was calculating how far his plane could fly and where it might crash. If so, his thoughts were interrupted by another shout.

"She's comin' back!" It was true. The biplane was tracing a wide arc. Where to run?

"Don't panic," cried Joe. "Stay put for now and watch; she may pass us altogether." As it bore down on the wharf, we all scattered like hens at the sight of a hawk. One of its skis hit a ballicader, sending the aircraft toward one of Uncle Harold's boom piers. Rock-filled, cross-braced, frozen fast in foot-thick ice, the pier awaited the Moth, that flimsy collection of balsa and canvas, its only durable parts the engine, cables, propeller, and skis.

The splintering collision smashed the engine and curled the metal propeller beyond repair. Gilmore waded in and untangled the shredded canvas, and balsa scraps, removed the cables and wrote off the rest. Then he went to the post office and wired for a new motor, propeller and battery. He also ordered canvas, balsa wood, waterproofing dope, screws and glue. By the time they arrived, he planned to have the fuselage ready.

Soon a big Norseman brought the repair goods and two technicians. The next two weeks were tantalizing for me. Every day after school I spied on Fox Moth VO-ADE's resurrection. Nobody would let me in. I peeped through the various windows. If I squinted it was as if they were building a model airplane. When they opened the doors on mild days to clear the vapours from the water-proofing dope, I'd stand outside and sniff.

Ten days later, the Norseman unloaded a new motor and propeller. Three weeks after the accident, Joe Gilmore flew the biplane back to Norris Arm. VO-ADE was lucky. Its sister biplane, flown by Pilot Sullivan on a seal-spotting mission to the Front, was never seen again.

The second incident involved a Norseman in the role of victim. The plane came one day in January 1945 to airlift a sick woman, Susie Gillingham, to Gander. They say she had acute appendicitis. The pilot, Group Captain David Anderson, believing she lived on the south side, landed first near Georges Point. Realizing his mistake, he began to taxi across at high speed in case the ice was thin. Nearing the north side, still unsure of where Miss Gillingham lived, he spotted a man, likely Reg Bath, walking on the ice not far from shore. He stopped to ask directions.

It was a near fatal mistake. The skis broke through. In seconds the heavy metal aircraft was nose-first in the drink. Only its wide wings saved it from going to the bottom in fifteen feet of ice-water. Anderson and his engineer barely had time to unbuckle and scramble up through the escape hatch before the cabin filled.

I never saw the Norseman land. But I got to watch its salvage, for my father had the contract. They had no time to lose. A sudden thaw could take the plane to the bottom. Dad set up two 24-foot spruce poles on opposite sides of the cockpit, joined them with a heavy cross-beam and ran guy ropes to short logs set crosswise in holes in the ice. To the uprights he spiked scaffolding and steps. He then rigged a double-sheave block and tackle from the cross-beam and hooked the chain to the aircraft's four lifting rings. While a dozen strong men spread out on a long hawser, they axed a circle of ice around the skis and stood back.

"Hoist away!"

Whether they sang the "Jolly Poker" I don't know. The drowned plane, like Lazarus emerging from the grave, rose inch by inch from its icy tomb, water cascading from its cylinder cowling, its exhaust pipes, its windows. When the skis snagged, a man nudged them free with a pole. The moment they cleared the water, Dad and his men slid long two-inch planks under them to bridge the hole and give the plane a platform to rest on. Gently the rope crew lowered it onto the platform. It sagged but held. Everyone cheered.

I missed the hauling ashore but not the rehabilitation. The site was just south of Point Head, about where the causeway comes ashore today. Group Captain Anderson had two mechanics flown out from Gander; one of them stayed with us. I remember he gave us his pea-soup K-rations (very bitter), and that Dad took me back with them to the site one Saturday.

The makeshift hangar covering the plane's front end was the biggest tent I ever saw. Inside, several gasoline fans were blowing hot air over the stripped engine. "What saved it was the fresh water," the foreman told us. "Sea water quickly ruins an engine. Here silt is our big problem; but we think we've got it all. Now we're drying the cylinders. After that, Joe Gilmore plans to fly it to Montreal for a new engine."

The other highlight of that week was seeing, up close, the tiny Piper Cub which Group Captain Anderson used as a taxi. It was a little jewel, too precious for the likes of me even to breathe on. Yet because the crew knew my dad, they let me touch its lacquered green and gold body, its varnished mahogany propeller.

Susie Gillingham was saved. A different plane whisked her to Gander hospital in time. Joe Gilmore was less fortunate. Flying to Montreal to fetch the new motor, he met a blizzard over Prince Edward Island and suffered a fatal crash.

Maybe I wouldn't be a bush pilot after all.

Other Pastimes

"Although I was hungry all the time, I could not bear to hold still and eat; it was too dull a thing to do..."

– ANNIE DILLARD, *An American Childhood*

Time. There was never enough of it. Had the management of time been up to us, childhood would have been one unbroken skein of adventure and enterprise, of pranks, exploration, risk-taking, whimsy. But no matter what we were up to or down to – indoor play, outdoor play, watching, listening, doing, undoing, teasing, traipsing, dawdling, aping – time foreclosed on us. Something – supper or weather or curfew or splinters or sore throats or homework or punishment – always intervened.

Grownups called our doings "pastimes." Pastimes they were not; anything but. They were our work. Unlike grownups, whose brains had finished growing, or were shrinking, we still had heads full of furiously firing neurons. Our brain cells craved the *frisson* of experience as fiercely as legs and arms craved glucose, water and oxygen.

It helped that we were poor in printed matter, poorer in radio, poorest in time-gobbling virtual pastimes. We had a bit of radio but no television, no Web, no cell phones, no Play Stations, no iPods. We had no electrical outlets. All we had were batteries, and not many of those. We had DC but no AC. Even if we had had electricity, the virtual pastimes it proffered would have paled before the plangent violence of forge and sawmill, the seductive multiplicity of nature, the endless opportunities for making and doing.

Summertime we lived the gypsy life. Pods of girls and packs of boys drifted across the greening landscape whenever chores allowed. Girls would picnic and skip rope and play hopscotch and dress up to be church ladies.

Boys might go sea-trouting on Point Head or Burnt Point. We might devote a whole day to making bows and arrows, to hunting hazelnuts by the brook, to teasing a ram or a billy goat, to luring blackbirds under a tilted box with bread crumbs, to catching bumblebees in bottles or flounders in a baited drop-net. On sultry summer days we prospected for gold along the alder-shaded brook and splashed cool water on each other. In the cool of the day, as the last raking orange light washed over the sawmill's silent pulleys and belts and posts, we listened to the saw filer stroke low fiddle-like notes from the big saws and high notes from the small.

We all, girls and boys, played pranks on friends and even on grownups. We gave each other "Indian burns" – wringing a bare arm alternately with both hands until the skin flamed red. Or we crept up behind someone and tapped their knees from behind, collapsing their legs. In late summer we sought out and destroyed hornets' nests. Come fall, boys made long-distance war with hard iris pods stuck on whippy alder throwing sticks.

To our shame we stood guard while older boys snitched apples off poor Mary Ann Gillingham's two trees. On November 5, Guy Fawke's Night, before we even knew the history, we built and torched magnificent bonfires. In early winter we vaulted over *rents* in the shore ice and fished for smelt in the cove. In early spring we copied ice pans.

It seems the only two things we didn't do were build tree houses and make gunpowder. I always regretted not making gunpowder. We were just too busy. Hungry or no, I often skipped meals. "That child lives on air!" my exasperated mother cried.

School was an interlude, but a good one when it came. It imposed order on our wayward lives. It broke up summer's cliques and claques. The 15-minute walk each way threw us together in new permutations and combinations of friendship. It gave shy girls and shyer boys a civilized excuse to mingle.

As for school itself, it foreclosed our gypsy wanderings but opened new vistas of knowledge and responsibility. It taught us to be on time. It taught us self-discipline. It taught us about community and cooperation: "If you want a warm classroom, don't forget to bring your daily junk of firewood."

Lest all this discipline kill our spirits, there was recess time. Boys wrestled and raced, tried and mostly failed to snare rabbits in the nearby woods. Girls played hopscotch and skip-rope and ring dances in season. We all played Blind Man's Bluff and roamed the landwash.

School gave us boys new ideas for making stuff. History for us was about battles. Sword-making and swordsmanship now consumed many hours. Any flat piece of wood – box board, mill edging, a bit of flooring – would do. You sawed it to length and whittled from there. Making the hilts was a challenge but worth the work. They saved your knuckles. My hilts always split or swivelled until I learned to use two small nails instead of one big one. For some reason we never used screws.

Duly hilted, we chased the Sheriff of Nottingham and King Arthur's evil nephew Mordred and any other scoundrel we knew of. We liked the lunge and thrust of battle, the woody clash of blade on blade. It was like that poem my brother was memorising: "And all day long the noise of battle rolled/Among the mountains by the winter sea…"

We also made bows and arrows. "Bow'n'ar," we called them, spoken in one breath like "ju-jitsu" or "jai alai." They were harder to make than swords, but appealed to some deeper instinct. After all, hadn't the local Beothuk twanged them in these very woods, arrowed caribou along that very River?

But how to begin? Making a bow and arrow was two challenges rolled into one. And no sense asking our elders – too busy. No sense asking my brother either; he now had Tennyson and girls on his mind. We'd have to make our own. A curved spruce limb was the simplest: cut it, peel it, notch it, string it. Making arrows was much harder. Nothing naturally grown seemed straight enough. Alder suckers *looked* straight – until you squinted along them. The tongue on a tongue-and-groove floor board was certainly straight, but it always spalled when we tried to cut it off.

Quivers we made from rolled birch bark or stitched canvas. As for fletching, we had lots of feathers but no glue strong enough to bind them. So we simply did without. This sent our missiles dangerously off-target, until we learned to weight the tip. Our results were a far cry from the English longbow that won the Battle of Agincourt. We didn't care. After all, we weren't out to kill Frenchmen, or to hunt food. We just liked the feel of it.

It was while eavesdropping on a Grade 10 history lesson that we first heard of crossbows. Mr. White was teaching about some battle or other where one side used this new and powerful weapon. They cranked it with a lever and shot armour-piercing wooden bolts instead of arrows. Crossbows had a rifle-type of stock and an arrow groove, he said, and so were simpler to aim. They required only three months' training compared to three years for a good longbowman. Everett and I liked that idea. Here was the solution to our arrow problems.

For the stock we each cut and carved a length of tongue-and-groove lumber. The groove was for the bolt. With Dad's brace-and-bit we worried a one-inch hole through the other end to hold the short bow. For string rests we carved three notches in the groove. For a trigger we nailed a small wooden toggle under the string. For arrows we cut and peeled short alder shoots and scorched their sharpened tips.

Teacher was right. Suddenly we could hit a soup can at twenty feet. As for birds, they always heard the bowstring and went to wing.

However, that crossbow nearly got me in deep trouble. One day after school, wanting to show off my new toy, I dodged over to Frank's where some friends of Susie's were gathered. The girls asked me to demonstrate, so I drew the bow to the first notch, inserted a bolt and was looking for a safe target…when the toggle slipped. The bow happened to be aimed at my cousin Zena Gillingham. She covered her eyes when the bolt struck her chest. I expected blood to spurt out and Zena to topple over; but it was my first crossbow and the missile fell weakly to the ground.

"You all right?" I said shakily. Zena peeked down her bosom.

"Only a scratch," she said.

"You'll tell your mom I suppose?" Her mother Millie was my mom's best friend.

"I might," she said. But nothing came of it. Fifty years later, at our high school reunion, she couldn't even remember the incident that had scared me so.

Windjacks were less lethal, more educational. Being in essence motor-less propellers, they taught us the rudiments of aerodynamics. You took a flat piece of soft, even-grained, knot-free wood like pine or fir, bevelled the opposite edges, drilled the centre and nailed it loosely to the end of a stick. If your blade refused to turn, you whittled the heavy end until it hung level. Then the slightest breeze would turn it. If there was no wind, you created your own. Running with the whizzing blade out front, you were an airplane.

Once I tested a submarine version. I nailed a tin propeller to the bottom of a wooden "outboard motor" and waded fast to make it go. If I put my ear to the wood I heard a nice twirling underwater sound, but clamping the outboard to a canoe was a mistake. Making it turn was just too much work. Instead of my pushing it, the motor should have been pushing *me.*

We toyed with stilt-making. My father had seen clowns walking on them in the States and showed me how. I took two long sticks, nailed on footrests, climbed on beside a fence, took a few steps, and fell off. "They needs toe straps," said someone.

No, said Dad, you were supposed to hoist them with your hands as you walked. He demonstrated, or tried to. The bystanders clapped. "But you got to lean forward," he said. He demonstrated, falling backwards. We cheered. But it was harder than it looked, more of an adult toy, the plaything of the week.

Long before we trouted seriously, we trained on Clarkes Brook. Our gear was simplicity itself: hook, line and alder pole with worms for bait. No need of sinkers or cork bobbers; they were for pond fishing. The first time I saw my Fogo cousins fishing with bobbers I snickered. Surely they must scare the fish. But without them my hook sank in the mud. If anything, bobbers *attracted* those Fogo trout. I caught some lunkers there.

When I was ten, my father, the professional river guide, made me a miniature salmon rod. He cut and peeled a whippy alder and attached wire line guides. From one of Mom's wooden thread spools he made a working reel, complete with tiny handle. He waxed black sewing thread and wound it on the reel. As a final touch he tied on a tiny Royal Coachman lure from his fly box.

"Isn't…isn't the hook kinda small?" I said.

"Yes," he said, "it is. It's only a number twelve hook; but you know, I've caught salmon on those. In angling, size matters less than how you presents the lure, how you plays the fish. But," he added, "don't try this rod on anything big. It might break – or the fish pull you in!" That rod and that lesson were among his best gifts to me.

In any case, half the fun of brook angling was in the ripples and reflections, the play of bright water over stones, the little boats of creamy *fob* that sailed around, the flights of mayflies, the antic skittering of water striders, the simple melodies of water. In later years, roaming farther upstream with longer rods, we'd find deeper pools harbouring foot-long specimens stippled in red and gold and blue. And in June we'd go after sea trout, silvery as salmon and some almost as big, catching them on peeled spruce poles with proper salmon lines.

We even brought our rods to school, fishing before and after classes and even during recess if the run was at its peak. None of us had licences; licences were for salmon anglers. Our teachers never turned us in. They liked the fresh trout we gave them too well. You might say trouting was on the curriculum.

Swimming wasn't. Too bad it wasn't; I might have caught on sooner. My parents couldn't swim, which made them nervous about deep water and me, and that made me nervous too. I didn't start out nervous. As a toddler water fascinated me. I was always getting wet feet. One time my father got so fed up he tossed me in, clothes and all. Fight water with water. Poor man, it didn't work. After all, on Mom's side I was part Waterman.

It is a curious fact that most rivermen couldn't swim. Neither could their saltwater counterparts – but they at least had a good excuse. The North Atlantic would chill and kill a person within five minutes. Dad did try to learn one time. He got a friend to push him overboard in the middle of the bay. "Don't save me unless I'm goin' down for the third time," he told him. The friend watched him flounder as long as he dared, then fished him out. From then on my father was convinced his body lacked the necessary flotation cells, that if he tried to swim he'd always sink like a stone. I half believed my body had the same flaw.

Maybe he was right. Falling overboard one night in deep swift river water, he did sink. His rubber boots actually touched the bottom. The only thing that saved him was his river pole. It was in his hands when he went under, so he climbed it for air and used is as a downstream prop to lever himself to shore.

My mother's injunctions didn't help. No swimming off the wharf; the bottom's muddy. No swimming off Point Head; the current is too strong. Had there been surf, she would have banned surfing too. To her mind the only safe place was the cove – except at high tide. One summer I tested the brook's deepest pool. Even in August, the water was icy – fine for trout but not for me. And, since I'd been wearing shoes for a while, the shale cliffs gouged my feet.

By age ten I was still a wading bird. I waded and splashed like any other youngster, but when older was always uneasy around deep water. Caul or no, waterman or no, the best I could manage was a sort of dog-paddling crab-walk, partly floating while touching the bottom with fingers and toes. Later I learned to swim under water, eyes open, until my air ran out.

One time I lingered so long that a strange euphoria came over me. I felt I could stay down forever. But it wasn't real swimming. Real swimming would have to wait a decade, until university, after lessons in a pool. There I finally conquered my fear – or most of it.

The most fun I ever had with water was the spring – I think it was 1945 – we were flooded out. Not in the foxy house, which stood on a rise and never got wet feet, but in the winter house. Our regular house was uninsulated and drafty. It got so cold on windy winter nights that my father tacked blankets over the windows and hauled mats against the doors. "That's it!" he said. "Next winter we'll be warm, guaranteed." That fall he cut logs and built the winter house.

It was a log cabin and he put it just beyond our back fence. He knew the land was a bit low, but with the brook 300 yards away, he judged it to be safe from flooding. It would have been too, had several blizzards and a February thaw and a March ice jam not combined to upset his calculations.

We should have known what was coming that March morning we woke to find the cabin door, our only door, stogged from step to lintel. Calvin was amused, I was tickled. While Grandpa and Dad shovelled us out, he and I, unwilling to be late for school, climbed out a window. We arrived late anyhow – but we had a grand excuse: "Stuck in the window, sir!"

Sometime after midnight a few weeks later I woke to loud splashing and a pair of strong arms scooping me from bed, blankets and all. Much as I liked water, much as I liked to see Nature kick up her heels, this was too much of a good thing. Dad whisked me out the door and across the garden and into the foxy house, where Mom had a fire going to make hot cocoa and toast.

In the weeks that followed we missed our cozy cabin. The flood receded, but left everything so soggy we decided to stay put. Anyhow, the worst of the winter was over. I did go back one day to skate through its curtained, echoing rooms. But we never wintered there again.

Most Aprils the meadow flooded in part or in whole for a few days. Yet it always startled me to wake and see water where I'd hunted grasshoppers short months ago. Such a flood occurred the year I was sick in bed with measles. I woke to a world strangely hushed. No birdsong from the meadow, no barking from the dogs. And no wonder – their puncheons were surrounded. Our hens and goats eyed the water with mistrust and wouldn't leave the barn.

Hearing a *tap, tap* at my window, I raised my head to see Calvin's grinning face gliding by. I sat up for a better look. His face glided back. A hand motioned me to come. He was standing in a canoe. When I lifted the sash he whispered, "Quick, wrap yourself in a blanket, stick your feet out and I'll help you down. I'm takin' you fer a paddle. Do you good; you've been in bed too long. Hurry now, before Mom comes!" But no sooner had my toes touched down than she grabbed me from behind.

"What in heaven's name are you two doing?!"

"Just takin' him out for some fresh air," said Calvin lamely. Which was true. Back she hauled me, slamming down the window so hard it cracked a pane. My brave brother paddled quickly away as I was ordered back to bed.

There were always boats to sail. Not real ones, but little whittled models. On the bay they had a habit of sailing over the edge of the world, but on

Grandpa's flooded meadow we could control them, somewhat. To keep my sailboats upright I wedged a slice of shale amidships for a centreboard. To make them go, I stuck a hen's wing feather in a hole drilled just forward of centre with its concave side facing aft. To steer them I slotted a bean can lid into the stern. After watching two of my creations sail clear across, out of reach, I caught on. By bending the rudder ever so little to port or starboard, I could, all things being equal, make the craft come back home.

The spring we left for St. John's, I whittled and rigged one last boat and set it gently in the running ditch beside the road. As I walked it along, guiding it with a stick, I was startled by a deep nasal voice: "Ahggh!" it growled, "you'm too big a boy fer playin' with boats!" The voice was that of Uncle Don, Dad's youngest brother, not long back from overseas, a place where even children had no time to play. Perhaps he was right. Perhaps I had explored Eden long enough. I only played with real boats after that.

At school we learned a new word: "Hallowe'en." The textbook pictured a pumpkin carved into a scary face. However, no pumpkins grew in Gander Bay and Hallowe'en was never celebrated. We never even put a candle in a scooped-out turnip. To us, All Saints Eve and Day were merely autumn dates in the Church of England's liturgy. Certainly we never went door to door in masks, trick-or-treating. For that, we had mummering and the twelve days of Christmas.

Our only autumn rite was the one Grandma sometimes recited:

> Please to remember the fifth of November
> Gunpowder, treason and plot;
> I see no reason why gunpowder treason
> Should ever be forgot.

"What do it mean, Grandma?" She told me it had to do with a plot to blow up the king of England and his government in London 300 years ago.

"Did they?"

"No, my son. They would have, but Guy Fawkes, one of the plotters, got caught planting kegs of gunpowder in the cellars of Parliament and told on his friends. Ever since, all over England and Newfoundland, people have celebrated with bonfires on the fifth."

None of this made much sense, but I liked the fires that blossomed on both sides of the bay on that night and the preparations that led up to them as my brother and his friends collected evergreens and driftwood and any other old trash that would burn. If anyone objected, they were reminded that their fathers had burned perfectly good toilets and boats on Bonfire Night.

One fall my friends and I got permission to cut small trees on Dolf Gillingham's land after school. Because lugging them out to the landwash was too much work, and the season for forest fires was past, we piled our shaggy cone of trees right where we felled them, on a hillside facing the bay. That way everyone would see it.

Felling sticky var with bucksaws and blunt axes in Indian summer weather was tough. For weeks we scoted after school like sled dogs. Our hands and clothes were tarry with resin that only grease and hard scrubbing would remove. At last the pyre was ready. To mark the occasion I knotted the top shoot of a young var. (Years later I'd find the knotted trunk, still alive.)

Night falls early in November month. Stumbling uphill through the dusky woods to the site, we felt like Druids on our way to placate some fierce fire god. It took us several tries and several matches to light our mountain of blasty boughs. But as the eager flames licked and roared toward the sky, they coloured our faces a lurid orange and shot satanic gleams through the woods around. We yelled and danced and sang dirty songs. When the flames faltered, we dared each other to jump through them. We sat in a circle and toasted bread on alder sticks and wolfed it down. We stared into the dying embers and thought of the dying summer, the coming winter.

Before leaving, I buried a bottle in the coals to see if it would melt. Then we hurried home in the dark and cold, curiously content. Next morning early my mother cried, "I smell smoke! Is the house on fire?" Then she remembered. "Oh, the bonfire last night. You smell just like Dad when he comes home from trapping." Another reminder to get a good job when I grew up. "Too bad you wore your new sweater; I hope there's no holes in it."

Coasting – in St. John's they called it "randying" – was also problematical. Our few hills were either too cliffy, too steep, or on the wrong side of the bay. Our best, Big Hill, was a half mile in the woods. So we sometimes coasted on the bay itself. We had heard tell of ice-boats. Dad had seen them in the States, a sort of sailboat on three skates, he said, which by quartering across a stiff breeze could skim along at nearly forty miles an hour. Perhaps, I thought, my Red Rocket coaster could, with a tree top for a sail, go just as fast.

Frank and I cut two bushy vars and lashed them to our sleds, but couldn't keep them from toppling over. The only solution was to sit and hold them in both hands between our knees. Then a January thaw melted every speck of snow and left an inch of water on the bay. And then everything froze solid. We had a sheet of ice, a shining plain without a blemish, as far as the eye could see. Or so it seemed. All we needed was some wind. It came one bright Sunday morning. We went down by the wharf, got on our coasters, pointed them downwind, gripped our bushy sails and shoved off. It was slow going at first. "No fears," said Frank, "once we gets out in the wind we'll fair fly!" A dozen yards out, the breeze took us.

"Hang on, me son!"

"Hang on yerself!"

Out past the pointy rock we flew, runners growling and scraping. Grandpa's wharf flew past on our right; on our left, church and bell tower sped away. Out in the clear the wind picked up, became a gale. Burnt Point with our old school fell behind, Horwood's barn and store and wharf were soon mere specks. The shouldering wind drove us along.

Now we were crossing the channel. It sobered me to think of the 700-ton steamer *Glencoe* anchoring here in summer. Six fathoms of black water under me!

We'd never been this far from home on our own, not even by boat. Webbs Island and Sandy Cove loomed ahead, and, beyond them, Main Point with French's sawmill, and the winter road to Carmanville. It seemed like we were leaving home for good. How would we ever get back?

"Think we should turn around?"

"I s'pose." I rammed my right boot hard against the steering bar, thinking to come about in a wide arc and stop. The Rocket Racer refused to obey. It ran straight on. Frank's sled did the same. Rudderless! The only way to get stopped was to down sails and ram something side-on. Any obstacle – a frozen patch of snow, a rent, a chunk of horse manure – would do.

Ahead we saw a ragged line of crusty snow along an old rent. Away went our tree-sails. We flopped on our bellies, dragged our toes and hands. The edgewise impact capsized us and sent us spinning like tops. It took us a while, slipping and sliding, to recover the sleds and each other.

We glanced back the way we'd come. Clarkes Head was but a few beads on a string. The only structure we were sure of was the church. Miles of level burnished ice lay between. The gale stung our faces and knifed through our clothing.

"'Tis a long way."

"Some ride, eh?"

"Yiss, my son. That it was!"

Faintly then, baffled by the wind, came a chime of bells. Not only had we skipped Sunday school, we were missing church as well. "Scandalous!" Grandma would say. With the wind against us we'd be lucky to get back by supper time. There would be explaining to do. There was always explaining to do.

We arrived home just before supper, our fingers scrammed with cold, our ears dusted with frostbite, but secretly pleased. It was the fastest we'd ever travelled, faster even than the sled-dog race when Frank's yellow dog nipped me on the arm from sheer excitement.

We were roundly scolded for taking off without a word, for playing double hooky. "But we couldn't help it," I told my father. "We never planned to go so far. The wind carried us away."

"I know," he said. "You had what we call a free wind. A free wind going, a contrary wind coming. 'tis often the way." That was all he said about it.

Overnight, Sandy Cove had become a known quantity, a place within our ambit. So when the whitefish – that is, smelt – returned to spawn in late January, we naturally wanted to fish there instead of on our side. We got permission, and collected our simple gear: twine and hooks and sinkers, fatback pork for bait, an axe to cut the hole and make a bough windbreak, a coaster to haul our gear. We even cadged a wooden box from Grandpa to put our fish in.

This time, with no gale at our backs, the trip took longer. The hardest part was cutting the hole. It had been a cold winter. We were down a foot before we saw a sign of water. Cutting the last inch or so was always tricky. Break through too soon and you'll flood the hole, making it next to impossible to cut it wide enough in time. The trick is to first chip a circle round the bottom and, at the last second, punch it out with the axe head.

Success! Jade green water boiling up, overflowing the hole. While Frank flicked out ice chips and slush with his bare hands, I went ashore to cut tops and boughs. They not only broke the wind but shaded the hole so the fish were less wary. We were almost finished when the tide swung the bottom eel grass the other way and the ice began to lift and boom. We baited our hooks, lowered our lines and started in.

Waiting for them to come, I wondered what the whitefish saw, looking up. A mother-of-pearl sky of bubbled ice and snow shadows, stark blue circle for a sun, our alien heads two dark moving blobs? Suddenly, immaterial as smoke, the little fish appeared. One, two, five of them down there, earth-green above like the rippled sand, silvery below like the rippled sky. Cautiously, sinuously, they glided into our dim skylight, vanished, then re-appeared.

That first tentative tug always electrified me. Soon we were hand-over-handing bright fish onto the wet ice. Their slender threshing bodies flashed lavender and silver. Minutes – hours? – later, three dozen of them lay flopping and freezing on the ice.

Time to go. We got to our feet. Stiff and chilled, we swung our arms for warmth and thumped our mitts together. Scooping our catch into the box, we shoved a spruce top into the hole to warn future travellers and trudged home in the gloaming. The sun swung low and the wind abated. We arrived at teatime, weary, wind-burned and elated. As we shared our catch we agreed that this had been the best day of our best winter ever.

ANIMALS WILD

It is November. I am five going on six. Wet snow falls from a leaden sky, each fat flake melting where it lights. My mother paces from window to window, wringing her hands. "Said he'd be back two days ago. That ol' Mianus engine can't be trusted…" My father and Uncle Harold have gone seabirding down to Dog Bay in the green skiff. Now she has me worried too.

Suddenly our dogs are barking. We rush to the windows; not a soul. Half an hour later Dad walks in the gate, ducks dangling from each hand, unfamiliar black and white and grey ducks, sporting green and yellow feet and bills. We go outside to greet him and I fall in step. "What kind are those, Daddy?"

"One king eider and two scoter ducks, my son," he says. "Take 'em to your mother while I helps Harold unload the rest." He plops the eider on the bridge and hands me the scoters. I grab the legs, one in each hand, and stagger proudly toward the kitchen, dragging their heads.

She steps aside, smiling at her little man. But her smile is mostly from relief, for it's the first fresh meat we've seen in weeks. It's been too mild for hunting caribou – the meat wouldn't keep on the long trip downriver – but sea ducks are plentiful on the Outside this year, so that's where the men are.

She lifts the scoters onto the table. "We had those in Fogo every fall when I was a girl," she says, showing me the white spot under each bird's eye. I go back to fetch the eider but it's too heavy for me. It is nearly as big as a goose. I drag it by its pale green head. "You're getting to be quite strong," laughs Mommy, taking it from me. "But let's not soil the lovely feathers. Later you can help me pluck them!" That night the feathers fly in a happy house. "I'll stuff new pillow cases with these," she tells my father as they sit in the kitchen before open sacks, happily plucking away, trading stories of their week.

Waterfowl and shorebirds, both saltwater and fresh, winged their way through my childhood. They graced our table, softened our beds, enriched our stories. That was how we came to know the oldsquaw, the murre (turr), the bullbird, the black duck, merganser (white-winged diver), and the blue-winged and green-winged teal.

Others we seldom saw and never hunted, knowing them more by sound than sight. The loon or loo was like that. Its sad, two-note, French horn cry came floating down from the sky as it sped to lakes unseen by us. Ravens were likewise remote birds, tossing down bell-like notes as they tumbled in aerial acrobatics. Snipes winnowed overhead in April or May, then contented themselves with a nasal *scaipe* all summer. Along the shore we often heard the stilt-legged auntsarey's harsh, scolding, one-note cry without seeing the bird. But the low-flying, long-necked *toggle* (cormorant) never seemed to speak. It skimmed the water as silent as an arrow.

So many songbirds came and went from spring to fall, wearing such varied plumage, calling such a medley of calls, it was impossible to know them all. "What a charm of birds this marnin'!" Grandma Saunders would cry. "Robins in the *medder*, swallows twitterin' round the barn, yellowhammers chirping in my rose bushes, hitchhspars digging – she said *firkin'* – in last year's leaves, and the chickadees singin' 'sweet weather-r-r…!'"

The only birds I knew by song were crows, robins, blackbirds, jays and chickadees. We never thought of eating any of them – though my father said his Aunt Sarah used to send him to shoot "a mess o' robins" for soup. Sundays in the fall I often woke to the blue jay's cry. Somehow they never seemed to come on any other day.

By age ten we were walking encyclopedias of animal lore, from centipedes to moose. Counting insects, we knew at least a hundred different animals. And our knowledge didn't come second-hand from books or movies or even from school; it came from first-hand experience and from storytelling – especially storytelling.

I cut my teeth on animal stories. Long before I ever laid eyes on a live weasel or a moose or a bear, these mammals romped through my mind. My father had a deep respect for wildlife and liked nothing better than recounting his adventures among them. One of my favourites was his tale of the flying weasel. I first heard it through the heat register in my bedroom:

"I was steaming down the river one evening when I seen this black duck trying to take off. Thinking it was wounded, I steered toward it, only to find something hanging from its neck. Coming closer, I saw a weasel biting the bird's jugular vein. As I was wondering how to rescue the duck, it went to wing. But the weasel never let go. When it finally did she was a hundred feet in the air. It hit the water with a splash.

"I cut the motor and coasted over. The weasel, tuckered out, was swimming slowly ashore. I dipped the paddle blade under it and it grabbed the blade and rested there, panting, its beady eyes on me. I lifted the paddle aboard: it didn't let go. But the second I laid the blade on the thwart, away it raced for the cuddy and hid under the painter. There it stayed until the keel crunched on the shore. Then it was over the gunnel and gone."

He also had moose stories. I liked the one about the calf moose. "I was dodging through an alder bed one drizzly day without a gun when I heard bleating nearby. Out came a wobbly calf moose, likely still nursing. Without thinking I knelt and began to pet it. It nuzzled me and soon stopped bleating. Then I heard heavy breathing and saw a bristling brown hump coming through the alders.

"I ran for the nearest tree. It was a birch, nice and sturdy but with no branches low enough to reach. With the moose pawing the mud and bellowing behind me, I started shinnying up. But the bark was smooth and wet and my thigh rubbers wouldn't grip. I did climb out of her reach, expecting to slide back down any minute. Then the noise stopped. She was gone. The calf had wandered off and she had followed."

He knew the story of the first moose ever brought to Newfoundland island. It was in September 1875, he said, twenty-nine years before the Howley introduction. Grandma Saunders knew the date because her step-brother John Gillingham, as a boy of twelve, had helped feed and water the animals that winter. She spoke of how British Navy seamen, shadowing French fishing vessels off Cape Breton Island, had at our government's request, captured the two, a bull and pregnant cow. How they'd brought them to Gander Bay on the Royal Navy's HMS *Eclipse* commanded by Captain J.E. Erskine. How Captain Erskine had landed the pair on September 13, 1875, at Bussey's Point on the north side, and had them penned in a spacious wooded enclosure for tending by a local salmon fisher. How Uncle John helped cut var boughs and birch browse every day to bolster their hay ration.

"Those moose not only survived," Dad told us, "but were in good shape when released on the Gander that spring. There could be no better moose pasture. By the 1920s people were seeing numerous tracks along the River. In 1938 we had the first open season. Pierce Francis of Clarkes Head shot one of the first, a 20-point bull."

Then there were his bear stories. Like the time he and Uncle Stan, muskrat trapping on the Gander one spring, returned to camp to find a bear coming out the cabin door sucking a molasses bottle like a baby. Or the time he was fisheries warden on the river and a bear reached under his tent wall and tried to take some fried salmon. How he'd clobbered its paw with a junk of birch, only to have the bear come back later growling, forcing him to light a candle, run for the canoe and sleep across the river. In the morning, he'd found his tent and campsite ransacked and his provisions gone.

I grew up on such stories. Sometimes they weren't just stories. At age seven or eight he took me to see the great bear he snared while guiding for Dr. O'Leary's camp at First Pond. This brute was stealing the anglers' salmon, upsetting garbage cans and scaring the guests, so my father volunteered to make away with him. On a Friday evening, after that week's guests and guides had left, he'd tailed a snare along the bear's trail in the nearby woods.

I was with him Monday morning when he checked the snare. He walked ahead, rifle in hand. I came behind. As we climbed the riverbank and entered the dense alders, he glanced at me and laid a finger to his lips. I half expected to see the beast rear up and charge. Instead I saw this dark form in the torn-up underbrush, huge, inert, already bloating. My father had taken it with a simple loop of braided wire tied to a heavy log. The stench nearly gagged me. The bear's summer pelt was useless. We buried the carcass.

Of course we youngsters never shot or snared anything. That would come later. For a nice while we simply poked and prodded and watched. Our only prey was small fry: insects and sticklebacks at first, then songbirds and sculpins; finally trout and snowshoe hare.

Our first prey was grasshoppers. We knew they were there. Down among the yellow buttercups and purple timothy in Grandpa's meadow they lurked. We heard their arid stridulations on sunny summer days, not early in the morning when the grass was wet with dew, nor toward dusk, nor on rainy days. But soon after the sun came out and a breeze shook the grass dry, then we would hear them.

"*Zstt! Zstt! Zstt!*" they went, dry and reedy as if they were thirsty but too lazy to drink. It was not a song that carried far, especially if a breeze rustled their grassy forest. Having once heard it, however, we were confident of finding the singers. The place to look was near the sunlit tops of taller stems. For this you had to wade knee-deep, then waist-deep into the billowing meadow. We found one after another clinging by their spiny forelegs like sailors on the swaying masts of windjammers, as if they hadn't a care in the world. But they *did* have a care, and it was us: Frank and Susie and Everett and Norman and me, barely able to see over the hay, but out to catch them anyhow.

At first our methods were haphazard. Swimming through the tall cool grass we came, closing in on our solitary singers. A few stops more, a wild lunge, a wilder grab. With infinite care I'd open my fist a crack and peer inside. Nine times out of ten I had caught only air.

Later, we learned to watch their pink herringboned hind legs for the first telltale tensing that foretold a leap. Then we found a better way, as simple as it was ingenious. We noticed that grasshoppers liked to sun themselves on a warm rock. Wouldn't a warm board serve as well? Poor deprived rural children we were, we did not lack for boards. Uncle Harold's lumber yard had thousands of stray pieces. The landwash was regularly heaped with slabs and edgings to be burned on the next rainy day, if no one took them for free firewood.

By trial and error we found their favourite sort, a wide, flat, half-round slab that settled into the long grass, right side up, like a boat. We'd go away for an hour or two – then creep back. Almost always we'd find several hoppers parked on it. How strong their muscular hind legs seemed, shoving against the moist prison of my cupped hands! It nearly scared me into letting go. But I knew they couldn't bite like beetles or centipedes. It helped to let them poke their heads out of the star-shaped crinkle in our fists. That way I could study their strange triangular faces while they stared up at mine.

We might as well have come from different planets. "Look at this," someone would yell. "'E's got a squish mouth like a flatfish!"

"No, no," someone else would say, leaning closer, "it's sideways like...like a rock crab!" And their oversized eyes had millions of tiny little windows that glinted with rainbow colours and never blinked. What did they do for tears, I wondered? If they skinned a knee or lost a feeler? Suddenly the grasshopper twitched its feelers, worked its jaws and spat out a dollop of molasses. By now we'd have believed almost anything about this creature – even that its ear was on its belly.

"Taste it!"

We did. It certainly wasn't molasses. It wasn't anything like molasses, or even Balm o' Gilead. We decided it was more like medicine, or even poison. It gave us more respect for this creature, and now we understood the verse our grandmothers taught us:

> Grasshopper, grasshopper,
> Grasshopper grey;
> Give me some 'lassy
> To put in my tay.

There were other small creatures to observe and examine: spiders that walked on airy webs; water striders that walked on water, like Jesus, but took six legs to do it; daddy-long-legs that caused rain if you squished them; orange shit flies that sipped horse manure; bluebottle flies that were once wriggling maggots in rotten meat. Under rocks and logs were quick copper-coloured centipedes whose curved jaws bit like fire. Along the brook darted dragonflies – we called them horse stingers, imagining they tormented horses, when in fact they were hawking for stouts and copperheads, and "horse" just meant big.

Then there were the bumblebees and hornets that could give you a poison sting, my son, and if you didn't slap wet mud on right away, like your grandmother told you, the part would swell up and drop off. Buzzing around in the dark of night there were shiny, shelly beetles of every size, little ones that laid weevils in your oatmeal and swift hunter beetles, pretty as a teal's wing. And, unfriendliest of all, the blue-black timber flies, long as your middle finger, that walked jerkily over the lumber piles on hot July days or flew about on rattling wings trailing long black stingers that could kill you in a heartbeat.

Exposed to such dangers, we were thankful for the peaceful tribes of daytime butterflies and night-flying moths – we called them *millers* for their dusty wings – that lived by sipping flowers and never hurt a fly.

Even in the dead of winter we found, behind windows, sleepy clumps of cluster flies. Under damp doorsteps there were slow-moving grey pill bugs or *carpenters* that curled into balls when you poked them. Sometimes I'd hear a dry ticking in my bedroom wall at night and know it was the death watch beetle and feel a chill. Thus we came to know the smallest dwellers of our continent of wonders.

Then there were the animals of the landwash and bay. We feared the swift charcoal-coloured wolf spiders that hid under the dried eel grass and flotsam, but liked its slow-moving eight-legged cousin the red sand mite. When it crawled over the wet sand at low tide, feeding on things even tinier than itself, it looked like a tiny Santa Claus.

Beyond the low tide mark was where the fauna of salt and fresh water mingled. The sand shrimp were almost impossible to see, let alone to catch. During the lowest tides of spring and fall we dug up chalky white moon snails the size of Mary Ann's apples. Mostly it was just their empty shells.

When not hunting sticklebacks in tidal pools, we'd look for baby flounders in the cove's shallow waters. Inches long, mud-coloured on top and snow-white below, they snuggled in the silt until all but their bulging eyes were hidden. Often we put our bare feet on them before we even knew they were there.

Baby sculpins hid from us too, staying under rocks and cliffs until they were big enough to hang around our community's three wharves. They were so easy to catch it was no fun. The only fun was tormenting them. "Le's ketch some ugly sculpins and tarment 'em!" We did not believe that anything so spiny, so useless, would mind. Moreover, sculpins interfered with our other fisheries. Just when a fine trout or eel was about to bite, along came a sculpin and grabbed the bait. The ensuing tussle drove away our prey.

They also bit our flimsy lines in two and made off with hooks and sinkers. If you stepped on one – never with bare feet for they had spines galore – it growled like a cross dog. But they had nice colours: dappled yellow ochre, umber and grey, superb camouflage for a life of ambush and gluttony.

Under the wharf lived eels, some of them three feet long. Catching them took patience. Eels would nose the bait many times before tasting. They would touch nothing but the freshest bait and had a tremendous sense of smell. They needed it to travel halfway round the globe the way people said they did. Usually I tired of waiting, jammed my pole in a crevice and left my baited hook dangling.

But it was the height of laziness to leave it overnight. Grownups frowned on it. The fish would swallow the hook deep and have to be cut open. Meanwhile, if you dozed off by your pole, a fresh-caught eel might coil its wet body round your arm, cover you with fishy slime and bite hard with its raspy teeth. The only solution was to mash its head with a rock. We never ate them; they were scaleless and the Bible said all scaleless fish were unclean. But the oldtime local Mi'kmaq used to. They called them a delicacy and speared and smoked them for winter grub.

Once, wading in the cove at low tide, I saw a blind eel or what looked like one. It undulated slowly past my bare legs, heading for the shore. Its thick body was as long as mine. I felt as if a shark had passed by. Oddly, its back was blotched with grey and its eyes were filmed with blue. It looked sick and I pitied it. Perhaps it was going ashore to die? Certainly it was taking a great risk, swimming in shallow water in broad daylight. Any cruising eagle or fish hawk could have snatched it. My father's pet eagle Jack used to catch and eat eels and flatfish all the time.

Yet here it was, lazing along, swimming in God's sunshine, bent on some errand only it knew. I wanted to catch it and show it off; but I knew it was too strong for me and that, confined to a bucket, it would only die. So I got in front of it and, jumping and splashing, tried to turn it back toward deep water. It swam on resolutely.

A poem about water-snakes by Coleridge which my brother was memorizing came to mind:

> Within the shadow of the ship
> I watch'd their rich attire:
> Blue, glossy green and velvet black,
> They coil'd and swam and every track
> Was a flash of golden fire.

Water snakes I knew nothing of; I thought the poet meant eels. My eel wasn't beautiful, yet it seemed so brave, so doomed, I couldn't forget it. Dad said it was a female – the biggest ones were always females – and likely getting ready to breed. When that time came, he said, they would do anything to reach the sea, even slither across wet meadows at night. He'd seen it himself.

"Where in the sea were they going, Daddy?"

"To the Sargasso Sea," he replied with a nod to the south. I thought if that's where my blind eel was headed, she'd never find it in Aunt Kathleen's turnip garden.

On cloudy summer days, dozens of black and white swallows might appear, skimming near the water, hawking after insects. Their backs glinted green and blue, their bellies were snow white. My father called them tree swallows and said that when they flew close to the water, rain was coming. Sure enough, rain came the next night.

One raw November day we had a visitation of squid. I was around seven. "Wanna come out in boat and jig some squid with me?" Calvin said. I nodded uncertainly, not quite sure what a squid was, though I'd heard the name in Fogo. Squid-squalls I knew – moon-eyed jellyfish that came every August – but they were different.

"Do they come up our bay?"

"Sometimes," he said, "like now. Dress warm."

Calvin poled the canoe out by the wharf and there they were, moving near the bottom, fat arrows a foot long darting over and under each other and sometimes shooting off in one direction like a flock of birds. Those near the bottom were the colour of mud; those higher up were almost red. Their eyes flashed white.

"Here's your jigger," he said, handing me a heavy tapered lead weight ringed with barbless hooks. "Watch how I holds the string now, and be careful you don't stick those hooks in your leg or mine." He grasped the twine, tossed the jigger out and let it sink among them. I did the same. "As soon as one grabs the jigger, yank it aboard quick before it lets go."

He didn't tell me about the ink. As I hauled the squid up, I leaned over the gunnel, got a faceful and dropped the jigger. The squid was gone. Calvin laughed and, as I splashed water over myself and rinsed the gritty black stuff out of my eyes – it didn't sting – he sang in his off-key voice, "One poor little boy got it right in the eye/But they don't give a darn on the squid jiggin' ground!"

"I wish you'd tol' me 'twould squirt," I whined.

"More fun this way," he said. "Next time hold the squid away from the gunnel until it squirts." After that we caught a couple dozen, enough to feed the dogs for a while.

The next day Everett and I found windrows of dead ones along the landwash. I kicked one over and gingerly parted its tentacles with a twig. Hidden in the centre was a beak like an owl's. "A feller wouldn't want that clamped to 'is cock," I said.

"And that 'e wouldn't."

Mammals moved like shadows through my childhood. Always you'd see harbour seals at a distance, black forms sliding off grey boulders as we steamed up or down the River. Because they, like us, preyed on trout and salmon, they were shot on sight. Our anglers had paid good money and come far to escape courtrooms and jangling telephones and hospital operating rooms. No thieving seal was going to stand in their way. That was the rationale. Dad shot them without remorse and left their carcases for the eels.

Later he would have other reasons to kill them. When the federal Department of Fisheries set up its first salmon counting station at the Gander's mouth in the mid-1960s, the salmon were so thick the counters couldn't keep up. And while the salmon milled around waiting their turn, harbour seals would come from miles around to feast on them. He said they romped among the panicky fish, slashing egg-laden females, tossing bloody heads and tails in the air, churning the waters to crimson froth. He always hated them.

Once time I saw a sea serpent. It was in the fall, with an east wind spitting cold rain. I was trudging to Sunday school when I saw this far-off line of shiny black humps, rising and falling in the choppy grey water, exactly like a long black snake. I was about to run and tell someone when I saw the tail flukes and the puffs of steam. It was just a pod of pilot whales, potheads as we called them.

Still, a rare sight. Years would go by with none, and then one day there they were. Nobody knew why they came so far up the bay, whether they were chasing prey or getting rid of saltwater parasites, or whether they were lost or dying. It made no odds to us. Free meat and good sport! Out came the guns and scythes and axes, away went civility.

One Monday morning I awoke to distant gunfire. Rushing to the wharf, I saw half a dozen riverboats out there, two or three men in each, blasting and hacking away, swimming in blood. Someone towed three dead potheads in and beached them by the wharf. Bullet holes dimpled their rubbery hides; long pink slashes streaked their domed heads. Dark blood oozed from their blow holes and toothed jaws. I walked the length of one. Even in death, its skin felt soft beneath my feet.

But now, having killed, the hunters seemed at a loss. These were no dainty harbour dolphins. The bulls dwarfed our twenty-four-foot canoes. Gander Bay had too few ice houses to store such a windfall of meat – and no ice to put on it till January at least. It had no flensing tools, no tryworks for rendering blubber, no market for the few barrels produced. Even so, here was a hoard of excellent fresh meat. But no one rushed to carve fresh steaks for supper. In the end some got fed to the dogs and the rest got towed out to sea to sink or rot or feed the gulls. I thought: So this was how that mysterious whale's rib I'd seen beside Clarkes Brook had got there.

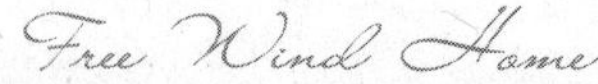

The Gander River Canoe

In 1942, the summer I was seven, my father took Mom and me by canoe to Fogo to visit her kin. To a riverman's son, the six-hour voyage by boat – the last leg across open ocean – seemed normal. Not routine, but normal. The only excitement came when, off Farewell Head, I spotted what looked like a bent stovepipe slicing through the calm water to starboard.

"Submarine!" yelled Dad above the outboard's drone. "One of ours, I hope." The periscope sank from view. I was too young to connect it with our coloured wall map which he and Grandpa Saunders scanned so anxiously during the BBC newscasts. Nor did I reflect that we were not far from the seaplane base at Botwood. Nor could we foresee that in two separate attacks that fall, U-boats would sink four iron-ore carriers at Bell Island near St. John's, killing sixty-nine men. Nor that on the night of October 14 they would sink the railway ferry S.S. *Caribou* on her North Sydney-Port aux Basques run with 137 lost, including some military personnel.

My father held his course for Fogo. But I've often wondered what those submariners, whoever they were, thought of our small craft so far out to sea. True, Newfoundlanders had been mucking about in small saltwater boats here for generations – but not in canoes. And while Dad thought this voyage in calm seas no riskier than running Big Chute with a load of freight, it *was* a bold, even foolhardy, feat.

Fogo's wharf idlers thought so anyway. Gawking down at us as we steamed past, they wondered out loud how we "Gander Bay Noddies" had managed to build such a craft and what with. "Oh, a few slabs and edgings, I s'pose." Their ignorance disgusted me.

This was not my father's first solo Fogo voyage by canoe. He had done it at least once before – a sort of shake-down cruise? – some five years earlier. Aunt Beatty said it happened when "you and Calvin were just little tykes." That would make it around 1937, when we were eight and two and she was twenty. We had come to Fogo via passenger boat, she said, and our mother waited for him to pick us up the same way. As the day wore on and no sign of him, she began to fret.

"Your mom did the wash and put it on the line to dry and kept going up and down the hill to see if the boat was coming. I would go with her. She was beside herself. Sick with worry. Grandpa Layman was trying all day to console her. Finally, still looking, she fainted. I ran for my dad. He got her in the house, laid her on the couch. I ran for Dr. Mackenzie. I can see Dad now, with brown paper dipped in vinegar, placing it on her forehead. She had a terrible headache. The doctor gave her some kind of powder. While she was recuperating, just lying quietly, who should walk in but your dad. Of course he was upset about your mom, but he was excited about the trip too. Believe it or not, in that little boat he came from Gander Bay! Said he kept close to shore all the way. Grandpa Layman was a very quiet man; but he wasn't too pleased that day."

The "little boat" would have been a good five feet shorter than our 1942 craft; that's how they built them then. Our particular voyage was much safer. Not much faster, but safer. The canoe – I remember it as dark green, the same colour as our water barrel – was not only longer, it was wider in the beam and deeper in the belly. And my father, having made the trip once or twice, had worked out island-weaving tactics for all weathers. By such arguments he must have cajoled Mom into chancing it.

As for me, the voyage seemed normal. River canoes were our standard mode of transport, as commonplace as motor cars today. I never questioned their presence, had no notion of how they came to be. Not until the 1970s, scripting a CBC documentary about my father's life, would it strike me how profoundly this craft had shaped our lives and how much it owed its development to the Saunderses.

Like most indigenous canoes the world over, ours had evolved to exploit a geographic niche. That niche was the Gander River, Newfoundland island's second largest stream, a sprawl of water draining 2,500 square miles of bog, barren and woodland south of the Notre Dame Bay archipelago. The Gander differed from its sister rivers, the Exploits and Humber, which have downstream waterfalls, in being navigable from sea to source without a portage – in the right craft.

My eighteenth century forebears had no such craft. When the Gillinghams arrived from Dorsetshire to net salmon and trap fur after the Treaty of Versailles opened the old French Shore in 1783, all they had were sailing shallops and luggers (How often did I "lug" water or wood, unaware of the word's nautical origin?) for heavier loads, and rowboats or rodneys for light work.

The rodney was deep-bellied, designed for tending ships, nets and weirs. At home on salt water, they were clumsy on fresh. They "drew too much water," ran aground on sandbars, and had to be coaxed and pushed and pulled like balky nags.

What my forebears needed was something small enough for poling up bouldery *rattles*, yet broad-beamed enough to float several hundredweights of venison over submerged sandbars. Something light enough for one man to haul ashore or to launch, yet robust enough to take hard knocks, rough water and serrated ice.

Above all, the craft must be buildable from local wood. That alone ruled out the admirable birchbark-and-cedar canoes which Mi'kmaw trappers were already bringing in from Nova Scotia and Maine. Not that the island lacked for big white birch – Beothuk builders had used it for centuries – it was cedar it lacked. The designers found a planking substitute in var, balsam fir, our next lightest wood. With that resolved, phase one of the Gander Bay Boat's evolution began.

The resulting hybrid was nimbler than a rodney but tougher than a birchbark canoe. Like the birchbark it was tapered fore and aft – hence "double-ender" – but longer and wider, close to eighteen feet long and over a yard in the beam.

Beyond that, it had more salt water in its design than fresh. Like the rodney it was planked with softwood *strakes* nailed edge-to-edge, carvel-style, onto sawn spruce timbers. The keel was carved from tough black spruce. Its seams were caulked with oakum – old rope enriched with tar. Like the rodney and shallop it boasted two sets of oars and rowlocks, though the latter were not Y-shaped metal inserts, but single wooden *thole* pins, each fitted with a braided viburnum *withe*, or ring, to anchor each oar. It also had a three-sided "leg-o'-mutton" sail and a take-down mast.

The resulting double-ender could be rowed or sailed in deep water, poled or paddled in shallows or rapids. Most of the time, our river being rocky and shallow and complicated, it was propelled by the adroit use of a ten-foot, sap-peeled black spruce pole. Gander river men would become master polers.

Double-enders had one bad fault. They were tippy – what rivermen called *cranky* – though not as cranky, being carvel-built and heavier, as a birchbark of the same length. Nonetheless, in time it would become our workhorse. For this reason people from St. John's to Port aux Basques to Labrador would come to call it the "Gander Bay Boat." And well they might. At one stroke this craft brought into our ambit everywhere and everything from Fogo to the Partridgeberry Hills.

Caribou, for instance. In the nineteenth century, Newfoundland island still had immense herds of woodland caribou, so many that on migration they often halted trains for days. These swirling seas of grey deer comprised several distinct herds, of which the nearest summered between Gander Bay and Wesleyville, on the so-called Southern Neck.

And because this herd poured past our doorsteps twice a year – Grandma told me she had seen it as a girl in the 1890s – swimming the River en route to the high southern barrens, it soon got decimated. These oldtime deer slayers seldom shot one animal at a time. That would waste costly powder and shot. Instead they raked the animals' legs with pea-sized SSG pellets fired from ambush. Each shot might fell a dozen. Then they'd wade in and axe them to death. Or they'd catch them swimming, brain them from boats and tow them ashore.

Once the Southern Neck herd was gone, Grandma said, hunters had to look farther afield. Then as now, the main eastern herd summered "in the country," meaning above Gander Lake on the high barrens along the River's Northwest and Southwest branches. Smaller groups straggled down the Lower Gander valley. But at the first whiff of snow, when venison was at its best and the weather ideal for storing it, the animals headed for the lichen-rich south coast barrens.

Though handy to south coast hunters, they were lost to my ancestors for another year unless they went in pursuit. The only way to follow them was to abandon their clumsy rodneys at tidewater and try to overtake the main herd on foot above the lake, over seventy miles due south. Then, after the kill, they had to wait for freeze-up to transport the meat home. Sometimes they put the carcasses in the water to drift, but this spoiled the meat. Their only other recourse was to winter inland like the Red Indians.

The double-ender changed all that. It let them intercept the south-bound herd above the lake at chosen crossing places, take what they needed and boat their winter's meat home with relative ease.

The new design also expanded the furring season. Most traplines were far upriver, well away from settlements. Traditionally, trappers like my great-uncle Stanley waited until January before mushing up the frozen river to their "fur paths" or traplines. Now they could leave before freeze-up, take a first harvest, return by dogteam as usual for the mid-winter season, and be back in May for muskrats.

A third benefit was tourism. When the trans-island railway reached Port aux Basques in 1898, rivermen could make a few dollars guiding rich hunters from Away. Some guides, like my father, would win international acclaim for their skill and lore. In the off-season they would ferry railway freight and passengers between Glenwood and the bay, a thirty-mile journey. The river became their highway, and the extra income freed them from part-time cod-fishing and sealing, further severing their saltwater origins. A hard-working riverman need never touch his forelock to a merchant prince again.

This phase of the boat's evolution lasted for over two generations. In all that time, builders like Ben Gillingham and his son Nat made only one major improvement. Because sawn timbers didn't "give" on impact, they replaced them with steam-bent tamarack ribs.

After the submarine sighting, Dad steered between Middle and South Dog Islands. This was to get some relief from the steady windlop marching down the long fetch of Dog Bay on our quarter. It was cold, too. But soon we were passing South End, Change Islands. Nonetheless, he trimmed every island, large and small, along that coast, from Woody Island to Hare Island, in case the motor conked and he had to hustle ashore for repairs.

Around Puncheon Cove near the north end of Change Islands he veered north-northeast, on a direct course for the high dome of Brimstone Head. This was the riskiest passage. We had nothing between us and Greenland but open ocean and Black Island and The Brandies – mere scraps of rock. Halfway across, the sea became oily calm and we felt the heave of an old storm passing under our keel, slow and majestic and vaguely menacing. For the first time we looked at each other, then looked away, unwilling to show how vulnerable we felt to be riding this defenceless cockleshell in all this waste of water.

Phase Two of the Gander Bay boat went much faster and Grandpa Saunders was in the thick of it. The impetus came from a new notion – the outboard motor. The first outboards appeared in Newfoundland in the mid-1920s. Their effect on canoe design was just as revolutionary as that which inboard engines had had on inshore fishing boats two decades before.

Grandpa almost certainly had the first outboard on our coast. Always in a hurry, this middle-aged shopkeeper, sawmiller and cannery operator found the weekly steamer service frustratingly slow and erratic. To his mind it wasn't much better than poling a canoe to Glenwood and back. At least that could be done in four days.

So when, in the fall of 1926, he received a flyer from John Barron & Sons of St. John's, announcing a 4.4 HP Evinrude portable gasoline motor that clamped onto a canoe, Grandpa wired for one right away. It was called the "Elto" – "Evinrude Leisure Touring Outboard" – but he wasn't interested in leisure or touring. He envisioned a one-day mail and freight link to Glenwood, with the couriers being his young sons Aubrey and Harold. (At this time my father-to-be was driving streetcars in New York.)

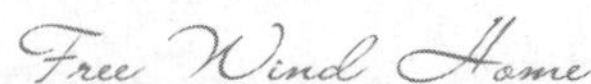

That spring the motor arrived. Clunky, a yard long from flywheel to *skeg*, it came with three dry-cell batteries for ignition and you started it by cranking a knob on top. Grandpa and sons were like youngsters with a new toy. There was only one small problem. It made the boat go in circles.

This was because these early prototypes could not swivel. Steering was a matter of working a joystick linked to the rudder by ropes and pulleys. So when they clamped the Elto on the gunnel, side-saddle style, and tried to steer, the wharf idlers had a good laugh. Evinrude did sell a cross-brace mount, but they knew it wouldn't stand up to the rough-and-tumble Gander.

What to do?

Grandpa consulted the Victoria Cove boat-builder Willy John Torraville, Harold's future father-in-law. Willy John said, "Skipper Frank, she needs a starn." No sooner thought than done. He sawed off one pointed end, built a broad stern and clamped the outboard to it.

Now the boat went straight – but its top speed was only five or six miles an hour. "Too much drag," yelled the wharf idlers. "Feller can row faster'n' that thing." Willy smoked his pipe and saw the problem: the stern was square in the water and raised a following wave.

His solution was a wine-glass stern that tapered evenly into the keel with no ledge. The effect was to echo the rodney's square transom above water but keep the double-ender's vee under water.

The improvement was dramatic. The craft's speed almost doubled. But at full speed it reared like a duck taking off.

"Yer hull's too shart to balance the engine," called the critics. This also was true. The former stern's bluff base had prevented that. Even with the operator sitting forward to work the steering ropes, it still reared.

Many more pipefuls of tobacco would be smoked before our several canoe builders managed, by trial and error, to strike a balance between engine weight and hull length. It was a lesson aboriginal builders already knew: The shorter your canoe, the deeper she floats. And finally they got it right. Not only right, but gained extra speed and cargo space and a shallower draft.

As outboard makers like Evinrude and Johnson and others built more powerful outboards, the Gander River boat kept getting longer. While the 1942 canoe that took us to Fogo was slightly longer than Grandpa's, by the 1960s young bucks would be racing 30-horsepower outboards on much longer boats. But the time they saved on the ponds was lost in poling and portaging, and they spent a lot of money fixing damaged hulls and replacing mashed propellers. By the 1980s everyone would have settled for a modest 15-20 HP. As always, the River had the last word.

And so our riverboat evolved toward the sleek profile I was seeing as a twelve-year-old: twenty-three to twenty-four feet long, eighteen inches deep, schooner-prowed, two thwarts amidships with cargo space between, raised floorboards to keep freight and feet dry. No more oars, no thole pins, no mast; just two river poles (one for a spare) and a spoon paddle for steering.

Another bonus of its evolution was improved stability. As an angler's fishing platform it was reassuringly stiff. This had a two-edged benefit. It helped prevent falling overboard, but also made it easier to crawl back in. Non-swimming rivermen liked that. I know Uncle Aubrey did.

One calm Sunday evening, I was up on Point Head when I heard a motor start. Presently, Uncle Aubrey's canoe nosed out from behind Grandpa's wharf with his eight-year-old daughter Patsy sitting in the bow. He was taking his eldest for a spin. As they moved out into the stream, trailed by herringbone ripples, he beckoned for her to come aft. Crouching low and holding onto the gunnels while she ducked past him in the approved way, he bent over while she slipped beneath him to take his place in the stern. But she moved too fast, and before he could reach the front thwart, Patsy opened the throttle and turned the tiller. This caused her father to fall overboard sideways.

I saw the splash – it was too far away to hear – and his head bob up as the boat sped away. Patsy was already turning the canoe and cutting the throttle. As she drew near, this non-swimmer calmly yelled out instructions. As I watched helplessly, he waited until he was amidships, then flung first one arm and then the other over the gunnel. When he heaved himself up onto his elbows, the boat tilted so high I was sure it must capsize – but it didn't. A moment later he had flopped inside, the craft righted itself and Patsy took him ashore.

Such "stiffness," plus shallow draught, made the boat ideal for freighting as well. And the loads it carried! Half a ton was commonplace. Drums of gasoline, a trussed-up Holstein cow and calf, firewood, the fuselage and wings of the Hawker Hurricane fighter which Dad and Uncle Harold salvaged for the RCAF in 1943. Quite a load to bring seventeen miles by canoe. When the project officer, a Sergeant King, questioned their ability to deliver it, Dad got vexed and said, "Sir, if your Air Force doesn't want the damned plane, say so! We'll fetch it anyway and put it in the meadow here for the youngsters to play in." The sergeant held his peace. By the time they had barged it to the steamer and got it safely aboard, they'd earned their $300.

I never saw the wings, but I remember seeing the fuselage by Grandpa's wharf, lodged tail-end forward on two river poles, lashed across two canoes with a splash tarp between. They talked about it for months.

Our war effort.

By the 1950s the boat's reputation would go international, spread by the hundreds of satisfied anglers and hunters whom it had ferried in comfort and safety to the salmon and trout, caribou and moose they sought. One retired U.S. admiral even carved a pine model. His guide, the son of Glenwood's famous one-armed guide Cecil Pelley, eventually passed it on to me.

We made it to Fogo Island in one piece, steaming past Brimstone Head, past Seal Cove, through the canal, past Long's and Earle & Sons' fishing premises and around the point into Little Harbour, Mom's home port. We tied up at the wharf of Tom the cooper, Mom's older brother. We would have canoed back home too, if a sudden storm had not forced us to go by steamer, canoe and all. The sea was so mountainous, my father had to lash the canoe to the S.S. *Glencoe*'s deck. I was too seasick to notice.

Even so, the adventure would stay with me, although whatever it was we did in Fogo, that trip was blanked out. My Fogo memories come from other, safer occasions. All I recall is that we went to sea in a pea green boat and lived to tell the tale.

Fogo

Fogo was my mother's world. Fogo was magical. An island world, a glacial rockyard, a place of lofty perspectives and sparse forest, as different from my father's world as chalk from cheese. A place of beetling iron cliffs, not gravelly banks, of thundering seas, not gentle steadies, of dizzying green deeps, not blonde pebbly shallows, of salt-bleached *cronnicks,* not lofty pines, of tangled stormwrack, not undulating river grasses, of turr not teal, of cod not caribou.

Here one saw trap skiffs, not canoes, heard the stutter of make-and-break inboards, not the bumblebee hum of outboards. Here the water tasted truly salt, not brackish. Here the landscape was more grey than green, an abraded terrain of extruded volcanic stone, where mats of crowberry and mountain cranberry struggled to cover the crumbling bones of ancient sea-mounts.

Even so, the island's hinterland was as lovely as anything along my Gander. It had peaty lily ponds that flashed silver in the salty winds; it had rushy hollows starred with marsh cotton in summer and haunted by the cries of willets and auntsareys every autumn. Only the wind-bent tamaracks and var were inferior.

Here, sleeping in my mother's sister's house, I woke to the crunch of iron-rimmed coal carts toiling up Jack Baker's hill, not the muffled creak of Silas Fancy's sawdust cart. Here, one heard the screams of gulls and stearins, not the wail of Uncle Harold's sawmill. Here, I fell asleep to a yodel of *crackies*, not to the sleepy flutings of deepwood thrushes.

And all these differences I cherished.

The view from the kitchen window of Aunt Fanny's and Uncle Jabe's trim, white two-storey house was heroic. It overlooked the flooded and eroded crater of a volcano that had blown its top eons before there was an Atlantic Ocean. The crater had three distinct notches which generations of fishermen had named Western, Middle and Eastern tickles. The house also overlooked a smaller bowl called Little Harbour, sheltered from the main harbour by Wigwam Point. In between lay Earles' fishing premises. Northward, across the crater, could be seen the rooftops of the Newfoundland & Labrador Export Company where Jabez Hart worked.

Uncle Jabe was a quick, short, slight man of ready wit and twinkling eye. Aunt Fanny was also small and quick, birdlike even; they were a good match. Weekday mornings he'd be gone before I got up. Sometimes I'd hear the gate latch click, more times I'd glimpse him striding west, hand-rolled cigarette dangling from his lip, lunchbox swinging, rain or shine. He and Dad got on well.

Fogo was antique and smelled it, especially on hot days with no wind. In Clarkes Head our worst outdoor smell was the sulfurous reek of rotting tree bark at low tide. In Fogo low tide lofted the stench of more than two centuries of rotten fish guts, seal blubber and rancid cod oil. One reason I preferred to roam the hinterland.

Back there my nostrils smelt nothing stronger than cool, mushroomy peat moss and hot resinous crowberry mats baking in the sun. One could fish there too. Roseate mud trout lazed under banks of mountain alder and Labrador tea and breached for gnats and damsel flies. So different from my dappled mossy woods, my salmon-haunted River – yet magical.

Because, unaccountably, Fogo *felt* like home. Had my mother stayed a fortnight longer in November 1935, it would have been. But she'd lost her nerve and hurried back to Gander Bay. I liked not only Fogo, but our journeys to and from it. Except for the 1942 expedition, we always came in Grandpa's passenger boat. It had a wheelhouse for dirty weather and a snug cabin with a drop-down table and a little cod stove for making tea and cooking simple meals. Home comfort.

The distance to Fogo was reckoned as twenty-five miles from Grandpa's wharf. Unless the trip was urgent, you waited for calm skies and a westerly breeze, not too brisk. Then you'd steam past Victoria Cove, Charles Cove and Farewell Head. Approaching Change Islands, you'd normally run along its rugged eastern shore. But if the wind veered easterly, it was more prudent to take the west side, passing through Main Tickle before tackling the five-mile run of open ocean to Fogo Island.

Once in the lun of Brimstone Head's nearly 400-foot dome, it was but a short steam down past Seal Cove to the man-made canal which served as the back door to Fogo Harbour. Again, if the wind was contrary you'd veer west around Brimstone and detour past Back Cove and along Fogo Head to sneak in through Western Tickle. And if dirty weather overtook us anywhere en route, we'd anchor in some sheltered haven or betwixt two islands for the night. The Notre Dame Bay archipelago had havens galore. There is no sweeter sleep than on a gently rocking boat with water chucking under her bows all night.

The worst was when a squall caught us in the open. Then Dad would send Mom and me below, close the hatch and wheelhouse door and take the lops on the quarter, slantwise to the troughs and hills. This would cause the boat to roll, and that would have Mom and me seasick in no time. There are few worse feelings than cold sober vomiting below deck with no fresh air, on a rolling boat with no relief in sight. You want to die, to jump overboard, anything to ease the torment.

In due course, however, the yawing and pitching would subside and we'd look out a porthole to find ourselves at some wharf or other, glad again to be alive. Nothing tasted better then than a cup of hot tea and, in my case, an egg sandwich.

Most of our trips were uneventful. About the most exciting event would be the sighting of some kind of whale. I once saw something black and shiny rise alongside and spurt what looked like steam. "Puff-pig!" Dad yelled, meaning porpoise. Another time he pointed and yelled "Grampus!" (killer whale); but with the sun-dazzle and flying spray, I couldn't make it out. Other times we'd see rafts of sea ducks or a squadron of low-flying turrs or a flutter of storm petrels darting between the swells. Most of the time I watched the passage of half-bald islets, green above and white below, where scrubby trees survived on gull shit and crab shells.

Sometimes the sea's surface was at cross purposes, with the swells of an old storm running counter to the day's wind and waves. One time, off Hare Bay Head, the storm troughs were so deep the lofty pink cliffs vanished each time we dived between the crests. At such times my mother's mild face would be pinched with worry. As for me, I'd study my father's face. If it was serene as usual, I'd relax and try to enjoy the ride.

He never got seasick, even in the roughest weather. Perhaps seasons of operating a weekly passenger service from the mid-1930s until 1944, travelling to Twillingate and Fogo and ports between, settled his stomach for good. I was all right so long as I stayed on deck.

Approaching the canal, he'd throttle down to dead slow. Even so, our engine would echo off the high and enclosing walls with deafening volleys. Leaning over the rail, I'd watch the green and shelly bottom rise and rise under our keel until I was sure we would run aground. In Fogo the bottom was always farther down than I thought. Suddenly the racket ceased, the water deepened and the main harbour widened to embrace us.

We would make a clockwise circuit out around the Earles' premises, past Wigwam Point with its white, three-storey merchant's mansion, past the spine of rock that always broke in rough weather and so into Little Harbour itself, ringed with a cat's cradle of rickety stages and flakes and oxblood fishing rooms, and overlooked by trim houses behind neat picket fences.

My mother's birthplace.

Dad loved Fogo too. It was the salt water and boats that drew him. Often he wished for a schooner, nowhere more so than while operating streetcars in

New York, sweating in his prickly woollen uniform in the pounding July heat. He seldom came to Fogo without arranging to go cod-jigging with Uncle Jabe, his brother-in-law. "Need some rounders for the winter, b'y," he'd say.

Planning these expeditions, the expert river guide would defer to Jabe's superior local knowledge: "No, Brett, my son, Eastern Tickle's too risky with the wind in like this." Next thing they'd be poring over a set of nineteenth century sailing instructions. Two or three dozen rounders – small cod – and several meals of fresh fish and brewis later, my father would be gone, back to his guiding, promising to return in ten days' time, "weather permitting." Always that caveat.

From spring through autumn, life in Fogo fairly galloped. The fishermen were up and steaming for the offer grounds before daylight. By the time the sun leapt out of the sea they were already handlining cod, baiting trawl lines, hauling traps. They prayed for a tuck o' fish but if they got a waterhaul, so be it. By midday, with any luck, they had the midship-room half full of mottled, twitching, wide-eyed, big-mouthed cod. And a pot of fish and brewis steaming on the tiny stove for dinner. By three o'clock they were back in harbour, forking fish onto stageheads. By four or five their knives were flashing over splitting tables and pips were raining down trunk holes.

Sometimes on the longest days of midsummer they might venture out again for a second catch. Then for sure they'd be working 'till all hours, by lantern light if need be. They never quit until the catch was safely salted down, no matter if it took all night. Or I might see them after supper by the landwash in some cove, cast-netting caplin for bait or fertilizer or dog food or all three. Or, come August, see a flock of punts jigging squid and trading news and gossip. It was this very scene which 15-year-old Change Islander Art Scammell described in a ballad he published the summer I was nine:

> Some are workin' their jiggers while others are yarnin',
> There's some standin' up and there's more lyin' down;
> While all kinds of fun, jokes and tricks are begun;
> As they wait for the squid on the squid-jiggin' ground.

With the onset of good drying weather, acres of stilted flakes gradually whitened with creamy drifts of salted cod laid head to tail, tail to head. The cod was tended like toast by bent and kerchiefed women of all ages from dawn to dark. "Time to spread the fish, my son. Time to turn the fish, maid. Mercy; 'tis gonna pour; hurry and take the fish in now."

By late August the fish was all cured. Then the rush was on to load the boats and hustle to the merchants' wharves to settle up.

Long before that, the new spuds needed trenching and fertilizing with handbars of caplin dug in; hay meadows were ripe for scything; herring and squid bait came ashore and went again; bakeapples and blueberries begged to be plucked; root crops needed digging; sheep needed shearing; livestock needed shelter. And then it would be winter, that cloistered season of trap and gear mending, of spinning and quilting, or sewing sails to dress the fleet for another summer down on the Labrador.

A hard but good life if you didn't weaken and you didn't forget to pray and the "Good Lard" didn't forget to listen.

Fogo's women worked even harder than their men. Not so much Aunt Fanny, whose husband was on wages, but all her former schoolmates who had married into fishing families had the flakes to tend to, as well as elderly grandparents, babies and household chores. When they weren't down on their knees scrubbing muddy floors or up to their elbows in hot soapy water, scrubbing shirts and socks and pants on the washboard, you'd find them up to the clothesline, youngster in tow, to hang out the wash, or in the henhouse collecting eggs for a birthday cake.

Or they might dart in over the hill with a clutch of other women – almost a vacation – to sow root vegetables in postage-stamp gardens manured with kelp and cods' heads. Or they might be setting yeast for barm, kneading bread dough, fetching another scuttle of coal, coaxing the finicky oven not to burn the bread, milking the goats that bleated at the gate, walking to Jack Baker's or Mrs. Furze's for a reel of thread or a bottle of Sloan's Liniment, cleaning, trimming, filling the lamps against the coming night, mending cuffs and socks until "'tis time for the blessed bed." Not to mention dressing the youngsters for school, dressing their small wounds, knitting mitts and garnseys and, always, seeing their men off at daybreak with a mug o' tea.

My mother's world. The world she had escaped. Sometimes her people teased her for marrying a "Gander Bay Noddy," a reference to the fulmar, which nods its head in flight. In self-defence we called her people "Fogo Jumpers."

Fogo people *were* different. Faced with unique challenges, they had devised unique solutions. Their gardens, for instance. Overwhelmed with rock, they made gardens not where they wanted but wherever it was possible. That might be by the house or a gunshot in over the hills. To that precious plot they toted rockweed and caplin and hen manure in season until the soil was bursting with vitamins and vigour.

Handier ground they cultivated for kitchen greens, even a scattered rose bush, even strawberries. Aunt Fanny grew strawberries on the scrap of ground they had out front. By August the berries were miraculously fat and sweet. She reprimanded me once when I picked some without permission. "Those are for Sunday dessert," she explained.

Fogo goats, like Fogo hens, wore yokes for that reason. The goats were forever probing loose gates and broken pickets, forever gauging the heights of fences and stiles. The preventive yokes consisted of three narrow wooden slats fastened at the corners after being fitted over the goat's head. This frame they wore all summer. The slats chafed at first but they soon got used to it. Over time, the wood, darkened by natural oils and polished by rubbing, became handsome as ebony.

We could have used yokes like those the year our goats raided my parents' vegetable garden. All my father's hard work wasted. "Brett, don't worry," said my mother. "You make two yokes and they won't get in again, guaranteed." Yokes in Gander Bay? People would snicker. He raised the fence instead.

The house my mother grew up in was only a few minutes' west of Aunt Fanny's. The front garden, large by Fogo standards, sloped steeply down to the main road. By the gate they had gooseberry and currant bushes, but by my time they had gone bushy for lack of pruning. I could see the outline of a vegetable garden as well. Uncle Tom's cooper shop was just outside the gate beside the road, the same one his father had built after Prudence fell ill. When Grandpa Layman retired around 1940, I believe he willed the shop and house to Uncle Tom and his wife Carrie.

On one of our visits my parents took me to my grandparents' house. Instead of walking up the main road, which meant a climb down and another one up, we took the short cut along the ridge between, using a goat path. Dad opened the back gate, knocked at the porch door and entered. It was my first time and I felt awkward. Also there seemed to be some sort of tension in the air, something to do with Mom's father no longer living there perhaps, or some memory of her poor mother who had died upstairs in total helplessness.

The porch led into a spotless kitchen, from which Aunt Carrie's clear nasal voice rang out in hearty greeting. "Take off your shoes," Dad whispered, "or Carrie will follow you with a wet mop." We stood making small talk, then moved into the cool dim parlour for tea and fruit cake. Aunt Carrie, a head taller than Mom and very erect, opened the heavy drapes. I saw floral wallpaper, upholstered furniture and a wide mantelpiece crowded with vases and candlesticks and a large pink conch shell. A large bevelled mirror multiplied their reflections.

Uncle Tom, a swarthy, stooped, smiling man in his late thirties but looking older, explained how an ancestor had brought the shell from the South Seas long ago. Rough and spiky on the outside, inside it gleamed like porcelain. When he placed it to my ear, I heard the Pacific Ocean. One of the spikes had been sawn off, leaving a round hole. "Makes a good foghorn," he said. I made as if to blow it but my mother shook her head – germs, I supposed. He also showed us a fist-sized smooth white cylinder that had been a sperm whale's tooth.

My favourite object lay on the floor, a stuffed white baby seal on a polar bear rug. "You can play with the white coat if you're careful," said Aunt Carrie. So while the grownups chatted about this and that, I flopped beside it and stroked its stiff yellowing hair. It had limpid black glass eyes that looked wet and soulful. There was also a stereoscope with pairs of photographs to view. I would have liked to play with it, but wasn't invited to. That might have been the year my parents got me the Viewmaster for Christmas.

Grandpa Layman had built the small cooper shop down by the road around 1923, the better to care for my grandmother Prudence. At age forty-two she began to suffer splitting headaches and then to go blind. As Twillingate's hospital was a year away from completion, Henry had first taken her to St. Anthony's, an overnight boat trip. Dr. Grenfell referred her to a St. John's specialist. The specialist diagnosed an inoperable frontal brain tumour which was destroying one or both optic nerves. He advised my grandfather to take her home to die.

For a vivacious woman who loved poetry, literature and classical music, this was a hard sentence. A year or two later, one or more strokes left her wholly paralysed, unable to dress, feed or even clean herself.

Layman's original cooper shop was a sprawling affair which dated back to around 1850. That was when Henry's father, Thomas William Layman, already a master cooper at age twenty, arrived from England's West Country. He was trained for both "tight" cooperage (for liquids such as cod oil) and "slack" cooperage (for dry products such as salt cod). He could also turn out butter tubs, water barrels, nail kegs and net floats.

Thomas had come to the right place. Fogo had been a salt cod and sealing centre for a century, and though its inshore fishery was declining, Labrador was showing great promise. Apart from his coopering skills, Thomas had, or seemed to have, a tantalizing connection to recent English history. His father William was believed to have sailed under the immortal Lord Horatio Nelson during several successful campaigns. Nelson was supposed to have declared, on hearing a rumour that Layman was lost, "I'd rather lose a dozen ships than lose a William Layman!"

The connection seems plausible only if the elder William had lived at least four years longer, or if Thomas William had been born four years sooner. Even so, was it mere coincidence that Thomas had named one of his boys Horatio, and that two of his other children, Hamilton and Emma, were named for Nelson's longtime paramour, Lady Emma Hamilton?

An early 1900s photograph of the main cooper shop showed ten men standing outside against a wall of new barrels, four tiers deep. Henry Eldred, tallest of the lot, stands second from the right, stoop-shouldered, fortyish, wearing the canvas or leather apron of his trade. It was a seasonal trade but a demanding one, especially in late summer. Orders could pile up, and they had able competitors. Still, Layman's had a good crew and they all made a decent living.

Henry's decision to work from home did not lessen his productivity. When he fell behind, he worked longer hours. Once when his step-brother Hamilton was laid up sick, Henry toiled all night, doing Ham's quota as well as his own rather than let the customer down.

Neighbours watching him hurry between cooperage and home every hour or two, tending shop and wife, wagged their heads in sympathy. So much trouble at his door. By the time Prudence went blind, the couple had already lost two children: Baby Alma in 1919 and five-year-old Lydia Lucretia a year later. At forty-five his six-foot-four frame, already stooped from bending over hundreds of barrels, sagged a little more. And they still had three children at home to care for, namely Tom and Harry Jr. at about age fourteen and twelve, respectively, and little Beatrix at eight.

Meanwhile the eldest, Winnie, had finished Grade 11 at fifteen and worked as a messenger girl for the Fogo post office, where she soon picked up enough Morse code to relieve the overworked postmaster. At sixteen she took the Department of Posts and Telegraphs exam from Fogo's chief Marconi Operator Edward J. Myrick and scored a perfect grade. A year later she was post-mistress in nearby Change Islands, another bustling saltfish centre.

And no wonder; she was a natural. Being ambidextrous – fully right- and left-handed – she never suffered the crippling "telegraphist's wrist." This was a form of carpel tunnel syndrome caused by the constant pressing of the spring-loaded key that produced the electrical "dot and dash" static which land lines – telegraph wires – carried to the earphones of listening operators within a 50-mile radius.

Moreover, she scribbled like the wind. Every incoming telegram had to be transcribed into legible English. Her handwriting was also ambidextrous and designed for speed: no flourishes, no tall or deep loops, no ornate capitals, no periods even, just dashes.

When Change Islands offered her the post-mistress job, her parents at first vetoed it. Their concern was the large amounts of cash involved: duty on parcels, sometimes large money orders and C.O.D. payments, petty cash. Only after Mr. Myrick reassured them their daughter was qualified and capable would they consent. This made her the youngest operator in Newfoundland's postal system, and, according to her telegrapher brother Harry, one of its most proficient.

Her parents' fears were well founded. Only a few years later, working in Clarkes Head's post office, she herself would fall under suspicion. One day she relieved postmaster Paddy Farrell. That very night someone stole the office safe and a substantial sum of cash. Neither the 200-pound safe nor the culprit was ever found. Few suspected her or Dad – who was away – but the incident bred mistrust and troubled them for years.

That Mom started working so early suggests her family needed the extra income. Henry's decision to work from home likely hurt sales. In a good year a professional cooper working alone might expect to earn $250. His increasing medical and travel expenses, not to mention the cost of building and equipping a new shop and of transporting barrels the extra distance to

Earles' by horse and wagon, would have eaten into that.

Even with his boys helping after school in the shop, he might have been hard pressed to make ends meet. A few dollars from his eldest daughter would have been welcome. Besides, Fanny had married young and the couple were living with them, helping with Prudence. After about 1923, when Winnie became post-mistress in Clarkes Head, her contributions would have increased.

Having met my father in Gander Bay, in 1926 she invited him to travel with her and some Fogo friends to New York City. Armed with four years of experience and a reference letter from George A. Veitch, the colony's superintendent of posts and telegraphs, she soon became assistant wireless operator for the city's Postal Telegraphy Company, which had offices in the new Biltmore Hotel. This prompted her to send her younger brother Harry a postcard which read, "This is where I work. What do you think of it?" It was there she came to have Scottish tea baron Sir Thomas Lipton, who had a suite of offices, as a client.

Meanwhile, her mother was dying. Little Beatrix, Henry's youngest, saw it all. In 2006, aged eighty-nine, she responded by letter to yet another of my requests for information:

> Papa and Fanny took care of her. She was fed with a spoon until she passed away. She had to be turned over and changed several times a day. I could hear my mother screaming with pain, which I understood was headaches…I would get dressed for school in her room and kiss her before I left. After school I would go into her room, hug and kiss her, same routine each day. I do not remember her features. I do recall she had pretty red hair.
>
> I was ten when she died. My Sunday clothes were kept in a drawer in her room. I went in as usual and got on her bed to kiss her. She didn't respond…I ran downstairs and down the road to get Dr. Mackenzie. Harry was devastated. Aunt Lydia came and took me away with her. The last thing I remember, when she was in her casket, is Harry with a mirror, checking to see whether Mother was breathing.
>
> I sat next to Papa in church. Her favourite hymn was "When I Survey the Wondrous Cross." As we sang it, my Dad stood so tall, holding my hand, tears rolling down his cheeks.

> Thank God we were blessed with the best father one could ever have.

I hadn't known about the hymn; yet its pathos and poetry had always wrung my heart too:

> See from his head, his hands, his feet,
> Sorrow and love flow mingled down;
> Did e'er such love and sorrow meet,
> Or thorns compose so rich a crown?

After age twelve my Fogo ambit widened to include day-long expeditions to the hinterland's trout ponds and berry barrens. But the chief attractions were still its wharves, stageheads and landwash. And now I had a sidekick, my eight-year-old cousin Aubrey. With me playing big brother, he could rove where he wasn't supposed to go yet.

We found the saltcod premises irresistible. There was so much going on. Boat traffic was constant, with trap skiffs and bulley boats converging from Joe Batt's Arm, Barr'd Islands, Hare Bay, Island Harbour, Seldom, and Tilting. The wharves were heaped with incoming fish. Tempers flared as fishermen and buyers haggled over prices. We could have been run over or bumped overboard. More than once we were bawled out for getting in the way.

Two big attractions for us were the company store and catching conners. While the store contained mostly fishing supplies, it also carried sweets: peppermint knobs, suckers, common candy. Whenever Aub and I had a few pennies, we bought some before heading home.

It was Aub who taught me to jig conners, the small ocean perch that hung around all wharves eating fish guts. Brownish fish with blue bellies, they ranged from three to twelve inches long. We brought our own pole and net twine, picked some *wrinkles* (periwinkles) on the way for bait and each bought a Mustad Number 15 hook at the store. Then we'd flop on our bellies at the high wharf's edge, stick out our poles and dangle the bait.

Since no one ate conners, we laid our catches on the wharf as trophies. Their small mouths made them frustratingly hard to catch, so I bought a triple-hook jigger that easily snagged them as they crowded round. Tiring of this, we'd kick our trophies overboard and find something else to do. No catch-and-release for us.

When not making a nuisance of myself around the wharves and stage-heads, I was hunting rock crabs by the landwash. I spent hours catching and studying these curious crustaceans. They were something new. Aub had little use for them, perhaps because his mother disapproved of them. She wrinkled her nose at my researches. "They eat dead things, you know," she'd say. "You shouldn't be handling them." It didn't impress her that they could grow new claws when they lost one, or dance sideways on tip-toe. To her they were just scavengers with a nasty pinch.

Another Fogo novelty was tansy eels. Slender as pencils, they lived under rockweed and sometimes twined around my ankles, but never bit. Some called them blennies.

Somewhere between the landwash, fishing premises, berry barrens and trout ponds, I fell in love. At least it felt like love. She had a lovely name too: Willa Hart. Willa was near my age and lived across the way and was likely a cousin of Phyllis and Greta's. Sometimes she showed her pretty face in their yard.

My budding interest in Willa in particular and girls in general, however, perturbed my mother. Another infection to ward off, I suppose. If I lingered anywhere too long, even in a public place, she sent Greta or Aub to spy me out and nudge me home. This was annoying. Between summer's jigs and reels my undeclared love withered on the vine.

I took to climbing the higher hills alone, including Brimstone Head. I wanted to test the legend that if the wind was right you'd smell the Devil's sulfur up there. I never did smell any, but it was worth the climb to see the whole town of a thousand spread out below, clustered round its ancient volcano like barnacles on a cliff.

On some of the hills sat rusty cannons on pock-marked concrete slabs; relics, I supposed, of England's many wars with France. One of them crouched right above Aunt Fanny's house.

"American freebooters!" snorted Uncle Jabe when I asked about it. "Grandfather Hart said they was worse than the French. After the thirteen colonies broke away from England, and again during the war of 1812, they'd sail down 'ere from the Boston States and burn our stages, swipe our fish. A friend of 'is, Mr. Torraville, fired on 'em once and good for 'im!"

Youthful sailors celebrating their youthful nation – who could blame them? I climbed back up and sighted along the cannon. Its muzzle was still aimed square at Middle Tickle. There was talk of joining Canada. Grandpa Saunders, for one, was dead against it. All I needed was a match, a peck of powder and an iron ball to fire a shot for *my* country, Newfoundland. But someone had stogged the muzzle with rocks.

Mishaps and Misdemeanours

Thank God Mom saw the smoke in time. It was the first indoor fire I'd set and I stood transfixed as it blossomed golden on a bench in the woodshed. My parents lit fires all the time; what was wrong with it? I was torn between exultation and fear. What would happen now?

My plan had gone well until she came. Now she was standing behind me, hands at her temples, speechless, blocking my escape. "Naughty boy!" she cried, thrusting me away from the crackling blaze. "Don't you move one inch until I tell you!" With that she ran for the porch, grabbed a bucket, filled it from the water barrel and raced back. My lovely fire died in a hissing cloud of steam.

Then she frisked me for matches and lashed me with her tongue. When my father came home she told him and he laced my bottom with an alder switch. I was sore for a week. But I never set fire to the woodshed again. A good thing, as it was less than four yards from the house. Where had I found the matches? They decided I must have climbed on a chair. Or found them in Dad's pants pocket while he slept – he was still smoking then. They shook their heads in dismay; their little boy had become an arsonist. They took steps to fire-proof me.

Years later, noticing a small ball-peen hammer with a blackened handle, I asked my mother about it. "Don't you remember?" she said, "That time, when you were four, that you set fire to the woodshed?" I nodded. "The hammer was on the bench when the fire started. It only scorched the handle so Dad kept it." Then I remembered how it got there. I had tried to light my first match the way Dad did, by stroking it across the nearest surface, the bench cover. When the first two broke and failed to light, I'd whacked the third with that same hammer.

Another burnt handle came to mind. It happened that winter. Company was coming, and Dad had lit the stove in the inside room and Mom had set the table with her best bone-handled cutlery. While she got supper in the kitchen I took one of the knives and poked its blade through one of the stove's mica windows to see how hard they were.

The blade buried itself to the hilt. In moments the bone handle was too hot to touch. It began to smoke and stink, which brought my mother on the run. Swiftly she folded her apron over the handle, yanked it out and laid the ruined knife on the fender. "Don't touch!" she cried, and rushed to greet the guests. Before being sent to bed I noticed how the hot blade faded from gold to lavender to blue. Later, a third of its handle eaten away, the knife became a paint scraper. It was around for years. I often wished they'd thrown it out that night. Every time my parents used it I relived my crime.

It didn't cure me though. One fall when I was five or six and Dad was getting ready to guide moose hunters, packing his canvas tent and tin stove, I decided to make a stove of my own. Using a can opener, I worried the end out of a large juice tin without cutting myself, and using a big nail and a hammer, punched a smoke hole in the other end. Somewhere I found a match – being an inch or two taller helped.

With my stove and kindling hidden under my coat, I strolled nonchalantly toward the back gate as if to use the outhouse. Once there I ducked behind the goat shed, where I hoped no one could see me from any direction. The only witnesses that could were our three dogs, who wagged their tails and strained at their chains as I passed. But they wouldn't tell.

Propping the can against the shed, I stuffed it with birch rind, scraped my match on a rock and plunged the spurting flame into the tinder. As tongues of fire licked up through the fuel, I sat back to watch. Suddenly my mother's shoes appeared beside me. This time she was less charitable. With a stick she lifted the hot can clear and dumped it in a puddle. She marched me to the house and again fetched Dad. He made me bring my pretend stove, and, while I watched, squashed it under his heel. This time he needed no alder switch. One pained look from his sea-grey eyes reduced me to tears. I never played with fire on the property again.

But how had my mother known? Had she been short-taken and hurried to the outhouse? She could have seen me from there. Then I remembered the dogs. She must have seen their antics from the kitchen window and known something was up. However it was, she saved another building that day.

It was around this time I chewed my first tobacco. I would probably have smoked it too, for I'd often seen my father roll a cigarette and light it, but all matches seemed to have disappeared from our house. His favourite tobacco was called Hi-Plane and came in a slim, pocket-sized turquoise tin with a hinged top and an airplane winging across the side. He kept it on the radio table. Turquoise was then my favourite colour. I took tin and tobacco into my hideout under the nearby table to study.

I had seen men chew tobacco down at the shop. The old men who sat around there yarning did it all the time. Seemed to be enjoying it too, squirting brown juice precisely into the bucket no matter what the angle. They chewed Beaver plug tobacco. I liked to watch them pare off moist brown flakes of it with their pocket knives, rub them between their calloused palms and, pausing in mid-sentence, tuck it in their cheeks. I would try that too.

Hiding behind the green tablecloth, I took a large pinch and tucked it into my check. The tobacco was loose and dry, and took some time to moisten. As my virgin membranes felt the sting of nicotine, saliva welled up under my tongue. I needed to spit, but had no container. I swallowed instead. Immediately my gorge rose. I dropped the can and crawled toward the kitchen retching. Whether Mom stuck a finger down my throat or made me drink salt water or both, I don't recall. All I know is that the tobacco juice came up, and came, and came.

From fire I went to water. Water enthralled me from an early age. I'd start with meltwater puddles, cold as they were. I would dodge along the wet meadow, bending low to see my dark reflection, finding small underwater treasures: a lost coat button, a dropped penny, a comb, every object glowing with microscopic clarity. So clear, I'd reach to pick something up and wet my sleeve to the elbow. Or I'd take a step and fill my shoe. And because it was spring, cold and muddy, I'd come home spattered and shivering. Spring rain was nice too, with water chuckling everywhere and each puddle like a bright eye staring up. Summer rain was the best because the water was warm and I could wade barefoot.

Decades later, Aunt Beatty wrote me about my addiction:

> I was always trying to keep your feet dry. You loved to wade in any drop of water you could find. Your mom used to be worried sick. You were always either leaning over the wharf or down on the landwash, even though she told you not to go near either.
>
> Your dad wasn't so patient. One day he declared he'd had it with you being around the water. So he threw you out! Of course he could reach you and it wasn't deep. I presume he thought he could scare you off it. I shall always remember it. Your mom and I talked about that many times.

No, fighting water with water didn't work. The long rubber incident proved it. Most rivermen wore long rubbers. They had to, being in and out of boats so much. The boot they swore by was a version of the British Wellington, made of synthetic rubber, lightweight yet durable and reaching to the thigh. They were just stiff enough to stay up without being strapped to one's belt; yet they could be snugged tight against rain or twigs by a short buckle. On land or in boat they wore them neatly rolled to below the knee. In cold weather they wore a felt inner sole with two pairs of socks. You could wear them all winter that way. A very practical boot.

To a Gander Bay boy it was much more. It was a badge of manhood, the mark of a true riverman, a licence to wade deeper; which is why my brother was so tickled, at age seven or eight, to be presented with his own pair. So tickled, in fact, that he went down to the beach and waded in over the tops. When he came home, sheepish and sopping wet, our father punished him in a way he never forgot. Dad pulled the rubbers off, slapped him with them about the shoulders, lopped them down to knee length and handed them back.

"My timing was bad," said Calvin years later. "He was in the middle of taking out our old Waterloo stove and trying to install the new Bridgewall range. The floor was all sooty and Mom was naturally upset." I was too young to witness his humiliation – if I had, it might have kept me out of further water trouble – but the episode likely convinced Dad never to buy me a pair. If he had, perhaps I wouldn't have borrowed his.

It happened one spring when the meadow was flooded. I'd noticed his rubbers standing in the porch, doing nothing. They were twice as tall, even rolled down, as my knee boots. I'd never get wet in *them!* When no one was watching I tried them on. They were so big no amount of socks would ever make them fit me. But if I held onto the rims and hoisted them at every step, I could waddle along.

The shimmering meadow beckoned. Soon, mesmerized by sky reflections, walking on clouds, I stepped in a mud hole. First the right boot stuck, then the left. Pull as I might, they only sank deeper. Too proud to call for help, I was forced to abandon them and wallow ashore in sock feet. Dad's boots looked forlorn standing out there empty, but I daren't go back. Wet again, punished again – but at least not drowned. Someone else must have rescued his boots.

My most embarrassing water mishap occurred one Sunday in late summer as my parents were preparing to visit Aunt Marion and Uncle Roy Reccord in Victoria Cove. I was to come too. While they got ready I went out on the wharf. Thinking we were going in Grandpa's motor boat, I stepped aboard it. After a while, for something to do, I started pacing the gunnels. My object was to walk clear around without losing my balance. The second time round, I stepped on a smear of engine grease and fell in. I surfaced soon enough but couldn't reach the rail. And my heavy wool sweater kept dragging me under. The wharf was only a short swim away but I couldn't swim. Gulping water, I started dog-paddling, making for the wharf ladder. On the way, I remember thinking, this must be what it's like to drown. So much for my magic birth caul. At one point I wanted to just sink. At last, exhausted, I hauled myself out and crawled onto the wharf.

That was when my parents arrived. It turned out they had planned to go by canoe. As I came dripping toward them, my father eyed me narrowly. Mom wanted me to change into dry clothes but he said, "No," quivering with anger. "He got himself wet, let him stay wet till we gets back. Teach him a lesson." If she dared not gainsay him, I certainly wouldn't. Silently I climbed into the bow. He picked up his river pole – was he going to hit me? –

and shoved off.

It so happened Mom had brought our Gerald S. Doyle blanket. She often brought it on boat trips. It was a double wool blanket, dark blue on one side, olive green on the other. We called it that because Mr. Doyle himself gave it to her on one of his trips selling patent medicines around Notre Dame Bay. Dad sometimes guided him on salmon fishing trips, and no doubt Grandpa's store bought his products. In the early 1930s this kind man would lend my father his outboard motor until Dad could afford his own.

The wind that day was raw, Victoria Cove nearly an hour's steam away. As soon as Dad was distracted, bailing water or something, Mom folded me in the blanket. Even so, my teeth were chattering when we arrived. But Aunt Marion cajoled her stern brother into letting her lend me a shirt and pants of Uncle Roy's. So the return trip was not so bad; I didn't catch pneumonia.

Why, I often wondered, was my father so fearful of water? He couldn't swim – but then, few Gander Bay men could. I decided it must have to do with Uncle Stan, Grandma's younger brother who drowned in 1924. Poor Stan, as they called him, was only thirty-two at the time. His death puzzled many because he was a strong swimmer, a skilled woodsman and a seasoned river driver. People said Stanley could jump on a floating log, stick in his pike pole, run to the other end and stand there as if on solid ground. "Like the cat," they said of him. It was said that he had once dunked the legendary boss of the Exploits River drive, Ronald Kelley.

Uncle Stan had not only introduced my father to muskrat trapping, he had shown him how to catch winter beaver – though the season had been closed for years. Stanley would roll the illegal pelts in an old sail and hide them in the shop cellar to sell on the sly. On one of those expeditions, Dad fell through the ice. It was nighttime and he was sure he'd have drowned had his uncle not rescued him.

But in the spring of 1924 my father was bound for Toronto, so Stanley had to take another muskrat trapping partner. On the way up Second Narrows, a gust of wind capsized their canoe. The partner survived but Stanley drowned. Oddly, the man spent that night alone in camp and then left for home without even looking for the body.

My father joined the search party. They found his uncle's bloated body floating face-down in the eddy below the Narrows. When the searchers returned to Clarkes Head, the crowd on the wharf heard them singing "Nearer my God to thee" as they paddled ashore. Sorrowing in the crowd was Grandma. The hymn was a sign they'd found him. My father embarked for Toronto after the funeral, taking his grief with him.

For a long time I was a sugar addict. The minute my mother was out of the kitchen I was into the stuff. I'd spoon it in and savour its melting, let it dribble down my throat. After she hid the sugar bowl, I'd dissolve my fix in warm water and drink it that way. It had less kick, but by swishing it around I got some satisfaction. Breaking that habit took months, and only happened after I found a substitute.

It was called common (mixed) candy. Grandfather sold it from big flat-sided clear glass jars. From then on, whatever money I had went on common candy. If I had none I'd avert my eyes from the rainbow jars in the shop window. I was sure they were put there to torment me.

One Newfoundland penny – two cents – would buy about five pieces. Grandpa also sold unmixed candy. If you couldn't make up your mind, he'd wave his scoop at each jar in turn: "Peppermint knobs? Is that what you want? Or chicken bones? Gumdrops? Toffee? Licorice? Or just common candy? I haven't got all day!"

I always went for common candy because a penny bought more and you didn't have to choose. I liked the different flavours and especially the colours: red for cherry, yellow for lemon, black for licorice, white for almond – which I usually threw away – and orange.

The process itself was interesting to watch. After peeling a small brown paper bag from its pile and snapping it open with a wrist-flick, my grandfather would twirl the lid off the jar and rummage with a tin scoop until it had about the right amount of the sugar-dusted candies. Then he'd shake the exact number into the bag, dump the surplus ones back, close the lid and fold the paper over itself exactly twice. He'd punch the price into his ornate chrome cash register, yank the lever to open the till and drop my penny in. Then he'd bustle into his office while I dodged down to the landwash and sat on a rock and decided which colour to eat first.

A few days and I'd be back for more. One day Grandpa said, "How'd you like to earn some money?"

"I wouldn't mind, sir."

"Well, I need two boys to sweep out the Number Four store tomorrow before the steamer comes."

"If Frank will help, I will."

"Good. Go ask him and tell me what he says."

That was my first paying job. I was nine or ten. It was a big job too, even for the two of us, to sweep out a store at least five yards by ten. We swept every foot of it except the rat-proof wire pen where he kept flour and oatmeal and livestock feed. We kept at it all morning and didn't fight; around dinnertime we were back at the counter, flicking sawdust out of our hair, waiting for our wages.

"Well then," said Grandpa. "You swept it all clean?"

"Yes sir."

"Even under the benches?"

"Oh yes."

"And dumped all the dust off the wharf?"

"Yes sir."

"Good then." He went to the candy shelf and gave us each a sucker. Frank and I traded a glance. A sucker didn't seem like much for a whole morning's work, coughing on dust, our shirts and scalps prickly with sweat. We could have been trouting or something. We went home in a bad mood and tried to forget.

I couldn't. It wasn't just that I was an addict, it was the injustice of it all.

I hatched a plan and put it to Frank. Why not steal a whole jar of candy, whisk it to a secret place and share the loot? Frank, more honest and less addicted than I, knitted his thick black brows in thought. But the prospect of having all the candy we could eat overcame his doubts – to a point. He would stand guard for me.

Grandpa was serving a customer when we peeped in. We waited until he went back in his office. With Frank scanning the road, I slipped behind the counter, snatched the full jar in both hands – it was heavier than

I thought – and hurried out. Where to go? We stood whispering alternatives. Frank was for hiding under the shop. I was for hiding in the tepee of firewood stacked behind the cow barn. His plan was better; but I had the candy.

Unfortunately, my route led right past Grandma's windows. Had it been winter I could have hid the jar under my windbreaker. As it was, I was wearing a singlet. So my cousin and I walked as nonchalantly as possible with the jar between us, hoping against hope she wasn't looking.

We made it through the back gate, ducked into the hideout and were sharing it out when a shadow fell over us. Grandma's form filled the opening. Her normally benign and mirthful face looked cross and sorrowful.

"And what are you two up to?"

"Nothin', Grandma."

"Where did you get all that candy?"

"From the shop."

"Does Grandpa know?"

"Errr…"

We waited for the thunderbolt. Instead she lifted the jar, replaced the cover and stood up.

"This is stealing. Stealing is wrong. It hurts other people and, what is worse, it breaks one of God's commandments. Shame on you. But since you wanted candy so badly, I'm leaving you a handful each. While eating them, think on what I've said. But first you must promise never to take anything from the shop without permission again. Do you understand?"

"Yes, Grandma."

"Yes, Ma'am."

Not another word was said about it. Her act of mercy left me so ashamed and grateful I was never tempted to steal candy again. It was true she caught me stealing turnips from her garden years later, but that was different – an experiment with bow and arrow and twine that she laughed off.

As for my other misdeeds in Clarkes Head in those years, they either went undetected or were too petty to bother with. Of the latter, I can think of several that amaze and embarrass me still.

Drinking my own piss, for example. It started as a dare between six-year-old male cousins, then took on an aura of science and ended up as a horrible taste. We conducted the experiment in Uncle Harold's woodshed. It was all over in a minute: pee in to the bottle, brace the stomach, swallow. I drank mine, all the way down; he spat his out. It was exceedingly bitter – and surprisingly warm. Had we waited for it to cool, we would have lost our nerve.

That same summer, in the same spirit of scientific enquiry, we tried to solve the riddle of sex. I politely asked two younger female cousins to display their private parts. Not in those exact words, of course. What I actually said, using our native West Country dialect, was "Lemme see yer *ding* (thing)." I wanted to compare the two. One girl giggled and demurred; the other said yes – "for a penny."

The compliant one dropped her bloomers and lifted her short dress. I remember feeling vaguely disappointed. Nothing much to see there. Like the conquering Roman general who barged into Jerusalem temple's Holy of Holies expecting to find Israel's God, only to find a carved box with two angels on the lid, I'd expected more – but wasn't sure quite what. The same thing happened when I hid under an outdoor toilet for an hour one afternoon, to be finally rewarded with the sight of a wavy pink slit bisecting a hairy moon that gave no light. Was this what all the fuss was about?

To satisfy our curiosity once and for all, a pack of us cornered a ewe in the privacy of an alder bed, and lifted her tail. This confirmed the rumour that female mammals did indeed have two openings to our one, but as for which orifice was for pee and which for sex, we could not determine without holding her a long time. While waiting, we puzzled our heads over the question of how a ram, let alone a man, could enter such a tiny opening. For rumour had it…On being released, the ewe bounded off with an offended *baa-a-a*, shaking her head.

Some misdeeds were mere mischief. One day, opening a fresh stick of gum, I noticed how much it looked like the grey cardboard inside a cereal box. What if I cut a stick of cardboard, dusted it with icing sugar and re-wrapped it, foil and all? For added realism I put the finished item back in the package with the real ones.

"Want a stick o' gum?" I'd say, proffering the fake one.

"Sure." I'd stay just long enough to see them bite on the cardboard, then bolt before the punch or kick hit home. Another prank was to take some item of value, say a pocket knife, and lay it on the road with a hidden thread running to some nearby hiding place. Soon someone would happen by and stoop to pick it up, only to have it skitter out of reach. Most people caught on right away, others would keep trying until they heard me laughing. A few, perhaps embarrassed, would lose their tempers and I'd have to apologize.

One June, on the outs with Frank again, I took a pickle jar, filled it with live bumblebees, opened his screen door, emptied them inside and ran, wishing multiple stingings on the whole brood – except Susie. The last I saw of my bees, they were writhing in slow motion on the floor, with some damp ones struggling away from the wreck. Not one flew or stung anyone.

I had a mean streak, no doubt about it. Ted Reccord confirmed it years later during a sentimental New Year's call. Telephoning from California, perhaps slightly drunk, he asked, "Do you remember the day when some older girls were tormenting you out by the mill?" No, I couldn't. "Well, suddenly you grabbed a piece of whippy edging and cracked the ringleader across the knees!"

"I did?"

"Oh yes! She ran home howling!"

I did recall making Susie cry one day. Frank and I were heading to the Sawdust Road on some quest or other and she kept trailing us. He told her to go back, but she kept coming. To discourage her I tossed a piece of bark in her direction. It smacked her right in the head, surprising me as much as her.

Ted knew nothing of that, but could have said much worse things of me. He could have told how my friends and I sometimes mistreated *him*. For Ted, long before we knew him, had contracted rheumatic fever as a toddler. The disease damaged his heart, which sometimes left him short of breath, unable to keep up with us.

More than once, in our cruelty, we left him behind. He in turn would curse and yell at us and call us names from a safe distance. Already an outsider by virtue of living in the States with a single mom, the last thing he needed was for us to rub salt in the wound. I, soon to become an urban outsider myself, could have prevented that by reaching out to him. Instead I joined the mob.

Not that Ted and I were ever enemies. The year he attended school in Clarkes Head we had a lot of fun together. It was Grade 3, and by then we both could draw fairly well, especially cartoons. I could toss off a Dick Tracy in seconds; he could do the same with Superman.

That year they made the mistake of sitting us in the same row about four seats apart on the landwash side. On drowsy spring afternoons when the shore ice was melting and all outdoors beckoned, we'd doodle outrageous faces and secretly get our classmates to pass them between us.

Soon our warty geezers and toothless hags were detouring into adjacent rows. We could hear stifled giggles. Next we competed to see which of us could make someone laugh out loud first. Presently, Mr. White would catch on, seize our drawings and chastise Ted and me for disrupting the class. What class? we thought, as he mumbled on. At least now everyone was wide awake.

Never mind, we were heroes for the moment. Next week, God willing, we'd draw some more. Ted would later become an architectural draughtsman who designed American supermarkets.

Certain youthful episodes defied classification. Among these was poking fun at people, especially the old or simple-minded. In St. John's there was a youngish man who rode the buses continually; one seldom saw him anywhere else. The city must have issued him a free pass. He had a great mop of unruly hair, seldom shaved and wore a long black overcoat summer and winter. He smiled a lot, as if he found the world amusing, and seemed as gentle as a lamb.

What his real name was none of us knew, but we called him Silly Willy, even to his face. At first I couldn't do it. At home we called any adult "sir" or "ma'am" without exception. As time went on, however, I joined in the mild heckling and have been sorry ever since. Willy, saint that he was, just smiled on.

In Clarkes Head there was an old retired gentleman – Paddy Farrell's father, "Son" Farrell they called him – who lived next door to us for a year or two during my childhood. A seaman all his life, he "missed the ocean somethin' turrible." He'd sit outside Paddy's house in the hot sun wearing wool mitts. A lifetime of jigging cod and hauling nets had ruined his circulation. He would moan to passersby, "Oh, the *say*, how I misses the *say!*"

We boys poked secret fun at him, especially after a spectacular blood-red display of northern lights convinced him the end of the world was nigh. For this my parents scolded me severely. "You've no notion of what it's like," said Dad. "In New York City I missed the River day and night. You see, for Mr. Farrell, being surrounded by trees is the end of the world."

There was a similar episode that could have turned out worse. It involved a Métis girl, and took place one summer in the sawdust field where Silas dumped his loads. She was just a slim, dark-skinned girl with an axe, minding her own business, perhaps going to cut an alder fishing pole as I myself had done so often. She hadn't counted on meeting several older boys. When she did, she stopped and faced us. When one of us asked where she was going, she gave no answer except to brandish the axe. This annoyed one boy, who hurled a racial slur. I told him to shut up, which he did, and, stepping forward, asked her to give me the axe before someone got hurt.

She refused and raised it threateningly. Seeing fear in her eyes and figuring the axe was dull, I extended my left hand to take it. The blade fell, slicing the inside of my thumb deeply for half its length. She might have done it on purpose, or it could have been out of panic or fatigue. I never found out. None of us teased her after that. I went home with my thumb bloodied, she with her dignity intact. I still have the one-inch scar.

My other mishap with an axe was even more humiliating. I was skating up at Zena's meadow. I'd brought along a small hand axe, for testing the ice perhaps. Feeling hot and thirsty, I knelt and chopped some ice chips to suck on. In scooping them into my mouth, I touched my tongue on the blade, which instantly stuck. To make matters worse I dropped the hatchet, which yanked my tongue so hard I felt the root stretch.

It is hard to call for help with an axe hanging from your tongue. In any case, you don't want people to know. So there I was, bent over, a drooling idiot. It was easy to remedy the situation – just yank the axe blade off. I didn't have the courage. Yet the more I delayed, the more painful it would be. Surely, I reasoned, it couldn't be worse than pulling a tooth by tying it to a swinging door? So I yanked. The frozen steel came away, taking a postage stamp of my tongue with it. For a week I could eat or drink nothing hot.

It was in St. John's that I finally cured myself of stealing. This time, temptation caught me by surprise – and on a Sunday too. The victim, though I didn't like him, had never deliberately wronged me. It was not his fault that his family was well-off, that his parents gave him a weekly allowance while the rest of us had to beg for every copper. But he could have flaunted it less.

One Saturday afternoon a bunch of us were playing in his yard over on Casey Street – playing hide-and-seek, reading comics – when the kid announced he had lost a 50-cent piece. He said he needed it right away because the family was going out to Topsail Beach that evening after church. He didn't outright accuse us of picking his pocket – he just hinted. We made a show of hunting for it, then drifted home.

All through supper that coin sparkled in my brain. "Son, you're just picking at your food," said Mom. "What's wrong?"

"Nothing," I said. But mentally I was totting up the matinees and comic books and chocolate bars fifty cents would buy me.

That night in bed I made a plan. I'd get up extra early, go over to their place and do a thorough search. I was back with the coin in my pocket before Mom or Calvin woke up. After a decent interval I spent it – all on myself. Finder, keeper, spender. Despicable – the more so since no one suspected "such a nice boy," and since no confession or restitution was ever made.

The Christmas tree incident was the fault of both my brother and me. I was five or six the year Dad brought our first tree home. Having a house tree was unusual in rural Newfoundland in the 1940s, though my parents perhaps practised the custom while living in the States. Americans were doing so some sixty years before Prince Albert brought the custom to England. German mercenaries fighting the rebellious colonists had introduced the custom to the eastern seaboard, where it was soon adopted by both sides.

Our mother, always keen to try new things, likely asked him to cut it. She'd been the first woman to wear shorts in Clarkes Head, braving the censure of its pious elders to do so. A nice fir would brighten her meagre decorations, namely two crossed garlands of twisted red and green crepe paper with a red paper bell in the middle.

After Dad had set the fir tree up in the inside room, he handed Calvin and me a shoe box of ornaments and left us to decorate it. We started out amicably enough, winding ropes around the base and hanging baubles. However, when we got to where I could no longer reach but he could, tempers flared. Soon we were in a tug of war.

Our yelling brought Dad to investigate. He took one look at the tangled tinsel and smashed ornaments, grabbed the tree, strode through the kitchen and chucked it out, tinsel and all, into the snowy darkness. I wailed. Calvin slunk upstairs to his room. Mom sobbed. Dad sulked. We later hung our stockings; but the magic had fled.

After that, the foxy house saw no more Christmas trees. Our presents, if they wouldn't fit in a stocking, were left on a table. One year – a very good year for gifts – mine were left in a flour sack by my bed. From that day until I had children of my own, the season would taste bittersweet.

Gilbert Street

After our spring and summer on Bennett Avenue in 1946, after Calvin's decision to go back to school, after my parents' decision not to go back to Clarkes Head for the time being, we packed up and moved about a half-mile across town to cheaper lodgings for the winter. A half-mile across town, but a century back in time. It was here the old city got into my blood.

The actual taxi ride to number 47 took but minutes: east on LeMarchant, south on Springdale, east onto Gilbert. They picked Gilbert because it was close to Prince of Wales College, Calvin's new school, and even closer to Springdale Street School, where I would take Grade 5.

Dad, guiding on the River all summer, would be coming in late October, but not to stay. He'd be taking up new duties with the Newfoundland Fisheries Board, this time on the south coast. Whether he got home for Christmas I cannot recall. Christmas 1946 is a blank.

What I do recall, with almost mystic clarity, is the arrival about this time of a barrel of dishes and kitchen utensils he had shipped from Gander Bay. I remember because the barrel was so new its pale yellow staves still smelled faintly of wood smoke from the flume, as if Uncle Tom had just made it – which he likely had.

Heavy! Calvin and I, wrestling its awkward bulk up the steep and narrow stairs, both determined not to let it roll back and smash every dish we owned and perhaps us too, had to take several spells.

At last the barrel stood on the kitchen's scarred linoleum floor, like a new and inscrutable member of the family. Mom regarded it doubtfully, as if it cradled her hopes and fears for this move – which in a way it did. She knew her husband was an excellent packer, that he would have carefully wrapped each item in paper or tea towels, but she also knew the ways of freight handlers.

"Well," said Calvin, "le's not stand 'ere like it was the Trojan Horse."

A few hammer taps and the upper birch hoops were off, a few more taps and the head boards were free. Out came the crumpled sheets of *Family Herald*, which Mom carefully set aside for lighting morning fires in the coal stove, our only source of heat.

Out came the first item. I held my breath as she peeled off the paper. Our green water pitcher was intact! So were the matching tumblers. She unwrapped a stack of saucers – also intact. The next item, a gravy boat wrapped in *Tarzan*, was missing a handle. One heirloom gone. But the next half dozen plates were whole. And so it went, layer by layer, item by item, whole and broken, to the bottom. The saucepans and frying pan and cutlery were all right, of course.

"Could have been worse," said Calvin.

Mom sighed deeply, set aside the mendables and dumped the broken pieces into the garbage can. The remainder she rinsed and stacked on the newly scrubbed kitchen shelves. "Every move takes its toll," she said. A few things would have to be bought, but she would wait until Dad got his first paycheck and sent the first money order. Until then, every spare penny would go on rent, food and school supplies. School was only a week away.

I used the week to look around. Our flat occupied the attic floor of a three-storey row house, so called because it was joined end to end to other houses except for the occasional narrow fire break. Our floor had two windows on the street and its own door. The roofs were of the Mansard type, flattish on top with steeply concave eaves, as if wearing winter caps with the flaps down. Cut into the flaps were the dormer windows, each with its own tiny roof. Facing us across the street was a matching row. In fact every nearby street, Charlton above and John below, looked much the same, except the dormers had different designs and the houses were painted different colours. Each row house seemed to have its own coal chute.

Rowhouse living took some getting used to. We had really only three rooms: the kitchen overlooking Gilbert, two bedrooms at the back and a shared toilet. The kitchen's two dormers faced Gilbert; the bedroom windows overlooked a high-fenced yard sloping down to other yards and chimney-potted rooftops, which in turn stepped down, terrace-like, to the distant harbour and the South Side hills. The yards had gnarled and grimy trees whose leaves were starting to fall.

Mom's bedroom had a tiny balcony with a pulley clothesline which sagged toward a matching pole. There were two other clotheslines for the flats below. The balcony had a wooden fire escape. That first week, going to bed, we tried not to think about that.

To use the toilet you opened a small door in the west wall and went down three steps into a windowless cubicle lit by a bare 40-watt bulb with a pull cord. The cubicle had a tiny sink, a flush toilet and a towel rack. No tub. This vexed Calvin and especially Mom, since on Bennett we'd had one. It never bothered me much.

Our neighbours' door opened between the sink and toilet. It made me think of the fo'castle door of a small boat. Both sides knocked before entering, politely if possible. A grunt meant "occupied" – or was it constipation? Silence, in times of urgency, was golden. Urgent or casual, you were expected to bolt the latch on entering and unbolt it when you left. Those who forgot, as I sometimes did, soon got reminded.

Calvin, our historian, told us that most of these row houses were thrown up after two great fires, one in 1846 and one in 1892, that the fires left thousands huddled under canvas in Bannerman Park and in open fields for weeks while new housing was built. Building in rows speeded construction and minimized cost, since often one wall served two houses, roofs were more or less continuous, and one chimney served two or more flats.

The great disadvantage, aside from the obvious fire risk, was that greedy developers crammed in too many people, dispensing with porches, front yards and even doorsteps. Gilbert Street was a prime example. Out front it had neither tree nor turf. Grey pavement lapped the very doors. The only summer greenery was a scattered dandelion or plantain colonizing the cracks and crannies.

People compensated with paint: maroon, yellow ochre and kelly green. It gave each house a face of its own, at least until the perennial soot darkened it to grimy sameness, after which it was washed and repainted. Or the landlord waited for a good rainstorm.

My walk to Springdale Street Elementary School takes under five minutes. The school is Church of England like St. Michael's. On the near corner, where Dunford Street slopes steeply down, lives Bobby Chafe. We meet on our way to school – but not the same school. Bobby is pale and nervous with black hair. He points down Dunford and warns me solemnly about the John Street Gang. They sometimes raid our street, he says. He would gladly walk with me, but he goes to a Catholic school elsewhere. I suspect that in a scuffle, I'd have to defend myself and him too.

My new school is wooden and ancient, a turreted three-storey building painted battleship grey with rusty iron fire escapes. Inside is dusty pandemonium. Roused by a shrill handbell, herds of boys and girls swarm up and down, left and right, yelling above the trampling of leather soles on creaky floors and stairs.

At random I turn left, which happens to be correct, because the Grade 5 room is two doors down the hall. The unpainted wooden floors are so worn I can feel the knots and nail heads under my rubber boots. Once we reach our classrooms and the galloping subsides, the clouds of chalk dust and street mud gradually settle to await the next stampede.

My teacher is Miss Collie, a tall thin woman in her fifties with gold-rimmed glasses and a pleasant face. After roll call and the Lord's Prayer and "God Save The King," she hands out some textbooks, gets us to write our names in them, makes sure we've brought paper and pencils, and starts the morning's lesson.

Within a week, Miss Collie moves me to the front of the class. This is neither a promotion nor a demotion; but because, judging by my mediocre performance and the fact that I never ask questions, she surmises that I cannot read the blackboard. And she is right. Even so, I'd rather have stayed put, because now my classmates give me nicknames.

Back home we brushed off nicknames by chanting "Sticks-and-stones-may-break-my-bones-but-names-will-never-hurt-me." Here I don't dare, at least not yet. I want to blend in. At first they call me the usual, "Teacher's Pet." Then they switch to "Milky." The hint of infancy angers me. It is clever though; they got it from Pet, a popular brand of condensed milk.

A week later, the school nurse comes and checks my eyes. She confirms Miss Collie's guess, namely that I am near-sighted in both eyes, especially the right one. She therefore prescribes glasses. The first day I wear them to school, my tormentors switch to "Four-Eyes." This is not so bad, since I'm not the only one with glasses. And there *are* compensations. For the first time, my gauzy world snaps into sharper focus. Soon my class work and participation improve. A fortnight later she moves me back to my original seat.

Life on Gilbert settled into a routine. I liked to sit in a high dormer window and feel the pulse of city life. I watched cars splashing through puddles, carts delivering farm produce or milk, women airing babies, men in coveralls and salt-and-pepper caps trudging home with lunch pails. Sitting up there recalled happy hours spent in our attic at home in Clarkes Head, reading, watching, daydreaming.

I began to appreciate the horizontality of rain-slicked pavements, the verticality of telephone and lamp poles and chimney pots. I gazed down the long slope of roofs to the distant harbour's maze of shipping. On sunny fall days the fresh-tarred roofs glinted blue-black. In the surrounding back yards, clotheslines flapped with red shirts, yellow dresses, white sheets. On rainy days, light pooled in flooded roof corners, reflecting upside-down chimney pots and trees aquiver. I lost myself in the black-and-white geometry of new-fallen snow, so immaculate it almost made one forget summer.

School became less burdensome, almost pleasant. Among our few text-books was *More Stories of Newfoundland*, a slim slate-blue volume published in Canada in 1939 with Newfoundland's coat of arms on the cover. I liked it because there were many line drawings and maps and even some photographs, such as "Petty Harbour," "A Breton Woman" and "St. John's Today." The crisp drawings reminded me of *Chatterbox*. In the back were teaching suggestions, such as how to stage a puppet play.

Inside the front and back covers was a map of Newfoundland island, the first I'd ever seen. On it I quickly found Gander Bay and Gander Lake and the squiggle of river in between. However, only four places – St. John's, Lewisporte, Grand Falls and Corner Brook – had been named. Labrador and the names of all our bays were missing.

As soon as I got home, I pencilled in as many as I knew, and got Mom to help me with several others: St Anthony, Port aux Basques, Cape St. John, Bonavista Bay, Cape Bonavista, Notre Dame Bay. And of course I put in Gander Bay. In the coming weeks and months I scribbled notes throughout the book. If Miss Collie said "accurate" meant "correct," I wrote "correct" beside the word. "Letters patent" I labelled "document or grant," "royal standard" became "Union Jack," and so on.

I even doctored the pictures. On page sixteen, which showed the boy Walter Raleigh spellbound by a sailor's tales, I slung a bow over the man's shoulder, gave him an ornate quiver and stuck an ostrich feather in his hat. On page forty-nine I sketched, in colour, Superman, Batman (on a rope, flooring a masked man with a kick), an improbable Batmobile (at high speed) and the Green Hornet.

Calvin had far more homework than I. He was now swimming in shorthand, bookkeeping, typing, commerce, business forms – things I'd never heard of, but which he clearly relished. He'd always had a knack for business, always liked helping Grandpa in the shop. He had started clerking for him on Saturdays during the winter of 1942, a year with lots of woods work, when loggers were suddenly flush with cash.

Once when Grandpa was on a buying trip to St. John's, Calvin had manned the store every weekday evening by himself. One summer he even made and sold ice cream – a first for Gander Bay. After all, he told his sceptical grandfather, they had a milch cow, an icehouse and a hand-cranked freezer – why not? He found a recipe, cranked until his arm was sore, sold the ice cream for fifteen cents a dish and made a profit, stealing some customers from old Joe Peckford in the process.

Now, at Prince of Wales Collegiate, he was in his element. And our mother, despite her worries over health and money, was pleased. At least one of her boys would "get a good office job," not be a riverman like his father. How wrong she was.

November came, bringing snow flurries and my woodsman father. Sunburnt and lean from his many weeks guiding on the River, he regaled us over supper with stories of eccentric anglers and hunters, of bears and salmon and caribou. He was pleased the barrel of dishes had survived so well.

In a few days he'd be leaving for Placentia Bay to inspect fish shipments along a coast entirely new to him, as rugged as the west coast, much foggier, yet remarkably ice-free. As in Bonne Bay, Bay of Islands and other West Coast ports the previous spring, he and his fellow officers would be busy checking fish shipments, mostly pickled herring and salt cod, for weight, cure and quality.

"A bit like being a game warden," he joked, "except we're after crooked merchants, not poachers. They pack bad fish under good fish, cheat on the weight, anything to fool us." The officers would be cruising as far west as Burgeo. They had power to cull and dump and even to impose fines. Most of the time, even in port, he'd be living on the patrol boat. They had a cook and engineer.

It sounded wonderful. I wished he could take me with him. It reminded me of the time when I was six and he went caribou hunting without me but took Calvin; I'd cried until his canoe was out of sight.

After the taxi took him away, I lay on the bed my brother and I shared and tried to picture it: long days at sea in all weathers, poking through pea-soup fogs by compass and dead reckoning, tying up at strange wharves, outwitting crafty merchants. That winter, in letters from Arnold's Cove, Harbour Buffet, Belleoram and Fortune, he would recount his adventures. Some of the postmarks had lovely sounding names like Lamaline, Isle of Valen and Merasheen. In his firm and forward-sloping hand he wrote of fog and storms and calms, of dumping rotten herring, of attempts to bribe him with rum and cash, of bluff and bluster and even a threat to heave him off a wharf. But always, faithfully, he enclosed the blessed money order.

We settled in for our first St. John's winter. Because people now started burning coal in earnest – oil heat was a few years away – the downtown air began to smell like train smoke. On windless frosty mornings, the pall was so dense it stung the eyes and throat. Every second day it rained or drizzled, causing Mom to rail against the "smut" that begrimed her clothesline and her washing. She'd come stamping in from the balcony, lugging the laundry hamper and mutter, "Well, that was a waste of time and hot water. All my whites to scrub again!" Wiping the rope helped, but no Gilbert Street wash was ever to her liking. Her list of foes now included soot.

I was no fan of coal myself. With Calvin busy and Dad away, the task of lugging it from cellar to kitchen fell to me.

"That coal scuttle's nearly empty again!"

"Awww…do I have to?"

"You don't expect me…"

"I'll go." Down the stairs I would clump, shuttle and scoop in hand. I'd hoist the bulky hatch at the foot of the stairs, clamber down the three steps and grope in the pitch black for the pull-cord. Always, for a heartbeat, I imagined hearing the scurry of rats' claws over loose coal. They could see me but I couldn't see them. What if one sank its filthy teeth into my ankles? Just in case, I always banged the bucket against the steps. The dusty bulb gave more comfort than light. The very air seemed dark and pestilential. Rapidly I'd scoop the scuttle full and, choking on the dust I'd stirred up, scramble back to safety. All winter my handkerchiefs were tinged with black. Would my two lungs blacken too? I ruined several shirts by forgetting to wear an old sweater. Never again would I resent woodbox chores. Firewood might be messy but at least it wasn't dirty.

Outside in the street and during recess, I was learning other lessons. Suddenly it mattered what street I lived on, what clothes I wore, how I talked, where I came from, what my father did for a living, what church we did or did not go to. Kids made fun of my rubber ankle boots. So did we – but we had a right; "lumps," we called them, referring to the black stubby lumpfish that moped about wharves. But they were long-wearing, waterproof, mendable and cheap, thank you all the same.

They called me "bay-wop." "Bay" I knew. What was "wop"? Some kind of hornet? It was the way I talked. Among these scions of Waterford and Galway, who said "ye" with every second breath and were always "after" doing this or that, my Dorset accent was a joke. So was my religious denomination. Before coming to Gilbert Street I had thought Catholics were Mi'kmaq or Mountaineer Indians with surnames like Francis, John or Jeddore. Unfathomable.

I began to fret about John Street. Perhaps Bobby was right. Perhaps the

Gang would waylay me between home and school. Simply by living on Gilbert I'd become the enemy of every boy on every street below. The fact that no John Street boy had ever harmed me, nor I them, made no difference.

Often I wondered what their street was like, what, if anything, they wore, what kinds of houses, if any, they lived in, what they ate. Bobby said they cursed like sailors and were good with their fists and boots. It was rumoured they never washed, that they carried knives and razors and didn't hesitate to use them. Their fathers were supposed to be drunks, their mothers whores, whatever that meant. But we never ventured down to find out. We ignored them, kept them remote, foreign. We wanted them worthy of our enmity.

Not that Gander Bay was without bigotry and fear. Ask any older girl or boy forbidden to "go with" this or that boy or girl. As for fear, ask my young Métis girl with the axe. But at least this bigotry and fear was our own, something understood on both sides. A modus vivendum, however unfair, had been worked out. In Clarkes Head my side just happened to be the stronger.

I began to detour on my way to and from school. No more crossing risky Dunford – too exposed. At any moment, even in broad daylight, The Gang might come swarming up it. I knew Mom would gladly have walked me across – but it would never do. Fear became my shameful secret.

My detour took me up Springdale, east on Charlton and south down Casey. It was tiresome with a heavy bookbag and as a result I often got home late. "Why is it suddenly taking you so long to get home?" asked my mother one evening. "Sure 'tis only a hop, skip and jump away. Something the matter, my son?"

"No," I lied, aching to tell her, "nothin'."

After a fortnight or so I stopped this foolishness. It happened after a strange boy my age showed up on our street. Three or four of us were standing outside the corner store on Casey, eyeing the comic books display, when he slipped in. We somehow knew him for a John Street boy. When he came out we blocked his way, crowding him against the wall. After some scuffling – we didn't quite know how to beat him up – we let him go with a stern warning not to show his face on Gilbert again. He whimpered and nodded and scampered off.

This episode buoyed my courage wonderfully. I felt tough. Those John Street sleevens weren't supermen after all. Life was good. However, soon after this episode, as I sat on the day-bed studying after supper, a rock crashed through the window above me, spraying shards of glass over everything. Half expecting another missile, I jumped back, then lifted the blind and scanned the street below.

Not a soul in sight. Whoever slung the rock must have immediately hidden or run. My mother, hearing the tinkle of glass, rushed from her bedroom. I chose that moment to tell her about the John Street Gang – but not about the scuffle. I did tell Calvin though. He thought for a moment, then asked, "But did they know our house?"

I didn't know. "Unless," I said, "the corner grocer saw us rough the boy up and told them." Again my days were clouded with menace. Yet nothing more came of it. My brother bought glass and putty and fixed the smashed pane. Neither Bobby nor I bothered the John Street boys again, and they never bothered us. It was all foolishness anyway.

For all its faults, Gilbert Street had something which genteel Bennett Avenue lacked: texture. As for me, the mild social ridicule and modest risk made me feel more alive than at any time since leaving Gander Bay. Running errands helped. I got to post some letters in the rain, to fetch trifles from the corner store. I was learning weights and measures. Sent to buy spuds and a cabbage from the grocer, I learned that a gallon of potatoes weighed six pounds and never forgot it. I was learning about household budgeting too. If Mom sent me to the butcher for a soup bone, I knew funds were running low. If she ordered stewing beef, things were looking up. If she ordered a whole pullet, the money order must have come.

Coal took a fair slice of the budget too, but we had to have it. If the coal man was coming on a Saturday I'd watch for him. At last he'd come toiling up Casey, turn the corner and halt just beyond our hatch. Climbing down from his cart, the sooty-faced driver would rap on our door and I'd be sent down the cellar to unhook the hatch.

Then the man would murmur, "Back up now, Nellie." If Nellie didn't move, he'd clack his tongue sharply and jerk the reins. "Stand clear now, lad!" he'd shout to me as he unlatched the tailgate and hopped aside. I'd cover my ears as the cataract of glistening black rocks thundered down, and close my eyes as the chute coughed up a cloud of gritty dust. Grabbing a short-handled shovel, the coal man would hurry the remainder down, scoop up the spillage, latch the tailgate and close the hatch. I thought: Too bad it don't come up that easy.

"Take that to yer mum," said the man, jamming the bill in my shirt pocket. A cluck to the horse and they trundled away. Now that the cart was empty, its steel-rimmed wheels grated noisily on the pavement. I thought of old Silas' muffled passage on the Sawdust Road.

Leaving, man and horse took a different route. Instead of going down Casey, he headed west on Gilbert and turned up Springdale. "That's where Lester keeps the horses," explained my brother.

"Who's Lester?" I wanted to know. He said Charlie Lester ran a big cartage business and had a huge barn out on Hamilton Avenue. "You should see it," he exclaimed. "Two storeys high with a ramp going up to the second floor! They say it'll hold over a hundred horses. There's everything from Newfoundland ponies for two-wheeled carts to great big Clydesdales and Morgans for hauling two-horse *slovens.*"

Not all the carters brought coal. One time a farmer came with turnips and cabbage. One day, making his rounds, he saw the horse was hungry so he strapped a brin bag over its muzzle and buckled it behind her ears. "What's that for?" I asked.

"'Tis past his dinnertime," he laughed. "Got oats in it."

"Do he need a drink? I can get one."

"T'anks all the same, lad, but I waters 'im downtown. There's a special fountain on Duckworth."

My friend Bobby knew a nose-bag joke. "There was this society lady, see, watchin' a coal man try to get the bag on a skittish horse. 'My good man,' she said" – here his voice went high and squeaky – "'you'll never get that big horse in that little bag!'" Bobby also knew a lot of "Pat and Mike" jokes. His worst one harked back to the days when teams of men toured St. John's at night collecting sewage in horse-drawn tanks and dumping it into the harbour.

"'Stop! Stop the feckin' cart!' sez Pat.

"'Why?' sez Mike.

"'Cos I'm after losing me coat in the feckin' tank!' Mike stops the cart and Pat roots in the shit. 'What in hell's flames are ye doin, Pat? Sure, your coat'll niver be fit to wear no more!'

"'Ach,' sez Pat, 'tis not me coat I'm after! I left me lunch in the pocket!'"

Then I discovered comic books. Comic strips I already knew of course: *Tarzan*, *Superman*, *L'il Abner*; but a comic book was better. For once you got the whole story, not a fragment. Besides, here were new characters like Captain Marvel and his sister Wonder Woman, the Katzenjammer Kids, and Popeye. My problem was money. At ten cents apiece, even one a week strained my budget. My friends were just as poor. So we read each new one 'till it was dog-eared, then traded for another.

Mom never quite approved of ordinary comics. "They interferes with your homework," she said. "And they fills your head with foolish notions like leapin' off tall buildings and such." Classic comics, though they cost a quarter each, she approved of, sort of. "They've got sensible stories in them, about real people," she explained. Now and then she even bought me one. Perhaps it was to compensate for never letting me borrow library books. One of them was *The Odyssey*, by some old Greek named Homer. Another was *Moby Dick*, about a sailor hunting a white whale that had bitten off his leg. I suspected she read them herself. Through those classics I glimpsed the world of literature.

The St John's winter faded earlier than in Gander Bay but also more wetly. Its banks of sooty snow melted and rushed into the harbour. Daylight lingered after supper.

My favourite after-supper game was Batman. What I really needed was a costume. No store or catalogue then sold them, and I couldn't afford one anyway. It was make my own or do without. "Why not wear your Penman's underwear?" said Calvin. I looked to see if he was joking. "No, seriously; it's grey and fits tight." This was in fact a brilliant idea – except for the trap door. I asked Bobby: Did Batman use a trap door? He didn't know. We would study the next *Batman* serial and find out.

"'Tis no odds anyway," said Bobby. "A trapdoor could come in handy on a long chase." For capes our mothers cut out cheap smoky cotton. For leggings I borrowed Calvin's black dress socks. We cut bat-eared masks from a corn flakes box and tied them on with garter elastic. In these getups we whooped and hollered through the long May twilight. We shinnied up power poles, struggled over fences, fell noisily over garbage cans, frightened ourselves in dark alleys until the street lamps came on and our mothers called us home.

It was movies, not comic books, that really inspired these shenanigans. Nearly every fine Saturday we hiked a mile to the Nickel Theatre up on Harvey Road, our longest journey. For a dime you could watch one or even two Disney cartoons, a 15-minute superhero episode and a full-length black-and-white cowboy movie.

The cartoons were mostly Woody Woodpecker with his manic laughter, Donald Duck with his garbled words and Bugs Bunny with his nasal "What's up, Doc?" They were funny – but also, unlike the other offerings, in full colour. The serials usually featured Batman and Robin or Superman.

On film, the Man of Steel was a disappointment. His costume had wrinkles. In the comics it was wrinkle-free, nothing but rippling muscles. It was all right for Batman's costumes to be wrinkled because he was human just like us; but a man of steel should look like steel. After that, Gotham's hero became mine too.

My favourite cowboy movies starred Hopalong Cassidy or Johnny Mack Brown or the Lone Ranger and Tonto. They were forever rescuing kidnapped damsels or chasing stagecoach bandits or fighting "redskins," and they always succeeded. Nor did their six-shooters ever need re-loading.

We children never questioned these Hollywood scripts and few grownups seemed to either. Perhaps after six years of brutal war, people hungered for such a tidy cosmos, such moral certitude. Certainly Jewish filmmakers like Mayer and Goldwyn did. Nor did we youngsters wonder why these cowboys had no fixed address, no family, no other job. Compared to real life it was pure fantasy, like the Big Rock Candy Mountain; but fantasy was what we craved.

Just to go to the matinee was exciting in itself. You were never sure you'd even *get* in. Often we'd wait half an hour outside, lined up down the sidewalk along the wrought-iron fence. On a fine day you could see ships threading the Narrows. If it began to rain, you saw the harbour disappear.

We pushed and shoved like shoppers at a sale. We fretted over missing the cartoons, not getting a ticket. Always there were boys lugging bundles of grubby comics, haggling like horse traders.

"Want dis?"

"Seen it!"

"Dis?"

"Go on, b'y! That's ancient!"

"What about…?"

Trading ceased the minute the doors opened. We got our tickets and poured down the sloping aisles, intent on sitting near the screen. Those with money bought Crackerjacks. There was much shouting and changing of seats and jumping about. As the tension mounted, bored ushers patrolled the aisles, threatening eviction.

At last the lights dimmed. A hush fell. All eyes fastened on the immense velvet curtain, watching for the first twitch, the first whirring of the mechanism. When it came, revealing the immaculate screen, a joyful shout burst forth. Then for ninety minutes we were lost to the world.

Afterward we'd burst into daylight, blinking like owls, momentarily unsure of where we were. Saturated with heroism, restless from sitting, we needed release. With two hours before suppertime, we'd race to the nearest vacant lot to hold imaginary reins and to fire real cap-guns. One day we rode farther than usual. I recall galloping around a strawy field, a desert with alders for cactus. We got home so late our mothers thought us lost for sure. And we were – but only in our heads.

There was one movie I almost wished I hadn't seen. On one of Dad's few visits, likely that spring, he took us to a theatre on Henry Street, The Star I believe it was. That week's movie featured a flying serpent which devoured people on whom its evil master had secretly planted one of its wing feathers. Loosed at night, the great flapping monster crashed through windows to devour sleeping victims, usually women. That evening and for weeks afterward I checked under my bed before risking sleep.

Despite city stimulations and entertainments, I felt homesick by times. Awash in Irish brogue, I craved my native speech. Mom had lost most of hers, Calvin was losing his. I needed to hear it from Frank and Everett and Susie as we swarved around mill and landwash.

One Sunday Uncle Harry suddenly showed up. Calvin was away and I was doing homework. My mother, greeting him warmly, took his raglan and hat and made tea. After laughter and small talk the conversation turned serious. I was doing homework but couldn't help but feel this was more than just a visit.

Was it about money? It was rumoured he and Marie were starting a hotel in Glenwood. Was it about Grandpa Layman? Mom's dad, now seventy-two, had been living with Uncle George and Aunt Beatty in town, but last November they had moved to Massachusetts and I hadn't heard where he went. Perhaps Uncle Harry wanted us to take him in? But since my parents spoke of moving to Lewisporte so Calvin could save on board and lodging, there might not be room. Whatever his motive, it was none of my business.

When the visit was over, Uncle Harry invited me to accompany him partway to his lodgings. This flattered me. Though he rarely visited, I always felt at ease with him. Perhaps this was because his name often came up in conversation, especially in Mom's. At thirty-four he was an urbane and well-dressed dude who kept his shoes shined and wore what Dad considered loud neckties. For a smallish man he possessed a surprisingly robust voice, a rich radio baritone which made all his stories riveting.

He was different from my other uncles – except perhaps Uncle Don – and totally unlike my father, who after all, was only nine years older. Compared to Uncle Harry, Dad seemed conservative, even straitlaced. He disliked flamboyance and prodigality and often said so. One Christmas he chastised Mom for sending Harry a box of chocolates and they argued hotly. Dad seemed to think his brother-in-law bent the rules and boasted too much. He had no use for either.

Our walk took us up Springdale and west along LeMarchant. The day was overcast and cool, the trees still winter-bare. We talked animatedly as we walked, and I did more than half of it. He asked me about school, about my drawing, my dreams. He seemed genuinely interested, not merely making conversation. He treated me like an adult, the first of my uncles to do so. Nothing could have been more empowering. He opened a window on adulthood, on manhood. He taught me that strong men need not be taciturn and hard. That walk welded a friendship which would endure until his death in 1993. Among the topics we discussed was church. Did I still go? I said no, not in town, that Calvin, when he went, preferred to take some girl. That, yes, my mother had nudged me toward a United church, but as she wouldn't come with me, I'd turned back at the door and she had dropped the subject. That I might resume in Clarkes Head when we got home. "You'll be getting confirmed soon," he said. On that note we parted, not to meet again for several years.

That spring of 1947, between the wrap-up of his fisheries board duties and the start of his summer's guiding for Murphy & Steele in Glenwood, my father reappeared. Time to go home. It was a happier homecoming than the last. Calvin had passed his exams with good marks. In fact he'd already left for Lewisporte to take up his work as a clerk in Bowater's office there. Mom's health had improved and her seizures came less often.

As for me, thanks to new glasses and some private coaching in fractions by Miss Collie, I passed Grade 5. I said goodbye to Bobby and my other friends and soon we were on a train chuffing up the Waterford Valley past Bowring Park, leaving the smoky, foggy, holy, wooden city, its ship-haunted harbour and its tiny tower behind – for a time.

The journey over the Avalon's moonscape was as interminable as ever. I snoozed and looked, looked and snoozed, until the Terra Nova River suddenly reminded me of home. It had the same tea-coloured water, the same grey boulders.

By the time we passed Alexander Bay Station's piney barrens, I was wide awake. As we toiled up the long grade past Square Pond and Benton onto the rolling plateau of spruce and birch, there were glimpses of Gander Lake to the south. Then we were coasting and swaying down into the River's wide valley and braking for the trestle bridge into Glenwood station. I stared out the grimy window, but could see nothing for rain. Anyhow, things never look the way we remember them.

The 30-mile river journey is cold and wet and miserable, but it makes no odds to me. I kneel in the bow on a coil of manila rope, warm and dry in oilskins, facing downriver the better to enjoy Big Chute and the rattles and steadies beyond. I play my old game of throat-humming to the motor's drone, finding and losing the harmonic vibrato. When the wind on Fourth Pond puddles my eyes, I face about and trace the herringbone patterns of our widening wake.

And I study Brett Saunders, the man at the helm. My father the riverman sits erect on his narrow after thwart, gunslinger eyes intent on downstream hazards hiding under swollen meltwaters. Rainwater streaming off his black slicker makes him glisten like a salmon's back. He looks supremely happy.

Our canoe, plunging through the chutes, rears and tilts; but he controls it and we settle in for the long labyrinthine run down to salt water. We thread islands of bare birch and glide under echoing aspen. Great rustling pines pass over us and fall behind, trailing dark reflections. I catch a whiff of exhaust. During my first months in St Johns, vehicle exhaust used to remind me of outboard motors back home. Now, heading home, it reminds me of loaded trucks changing gears as they labour up Casey Street. I've come full circle.

Church

"We have left undone those things which we ought to have done, and we have done those things we ought not to have done, and there is no health in us…"

– BOOK OF COMMON PRAYER

As a toddler I thought it magnificent. I marvelled at the sturdy white steeple with its circled cross, the clean white walls pierced by eight pairs of windows, the white belfry standing apart like a lighthouse, brass bell ready to give voice. Outside and in, nothing else I knew could equal it. Inside, I basked in the honeyed glow of wooden pews and ceiling, the sky-coloured pebble glass windows, the fluted pillars soaring up to join the flaring rafters, the faint scent of spar varnish in summer and of wood smoke in winter, the slightly breathless upright organ my mother so often played.

I especially admired the carved wooden eagle bearing the great tasselled bible on its half-open wings, the high six-sided pulpit where the preacher declaimed, gripping the rail as if in heavy seas. And always I pondered on what strange power might reside in the ornate font inside the door, too tall for me to see into. Here, squalling babies were held aloft and sprinkled with water and marked with a thumb print and declared children of God and inheritors of the Kingdom of Heaven.

Some years later it would dawn on me that I myself had been so printed. I tried to picture my impossibly young parents, Winnifred Jane and Evelyn Brett, thirty-one and thirty-two years old, standing by that font on February 13, 1936, and being asked the terrible question:

> Dost thou, in the name of this child, renounce the devil and all his works, the vain pomp and glory of this world, with all the covetous desires of the same, and the carnal desires of the flesh, so that thou wilt not follow nor be led by them?

And how, after they renounced them all and had said the Apostles' Creed and formally requested my baptism, after they had vowed to keep the Ten Commandments and had recited more prayers and promises, they had handed me, wide-eyed, into the waiting arms of surrogate minister Dan Bragg to be signed with the sign of the cross. Later they would have me christened, and after that only one thing remained for full acceptance into Christendom: confirmation at age twelve.

Until then, and for some years afterward, Christ Church – so grand a title for so humble an edifice – would be my spiritual home. It didn't matter that from age eleven I might sojourn elsewhere, first in St. John's, then in Lewisporte and later Toronto and Fredericton. The church was always there when I returned. It didn't matter that I was unaware of its petty animosities and scandals, its politics and rivalries and gossip: who was on government relief this winter, who wasn't speaking to whom and why, where the minister or bishop would lodge on his next visit, who was knocked up and by whom, who would get this year's road-building contract or not, where the new government wharf would go. Such things might be whispered in the pews and at Select Vestry meetings, but they had nothing to do with me.

Except to know that Grandpa Saunders had sawn and donated the clapboard and shingles for the church, had been on the committee that hired

Reuben Peckford of Gander Bay and Robert Small of nearby Summerford to build it, had helped to dedicate it and its little cemetery in April 24, 1910. That he and Grandma had their own paid-for pew halfway down on the left, no longer obliged, thanks to hard work and good planning and the grace of God, to travel by open boat to Fogo or Change Islands to have a child properly baptised – or buried, as they'd had to do with baby Gordon Earle in 1902 and baby Alma Edith in 1907. Even so – or perhaps because of these things – my parents were never regular church-goers. We didn't even have a family bible. There had been one in my mother's childhood home, but it had stayed there when her brother Tom was willed the house.

Not that they weren't believers. It was just that, having fled the suffocating piety of their upbringing for the religious freedom, however secular, of the big city, they were reluctant to plunge back in. At least my father was reluctant. Mom would have attended, she said, but she couldn't get Dad to. "No, Winnie," he'd say, "not until they lets me wear a hat. You women wears hats; why can't men?" I knew the dialogue by heart.

She: "You just wants to hide your bald head, that's all. Surely you don't think God Almighty cares?"

He: "He might…"

She: "Sure, you've been bald since for years and I never minded. Your own mother doesn't mind. Your own father is bald and he goes to church, goes every Sunday…"

And so on. It was no use; he wouldn't go. I suspect the real reason was more theological. We seldom had a real minister. Our real minister was based in Change Islands, whence he travelled by boat in summer and by horse and sleigh in winter. Even in summertime, Clarkes Head was lucky to see him once a fortnight. In between, the school teacher filled in – if he happened to be male. If not, Joe Peckford or someone else became lay reader, preacher and all.

So Dad didn't go, and my mother, unless asked to play the organ, generally stayed home too. Christmas and Easter were almost the only times we went as a family.

All this Grandma Saunders deplored. She and Grandpa always attended church – except on the Sundays when Joe Peckford was lay reader. Mr. Peckford, as manager of the Horwood Lumber Company store, was Grandpa's business rival. There was no way he was going to sit and be preached to by Joe Peckford. Like two roosters in the one yard, they often sparred. My grandfather was not above blaming him for business setbacks, even for acts of God like losing a boom of pitprops in a storm. One Sunday, thinking someone else was lay reader that day, he went to church only to find Joe preaching. He got up red-faced and huffed out.

However, sometimes my grandparents borrowed me for church. I don't remember anything particular about those times, except that we sat in their special pew. What I do recall was my grandfather's flatulence. He managed to contain it through the one-hour service, but on the way home he let out great, long-drawn horse farts all the way home. I was impressed. The most I ever managed was a squeak or two. To hide my grin and to stay to windward of him, I marched ahead. This episode humanized religion for me. I wondered whether God smiled too.

Sunday school was more educational. By age ten I'd learned a little about God and Jesus, knew some bible stories, could sing a few simple hymns and more or less follow the morning service in our Book of Common Prayer. However, I was still not tall enough to reach our kneeling bench without sliding off the pew. Sometimes I would accidentally topple off the bench with a clatter. Or, idly flipping through the heavy hymn book during an especially doleful tune, I'd lose control of it and have to retrieve it amid frowning adults. Although certain prayers and epistles stirred me, the antique English mostly went over my head:

> "Dearly beloved brethren, the Scripture moveth us in sundry places to acknowledge and confess our manifold sins and wickedness; and that we should not dissemble nor cloke them…"

Grandma chided my father for not "gettin' after Gary." She was not so naïve as to think souls were saved by merely sitting in a church pew and mouthing pious words, but she did know that the place to commence the Christian journey was within a worshipping community of believers.

She was never strident about it. One simply felt a gentle spiritual suasion, relentless as gravity, pulling heavenward. My absences grieved her. Perhaps, like the young St. Augustine's anxious Christian mother, she was already praying for my immortal soul, stained as it already was by countless sins, not the least of which were candy theft and cruelty to hens and goats and profanation of the Sabbath.

The Sabbath. Like Jews, they still called it that. But as to what the Sabbath was or how it came to be, I was still in the dark. It was simply a fact of life, like the fact that most outport churches faced east. When I asked my mother why, she said, "Because that's where the Holy Land is." Grandma's family bible had pictures of this Holy Land, muddy engravings of Mount Hermon and Jerusalem and the Sea of Galilee and "shepherds outside Bethlehem."

To me, the Sea of Galilee looked no bigger than Clarkes Pond and not as interesting. Its barren hills looked not so much holy as very old and worn, a lot like Fogo's. But I liked the Pool of Siloam because of Hymn 551:

By cool Siloam's shady rill
How sweet the lily grows
How sweet the breath beneath the hill
Of Sharon's dewy rose!

"Rill" meant nothing to me nor did I know who Sharon was, yet the hymn had the same sorrowful beauty that Calvin's textbook poems did. This, I thought, must be what holiness was like. I listened for and found it in other hymns:

Jerusalem the golden
With milk and honey blest
Beneath thy contemplation
Sink heart and voice oppressed.

My world too had beauty and sadness: sunrise on a window blind, my salmon's heart that died, a loon yodelling high in the night sky. But because they were found outside of church, no grownup seemed to think such things religious.

In Sunday school we'd begun to memorize the Ten Commandments. The fourth one said:

> Remember that thou keep holy the Sabbath day. Six days shalt thou labour, and do all that thou hast to do. but the seventh day is the Sabbath of the Lord thy God.

Might not an ordinary day be holy too, another day be the Sabbath? But grownups revered one day only. Moreover, they thought that "keeping it" meant above all attending church. This, they believed, would earn one admission into Heaven, wherever and whatever and whenever that might be.

By age five I was already uneasy about Heaven. I remember asking, "Mommy, is there a floor in Heaven?" My mother didn't bother telling me about golden streets. She simply said, "No, my son." It was as I feared. I was left, like Peter walking on the Sea of Galilee, with nothing solid to stand on, a crisis of belief. I would postpone Heaven as long as possible.

And what was my "work"? I would ask Grandma. We were in her kitchen one wintry Saturday afternoon when I brought the question up. I was munching a lassy bun and she was kneading bread. She paused and sprinkled flour on the sticky dough. "If God himself rested after creating the world," she said, "shouldn't we do the same?" The table resumed squeaking. I munched in silence. "That's why I'm making bread today and not tomorrow," she continued. "I don't need to; I've enough in the pantry to last till Monday. No, it's to respect God's command. The Bible says even servants and farm animals are not to work on the Sabbath."

"Not even youngsters?"

"Not even youngsters."

It had crossed my fallen mind that children were exempt anyway. At any rate, I was too little to make bread or lug water or fetch wood. She smiled and laid a floury finger on my nose. "My son, even throwing rocks is work; mark my words, every rock you sling on the Sabbath you'll have to pick up in the next life." And she resumed kneading. If that was true I was in trouble. Especially if God counted the skipping of rocks. I downed the rest of my milk, pulled on my boots and mitts, thanked her and, burdened with Sabbath thoughts, plodded home.

And yet I wasn't wholly reprobate. Early on it seems I took a lively interest in matters spiritual. Most children do. Wayward though I was, my parents and grandmother saw hope for me. Long before Sunday school or day school, my mother and Aunt Beatty had taught me the standard children's prayer: "Now I lay me down to sleep, I pray the Lord my soul to keep; if I should die before I wake, I pray the Lord my soul to take." By age seven, said Uncle Harry, I was saying the Lord's Prayer. It became my bedtime prayer. Wintertime, kneeling on the cold canvas, I'd scamper through the words and jump under the blankets. Summertime, I'd pray it phrase by phrase, sifting for the meanings as best I could.

Another winter, another spring, another Sunday evening. Clarkes Brook is swollen with meltwater; the tide is top high and from the bridge by Uncle John's I see dark shapes flashing silver in the water. Sunday or no, God's sea trout have returned. I run back home, grab my bamboo pole with the green and yellow trout fly and hurry back. After catching several, I sneak home, going by the landwash so Grandma won't see me. At home I lean my rod in the angle of the porch and go in for supper. Mom and Dad praise my fine fat trout.

During supper Calvin says, looking out the kitchen window, "There's something wrong with the white goat."

"Yes," said Mom, "she seems to be caught in the fence. Go see what the trouble is."

We find the nanny standing head down in the garden, weaving back and forth, trying to free herself from my rod and line, which are tangled in the fence. The line leads to her jaw, where my trout fly is firmly hooked. "She must have nibbled the lure for its salty taste," says Calvin. "You're after catchin' a goat!" He sends me for Dad's pliers and soon has her free.

In time, of course, Grandma got her wish. She had Confirmation on her side. Once I reached age twelve there was no avoiding it. By then all of my Sunday school classmates were memorizing not just the Ten Commandments, but the Apostles' Creed and the Sacraments. All were spelled out in the prayer book between "The Order of Baptism for those of Riper Years" and "A Table of Kindred and Affinity." So was the "Order of Confirmation." Leafing ahead, scanning page after page of questions and answers, I felt a premonition of disgrace. But our Sunday school teachers, volunteers though they were, worked diligently to train us up in the way we should go. Patiently, week by week, guided occasionally by our itinerant minister, they drilled us.

Reverend Roberts was a stocky fortyish man with a shiny pink complexion that reminded me of Aunt Carrie's conch shell in Fogo. His eyes were like my grandmother's, dark brown and mirthful. Before he came to us, our church had been served by a Reverend Davis and before that by Reverend Elliott.

From May to late October, Reverend Roberts came from Change Islands in his open motor boat. In summer we often recognized the sound of his inboard engine before his small white skiff hove into view. Bustling ashore in oilskins and sou'wester, he looked like a fisherman.

What a pleasant life he had, I thought. Out in boat every day, teaching and preaching from Birchy Bay to Carmanville, marrying and baptising, comforting the people. "Comfort ye, comfort ye my people." Burying them too – but I preferred not to think of that, having recently been a pallbearer for young Charlie Gillingham, Frank Gillingham's brother. Death to me was being put inside a dark and very heavy coffin.

Mostly the minister arrived on a Saturday evening, stayed at Grandpa's overnight, conducted Matins the next morning, and visited some sick and shut-ins. Unless there was a wedding or a funeral or he needed to instruct catechumens like us, he'd leave before supper for his next community.

For one whole summer I wanted to be a travelling minister. Now and then Reverend Roberts came to regular school to speak on some aspect of the faith. For this, our usual classes would be cancelled, so we were always happy to see him. By custom we rose when he entered and when he left.

His presentations were never dull. If nothing else, he deepened our knowledge of Mediterranean history – and the teacher's too perhaps. I especially liked his maps. Once when he spoke about Saint Paul's missionary journeys, he brought one three times the size of Dad's war map. It was so large he had trouble unrolling it. Two or us helped him hang it from the blackboard. He walked to and fro, jabbing his wooden pointer.

I could have listened to him all day.

Meanwhile we were bogged down in the quagmires of the Ten Commandments with all their grim "shalts" and "shalt nots," their clauses piled upon clauses. It was not enough merely to memorize them. We had to know what they meant. In time we learned all ten, by head if not by heart. At last we were within sight of the foothills of Confirmation.

My greatest fear was not the ritual itself – after all, we had rehearsed it – but my spiritual readiness for the Eucharist, the Lord's Supper. Doing without breakfast that morning would be hard enough ("What if our stomachs rumble?" someone asked) but we were also supposed to come "…steadfastly purposing to lead a new life; have a lively faith in God's mercy through Christ, with a thankful remembrance of his death; and be in charity with all men."

As for fasting, the minister advised us to think of it as simply a way to focus our mind and spirit. "Did you know," he said, "that our word 'breakfast' simply means to break one's overnight fast? You've been fasting all your lives and didn't know it!"

At last we are ready. I am not quite twelve but others are nearly thirteen and it is important to catch the Bishop on his autumn rounds. His yacht has arrived; he is already in the church. To honour him, men have trekked to the woods for evergreen boughs – "palms," they call them, because we use the same sort at Easter. The men fashion an archway over the churchyard gate.

From the narthex we process to our reserved pews, girls on one side, boys on the other. I glance over at the little girls I've grown up with: Viola Peckford, Zena and Nellie Gillingham, Edith Collins and the others. When I left for St. John's nearly two years ago, they were flat-chested and gawky. Since then most have blossomed into long-legged bosomy creatures I hardly know and perhaps never shall. We boys seem to be boys still.

The ceremony itself is as solemn as a wedding. Parents, godparents, family and friends are here. A raw east wind is blowing. We shiver as we wait in the unheated porch, especially the girls in their thin white gowns. His Grace the Bishop raises both arms and asks God to fill us "with the spirit of thy holy fear." As if on cue, my heart begins to palpitate and hot blood pulses up my neck and overspreads my scalp. My collar seems too tight. Breathing becomes an effort. My forehead and palms start to sweat.

Turning to the minister, the Bishop intones, "Take heed that the persons whom you present be duly prepared to receive the laying on of hands." To which Reverend Roberts replies, "I have instructed them and enquired of them and believe them so to be." Then each of us advances in turn toward the great man towering resplendent in his studded cope, waiting to clamp his large hands on our bowed heads. My turn comes. Through half-closed lids I see his right hand descend and hear him say:

> Defend, O Lord, this thy child with thy heavenly grace, that he may continue thine for ever; and daily increase in thy Holy Spirit, more and more, until he come unto thy everlasting kingdom.

It seems my neck will crack. Is he trying to shove me through the floor? Then he lets up and says, "The Lord be with you."

"And with thy spirit," I hear myself croak.

And there we are, confirmed. Nothing feels different, yet nothing will ever be the same again. We have studied for ourselves the meaning of things fundamental to the church's version of the Christian faith: the Creed, the Commandments, the Lord's Prayer, the Sacraments of Baptism and Holy Communion. Having studied, and having acknowledged that without God's help we shall fail, we have publicly pledged to do, as adults, what our parents and godparents promised for us as infants a dozen years ago. For better or worse, we have given our souls to God. Parents and grandparents and godparents and siblings and friends surround us to congratulate us, to wish us Godspeed. We the confirmed congratulate one another. For better or worse, we have come of age.

For the occasion Calvin sent me, from Lewisporte, a small morocco-bound, zippered King James Bible. Later Grandma and Grandpa Saunders would give me a pocket-sized Book of Common Prayer. These two books, I supposed, contained everything one needed to know. Wishful thinking on my part, yet for the time being true enough. I was like the student who crams for a final exam, passes the test, but within a month has forgotten most of what he learned.

Leafing through the little book Grandma gave me, I discovered it was in two parts. Its second half was called The Book of Common Praise. It contained more than 800 hymns. Leafing through them, I was surprised how many I knew. Some I had learned in school. Most of them I'd learned from hearing them so often, not only in church but from the lips of grownups, especially my grandmother's, as they went about their lives. Some, like Henry Van Dyke's verses, were sheer praise:

Field and forest, vale and mountain,
Flowery meadow, flashing sea,
Chanting bird and flowing fountain,
Call us to rejoice in thee.

Others, like Frances Havergal's "Take My Life and Let It Be," were veritable love songs:

Take my love; my Lord I pour
At thy feet its treasure store;
Take myself, and I will be
Ever, only, all, for thee.

Then there was Isaac Watts' "When I Survey The Wondrous Cross." Though less elegant than some, its sacrificial tone moved me deeply even then:

Were the whole realm of Nature mine,
That were a present far too small;
Love so amazing, so divine,
Demands my soul, my life, my all.

Thinking of hymns reminded me of Frank Gillingham. A third or fourth cousin near my age, Frank was the voice of our church organ. It was no pipe organ, but it needed more wind than pedalling could muster. It needed a strong back to fill its lungs. This Frank supplied. He sat on a stool behind a screen and worked the bellows with a wooden lever. During quiet hymns it was easy to forget he was there. But during sustained and turbulent passages in such hymns like "Onward, Christian Soldiers," we'd see his mop of curly blonde hair bobbing up and down like a woodpecker's crest, see his brow shiny with sweat.

As for my new bible, it would stay zippered for long stretches of time. Yet now and then, as much for Grandma as for myself, I'd flip through its pages. Alighting on a passage like Micah 5: 6-8, I would wonder why I didn't read it oftener:

Wherewith shall I come before the Lord, and bow myself before the high God? Shall I come before him with burnt offerings, with calves of a year old?

> Will the Lord be pleased with thousands of rams, or with ten thousands of rivers of oil? Shall I give my firstborn for my transgression, the fruit of my body for the sin of my soul?
>
> He has showed thee, O man, what is good; and what doth the Lord require of thee, but to do justly, to love mercy, and to walk humbly with thy God?

Likewise, with the New Testament, where in Matthew 16: 26, Jesus says, "For what is a man profited, if he shall gain the whole world, or what shall a man give in exchange for his soul?"

About this time, impressed with my apparent piety, grownups began to call me "a serious boy," and say things like "old for his age," "the makings of a minister." This stroked my ego and delighted my mother. But I was sailing under false colours and knew it.

One Sunday morning after my birthday, passing the offering plate, I accidentally spilled some change. As the coins crashed and skittered under the pews, I muttered, loud enough for half the congregation to hear, "Shit!"

People picked the coins up for me but I was too flustered to thank them. They saw me for what I was: callow, selfish, hypocritical. They likely forgave me, but I could not. At that moment I understood that true holiness, whatever and wherever it might be, was beyond beauty, beyond art, beyond my present condition; it demanded my soul. I was thirteen, with everything to learn.

LEWISPORTE

My parents had two good reasons for moving to Lewisporte in the late fall of 1947. First, the Newfoundland Fisheries Board had assigned my father to Notre Dame Bay for the winter. Second, Calvin, who had been working there since he left St. John's that spring, was fed up with hotel living. That the town had a good elementary school, even though it was United Church, was a bonus.

It would mean another winter of renting, but at least we'd have a roomy house with a bathroom to ourselves.

So after my confirmation, and after Dad had seen his last hunters off with their trophies and venison, we embarked from Victoria Cove with our trunk and suitcases and one pregnant Toggenberg goat aboard Lewis Porter's passenger boat. Mr. Porter serviced Twillingate on Tuesdays and Lewisporte on Thursdays. After six or seven uneventful hours we nosed into the town's railway wharf, where Calvin met us with a truck.

Mom hugged him tearfully. Dad and I shook hands with him. He looked somehow paler, softer. "Hotel food," he explained, "and office work."

The place he took us to was at the west end of the town, which seemed to be strung out along one unpaved main street along Burnt Bay's low western shore. We drove almost to its head some two miles away. The house had been the family home of Frederick Rowe, a noted Newfoundland educator and soon-to-be minister in Joey Smallwood's Liberal government. Dad knew Mr. Rowe from ferrying him once or twice between Glenwood and Gander Bay on government business. In the course of small talk he'd learned of the vacant house and arranged to rent it – sight unseen.

"There it is," said my brother, turning up a longish lane toward a stand of yellowing poplars with a chimney and a mossy roof poking through. Compared to our foxy house the Rowe place was a mansion. A run-down mansion by the look of it, but with life in it yet and perhaps a ghost or two. As we got out, Mom cast a sour eye over its peeling paint, its rickety verandah, the overgrown garden. My father busied himself with the back door key. When the door swung open he looked relieved.

"Well, here we are," he said, taking a deep breath and ducking his lanky frame through the low door. The porch was a dark clutter of absent lives. There were bamboo fishing poles, rusty gardening tools, a pair of women's skates, dented pails, a few ancient toys, assorted lumber. I saw a half-full coal bin in one corner. "At least we won't need to buy coal for a while," said Dad.

The kitchen smelled of neglect and damp. "A broom and mop will work wonders," said Dad.

"Yes," said Mom. "Too bad you won't be here to help." It was true. The day after tomorrow he would be on the Fisheries patrol boat, heading for Musgrave Harbour. He looked at her. "Winnie, I'll do what I can before I go."

"I know," she said.

The kitchen was large and opened onto the verandah. Swags of yellowing hop vine swayed along the eave, darkening the kitchen. The putty blue walls didn't help. A coat of bright paint would work wonders too, I thought – if the landlord would pay for it. After Calvin and I wrestled a few windows open, things smelled a little better.

The place did have electric lights. "The town council bought the Army's generator after the military left," said my brother. The generator didn't supply enough juice for electric stoves and such, but at least it gave the town lights and running water.

The rooms upstairs were musty but brighter. Everything we looked at needed attention: mattresses to air, bedclothes to be scrubbed, rugs to be whacked. Was Mom up to it? I knew that last year's operation still bothered her at times; a burning sensation came and went. Calvin and I would have to help her. He'd be moving in on the weekend.

"Well," he said, "gotta get back to work. See you tomorrow. Supper will be on me."

So there we were, in an old house with our luggage unopened because we wouldn't be staying just yet. Mom had Fogo friends in town, the Randalls, and they had offered to feed us supper and put us up for the night. All we had needed to do now was run some water to clear the pipes, unpack some essentials and find a shed or something for the goat. I went looking and found a perfect little barn out back. It even had some hay in the loft.

An hour later our stomachs reminded us that we hadn't eaten since breakfast. My father, busy with the coal stove, beckoned me over and handed me two 50-cent pieces. "Go buy us a large tin of Irish stew at that store we passed," he said. "I've got bread and butter in my lunch box."

The store was about ten minutes' walk down the main road. A chance to stretch my legs. The road was wide and I met some cars and trucks. It traced a gentle curve along the landwash, which was bouldery and seemed to have no beach. The houses were spread out. I noticed several newer ones on short side streets lined with skinny poplars. On the ridge behind the town gleamed several large white storage tanks. Aviation fuel for Gander, Calvin had said.

I found the store, bought the stew and in half an hour we were eating. The old stove wasn't throwing much heat. "Chimney likely needs cleaning," said Dad. "I'll check it tomorrow." The stew was lukewarm, but the sea air had made us ravenous and the tea and jam bread cheered everyone up.

I could see my new school from our west windows. I made a coloured pencil drawing of it: a squarish white two-storey building with a wigwam roof and green shutters. Next day, after dinner, Dad walked me there and got me registered. The school had four large classrooms, two downstairs and two up. Classes had been in session for weeks and I felt nervous and conspicuous. The principal introduced us to my Grade 6 teacher, Miss Marie Lane, who also taught Grade 5. The other teachers were Eileen Simms, Julia Greenland and Gwen Gates. My classroom was on the main floor to the left.

So I started school and Dad started his new assignment.

Because I lived near enough to walk home, there was no need to bring a lunch like most other students. This hampered my assimilation. Starting several weeks late like that was a decided disadvantage. It reminded me of my experience at St. Michael's. Most students had already formed their groups and teams and picked their friends. However, after drifting around the halls and playground alone for a few days, I was befriended by a freckled classmate named Roy Miles. Roy had buck teeth and a ready smile and introduced me to two or three other boys.

At least there was no name-calling or obvious bigotry here. Yet there was no cohesion either. The students came from all over Notre Dame Bay: Pilley's Island, Exploits, Leading Tickles, Moreton's Harbour, Herring Neck. And Gander Bay. Living in a place which was neither a real town nor a real outport, we were like show dogs jumbled together, trained to get along but suspicious of each other. As for me, I was half townie. St. John's had spoiled me for both. I was neither fish nor fowl.

Trying to figure all this out, I did a lot of walking. Walking asserted my independence – though I would gladly have surrendered it. But this was a new environment and I felt like exploring it. Besides, here I had few chores. In Gander Bay at age thirteen I'd have been almost too busy to explore – or would have already done so. Here, thanks to running water and a coal stove, I was fairly free. Fill the coal scuttle, tend the goat, run errands, do my homework and I could take off.

So, while the good weather lasted, I walked. I walked to and from school, ten minutes by the road, less by the railroad track. I walked with Calvin to the hilltop Quonset hut where he worked for Bowater's, the pulp and paper people. Up close, the fuel tanks were enormous. He gave me a tour of his desk, typewriter and filing cabinet. His view of Burnt Bay was spectacular. It was like a narrower Gander Bay with no houses on the south side. I walked to what they called the Downtown. One time I walked the whole way north along the track to the wharf where we'd landed, where the railway station was and Manuel's Hotel where Calvin had grown so pasty pale.

Listening to my marathon story, he told me one in return. It was about Grandpa Saunders and one I'd never heard. He said that before Lewisporte had ever had a hotel or wharf or railway station, our grandfather had taken much the same walk, looking for a plot of land to buy. The year was 1898 and he was twenty-two. He'd read in the *Twillingate Sun* about the new trans-island railway and, by his reckoning, big things were about to happen in Burnt Bay.

A branch railway was being pushed north from Notre Dame Junction and he was timekeeper for the project. The driving force behind it was Lewis Miller, a lumber baron with failing Swedish operations and government connections. Miller was, in fact, the boyhood friend of Scottish railway builder Sir Robert Reid, just then completing Newfoundland's line to Port aux Basques.

Grandpa knew that Miller was building a large steam mill on Red Indian Lake and a smaller one in Glenwood. The intent was to saw enormous amounts of white pine deals, three-by-twelve-inch planks, for shipment and re-sawing overseas. To achieve this, he was building on Red Indian Lake a veritable sawmill village: fifty homes for millwrights and loggers and their families, Swedes and Scots but also Newfoundlanders; a church, a school, warehouses, stores – the whole shebang. Hadn't the politicians promised to develop the interior? Millertown looked to be a prototype.

The key to this grand scheme was a deepwater port linked to Red Indian by rail. Burnt Bay had deep water and was only six miles from the main line at Notre Dame Junction. To link it all up, Miller was building a branch line from Millertown to Joe Glode's Pond, the future Millertown Junction. Wharf facilities were being built in Burnt Bay to accommodate the combined production of his Red Indian and Glenwood mills, forty million board feet per annum. All that remained was to lay two miles of dockside track to accommodate the production on rail cars. Overseas orders would be rolled directly onto waiting ships.

Grandpa was so enthused, said Calvin, that he'd quit his apprentice bookkeeper job with the saltfish firm of Owens in Twillingate and applied for the timekeeper job. And once he got it, he started saving for his dream: a general store in the future Lewisporte. He already had a nest-egg. It was in a leather bag hidden in his steamer trunk under the bunk in his caboose office. The bag contained 300 dollars in silver fifty-cent pieces his father had handed him on leaving home over a year ago. To Samuel and his wife Thurza it was a good investment. Frank was their soberest, hardest working and most robust son. His older brother Ned was too fond of poker; his younger brother Edward James was sickly. And Frank had a head for business. That was why they had sent him to Methodist College in St. John's.

Grandpa, my brother continued, was well on his way to doubling his nest-egg when the dream fizzled. Not that his nest-egg was stolen; it just wasn't big enough. No sooner had Miller's rails reached salt water than Burnt Bay was overrun with St. John's land speculators who knew the score and grabbed up the choicest lots. Prices soared. He had waited too long.

There was nothing for it but to take his last pay envelope and look elsewhere. His second choice was Georges Point, Gander Bay. It had been thriving for nearly a decade and still looked promising. J.W. Phillips' big steam sawmill had been sawing Gander River white pine lumber there on double eight-hour shifts since 1892. It was run by J.W's son George.

He went there right away, said Calvin, and promptly bought a plot of land. It was a smart move. By 1903 Lewis Miller was running out of prime pine. His overweight Scottish timber cruiser had grossly overestimated the standing volume. Unfamiliar with snowshoeing, he never even bothered to walk the pine stand beyond the lake, let alone Miller's 800-square mile woodlands.

By 1900 Grandpa had himself a modest shop. By 1903 Phillips, like Miller, was also running out of good pine – partly because his rival was buying up choice timber lots around Gander Lake. But our grandfather had seen it coming. The following year he moved across the bay to Clarkes Head, where Billy Gillingham, father of his new wife Mary, owned land on Clarkes Brook. There he'd erected his own sawmill, a water-powered rig to saw shingles and clapboards for buyers in Fogo and elsewhere – and, finally, built his cherished general store.

A lesser dream, but adequate.

"So you see," concluded my brother, "but for a timber estimating error all of us might have been born in Lewisporte!"

One evening Mom said we needed groceries. As it was a nice walk downtown and Calvin was out somewhere and there were no street lights at our end, she asked me to go with her. It had rained earlier, and traffic had potholed the road. Later, heading home with a flashlight, picking our way along opposite sides, I accidentally trod on one end of a half-buried plank, causing the other end to trip her. We were both carrying heavy bags. She fell heavily.

It was the last straw. As I rushed to help her up, she railed at the world, at herself and me especially. Collecting her spilled groceries, I was devastated. It was Bennett Avenue all over again. The memory of that Sunday in the playground, when she'd ranted about the midwife who had birthed me, washed over me liked a mudslide. But tonight I was definitely at fault. I apologised for the accident and meant it sincerely. When we got home she did likewise and meant it sincerely too. All forgiven. But how to forget?

Other trials were in store for her. One day after school I heard a scream from inside the porch. I found her standing over the flour barrel.

"What happened?" I cried.

"I put my hand in to get a bit of flour and grabbed a live mouse! I threw it over there," she said, jabbing a floury finger toward the corner.

"Did it bite?"

"No, but see if you can catch it." Of course the mouse was gone, but I promised to get some traps the next day. I did catch a few.

It was not long after this that she found the bedbug. "Loathsome creature!" she cried, squishing it underfoot on the bedroom floor. "I'd rather be stung by a dozen hornets! We'll have to move, I can't sleep here another night."

But where could we move? We couldn't afford a better house, and anyway they were scarce. After she calmed down we boiled the bedding. She took a knitting needle to the floor cracks. She scrubbed the upstairs floors and skirting boards with Lysol. We hauled the mattress and rugs outside and beat the bejeesus out of them. Only then could she begin to relax.

Thank God we had the Randalls. Like Millie Gillingham in Gander Bay and Aunt Beatty in St. John's, Mrs. Randall became her friend and confidante. As with many friendships, it was forged in adversity. That first night when we'd stayed at their home, Mom had suffered a grand mal seizure. The next morning, waking deathly tired, she knew what had happened – but prayed her hosts did not. When she learned they had witnessed the whole thing she was mortified.

Yet so gracious were they, so understanding, that the episode became a bond of sympathy and love. To my knowledge, the Randalls were the only people outside our family who ever knew of her affliction. This lifted a burden from us all.

In that climate of renewed unhappiness I found relief in renewed exploration. Having explored the town, I concentrated on the property, on things I'd missed during those busy early weeks. Indoors there was the porch and its paraphernalia, an attic and various closets. Outdoors there was the goat barn, miscellaneous sheds and various trees and shrubs. And wildlife.

The verandah itself was intriguing. We had never had one before. It overlooked a seedy rose garden haunted that autumn by several sorts of sparrows and warblers. After Calvin and I fixed the rotten boards, I found in the porch a couple of wicker benches and dragged them out there. During the Indian summer I'd sit and study out there after school, munching on a molasses bun, soothed by the papery rustle of the hop vine's seed pods.

After the summer birds had flown I kept finding their empty nests around the yard: dry grass bowls made by robins, clay and spittle constructions built by barn swallows under the eaves; a hummingbird's thimble nest camouflaged with lichens and fastened with spider webbing. A few straggling yellow-shafted flickers patrolled the lane, spearing ants and uttering their penetrating staccato cries.

"Mom, Calvin, come quick!" Perched on the verandah one morning was a puff of brown-striped grey feathers. Only when the bird swivelled its outsized head and glared fiercely at us with golden eyes did we realize it was an owl. Then I recalled the tremulous whistle, like notes on a descending scale, that we sometimes heard. Calvin guessed it was a screech owl. "But it didn't screech," I said.

"I guess screech owls don't," he said. "They whistle." Turning to Mom, who had one hand to her mouth, he added, "And they catch mice."

After exploring the garden I rummaged through the sheds, including the goat barn. The nanny didn't mind. Since I had started feeding and watering her we had become good friends. She really needed an outside pen, but we couldn't afford the fencing and didn't dare give her the run of the property. Besides, she was swelling noticeably. Come spring, there would be one or two kids.

One day I found an old bicycle. It was behind some trunks and boxes in the porch – a Raleigh. Covered with cobwebs and speckled with rust, it looked done for. My brother rode a bike to work, had ridden bikes for years; I'd ask his opinion.

Calvin squeezed the tires, tried the brake levers, flipped the bike on its back and spun the wheels to see if they ran true. "Seems all right," he said. He fetched his pump and inflated the front tire: "Well, that one doesn't leak." The rear one did. "It can be patched," he said. "But you'll have to clean the drive chain with a brush and kerosene," he said, "it's all caked with old grease and grit. You do that, and, come spring, I'll teach you to ride."

One day, in a large closet at the head of the stairs, I found a bone-handled folding razor in a slipcase. It was a cut-throat razor of the kind professional barbers used in St. John's, the kind that made me shudder every time I heard them scraping some guy's taut throat. They kept those razors sharp by stropping them on leather.

Unfolded, the razor's concave blade gleamed like a new mirror. Just looking at it made me shiver. But I coveted its wicked beauty. Its curved bone handle seemed meant for my hand. An Excalibur of sorts. Compared to my father's new-fangled "safety razor" this was a surgical instrument. Perhaps one day soon I'd have enough beard to use it on. I shook my head and put it back where I found it. Later, craving the sight of a beautiful man-made thing, I took it out and admired its flash and fire. Once or twice.

School and exploration and lemon lifesavers; that was my routine as winter came on. Winter was confining. It curtailed my friendships. Candy became a comfort. Loneliness was turning me back into a candy addict. This I knew would let me in for more agony down the road, more hours of holding my mouth open over the hot stove, of poking cloves into throbbing cavities, anything to quell the pain.

Lifesavers were a comfort. Every few days I bought a pack, lemon mostly. On really bad days I chewed the lot at once, as one would a candy bar. Mostly I sucked them one by one, savouring the tartness, the sweetness. I sucked them on the school playground and while balancing from rail to rail along the train tracks. Sometimes for diversion I'd place a penny on the track to see the squashed copper wafer next day.

What was I pining for? A girl? I would never have admitted it. Still, I was on the borderland of puberty, that landscape of biochemical upheaval, of wet dreams, of inchoate and exquisite yearnings impossible to communicate. What I needed was a girl-next-door; but where I lived there were none.

More wandering. I wandered so much that Mom and Mrs. Randall thought Sunday school might help. United Church people had already invited Mom to worship with them in the big church down the road. But Mom didn't care to; weren't they Methodist before the 1925 amalgamation? Instead, she and a few other Anglican women were just then forming their own worship group.

Her recent efforts to make a Boy Scout out of me had not gone well, so she hesitated to ask me. I had quit after only two sessions, bored by the uniforms and badges, the little promotions. I did like the knot-tying though. A different leader might have had better luck. Knot-tying seemed to be all he was good at.

To her surprise I said yes to the Sunday school proposition. Since my confirmation I'd had minimal contact with the Church. Even if we didn't plan to attend services, church school would give me something to do with myself on Sundays. Perhaps it would deepen my understanding of the faith I had so recently espoused.

There were no epiphanies. My teacher, another earnest volunteer, was soon forgotten. What I didn't forget was a small magazine which she handed out after each lesson. Printed on smooth white paper with good illustrations, it piqued my interest. There were articles, quizzes, quotations, cartoons and bible study homework. Some issues I read from cover to cover on the way home. Where it was published, I never knew.

From that little magazine I finally got an inkling of what the Old and New Testaments were about. I came to love the so-called minor prophets, ordinary men like Jonah, Amos, Hosea and Micah. Their passionate calls for reform and justice reminded me of the New Testament. Here was Micah again: "But thou, Bethlehem Epthratah, though thou be little among the thousands of Judah, yet out of you shall come forth…a ruler." Shadowy forerunners of Jesus of Nazareth.

Thanks to my mother and some unknown publisher and a volunteer teacher, I had rediscovered the treasure map I would carry all my life. I could picture Grandma Saunders smiling.

In school, now well integrated and confident, I'd begun to secretly write scatological and sexual doggerel to pass around for the titillation of certain boys I knew. It was the verbal equivalent of the cartoons which Ted Reccord and I had drawn in Grade 3 at home; a way to win their further approval. One day I wrote:

Where's your balls?
In your bag
On your cock
Between your legs.

The boys snorted with glee; the girls, not in on my joke, looked askance. Miss Lane, busy helping a girl two rows over, overheard the tittering and made the last boy surrender the paper. This wasn't my plan. My plan had been for him to read and destroy the note. Now she was reading it! Horrified, I watched from behind a textbook as her eyes ran over it, as her face flushed to the roots of her hair.

What must she think? Until that moment I'd been a quiet and tractable boy who excelled at drawing and English. "Who wrote this?" she demanded, scanning the class without lifting her eyes from the note. I raised my trembling hand.

"See me after school," was all she said. In the empty classroom, she told me how one could be expelled for such things, how disappointed she was in me. She wanted to know why I did it. I couldn't say. She made me promise never to do it again.

The episode raised my status with the boys, and even with some of the girls; but for the next few weeks I lived under a cloud. Had Miss Lane told the principal? Would she tell my parents? But nothing more was said. I was in her debt. Before the year was out my debt would increase ten-fold.

Christmas came, bringing home my seafaring father. He looked fit, had even gained a few pounds despite smoking a pack or two of cigarettes a day. Salt air and seafood had always agreed with him. Since October they had patrolled east as far as Musgrave Harbour and Doting Cove. In the New Year they'd work their way westerly through the archipelago perhaps as far as La Scie.

We listened to tales of narrow escapes, of characters he'd met and of the latest doings and sayings of Doctor John Olds of Twillingate. In Fogo he'd had a meal with Fanny and Jabe and visited Tom and Carrie. For the first time in many weeks, my mother was chatty and relaxed, her old self. He praised my drawings.

For Christmas I got a surprise gift. Besides the usual tin box of water paints, the socks and handkerchiefs and pyjamas, there was a small but heavy present. This one had a story behind it. A month before, poking through a roll-top desk upstairs, I had found a harmonica. Without thinking, I rushed downstairs to show Mom. "Where did you find that?" she asked, frowning. I told her. "I hopes you haven't put it near your mouth," she said solemnly. I shook my head. "You never know…"

"You never know who's been playing it," I finished sarcastically.

"Or what diseases they had!" she said, unamused.

"But it looks brand new," I'd countered. "And it's been in that desk for years; surely no germ could live that long."

"No, you're wrong; I've read that typhus germs can live for years. And surely you know that saliva is one of the worst carriers of TB?"

"Yes, Mom, I know. You've told me that a thousand times."

"Well, 'tis for your own good."

"I knows that too."

"Anyhow, put that thing back where you got it or I'll tell your father."

"All right." But trudging back upstairs, I blew a few notes loud enough for her to hear.

So now she was giving me a new harmonica. I was doubly tickled. This one was a ten-hole Hohner Marine Band, key of C. It came in a blue velvet pouch with a drawstring. The cover glittered with engraved images of prizes the band had won. When I looked up, Mom was watching me. I smiled my thanks. After dinner I stole away to my room to practise from the accompanying songbook:

Come and sit by my side, little darlin',
Do not hasten to bid me adieu
But remember the Red River Valley
And the cowboy who loves you so true.

The song became a mental movie. Campfire scenes always had harmonica music. Always you heard its plaint as the cowboy bedded down by his dying fire under the glittering stars. Harmonicas always had the last word. By February I could do passable renditions of "You Are My Sunshine," "Little Red Wing" and "The Squid Jiggin' Ground."

But my true redemption came through art. That we had an art class at all seemed a miracle. In St. John's, even at St. Michael's, I'd never had one. The initiative was Miss Lane's. Artistic herself, she wanted to share the experience. Brave soul, trying to teach everything from math to geography with scanty resources, she managed to make time for colour, line and value. And though the school had no budget for paints and brushes, somehow she obtained, likely with her own money, handfuls of coloured pencils and reams of cheap paper.

Once a week, on her dinner break, squinting and biting her lip, she would set up still lifes of bottles and fruit on an artfully folded tablecloth. Then, as she circulated round the room, we tried to draw them. If she liked something we did, she praised it and said why and pinned it up. Often my work was among those displayed. I basked in the attention, the apparent exoneration.

Toward spring, Miss Lane said that instead of drawing we were going to see an art film at the theatre downtown. "We'll be walking there," she said, "so after the film you can go home." We cheered. "So take your homework things with you." We groaned.

The theatre had folding seats and a small screen. As soon as we were seated, Miss Lane told us there would be two films: a sing-song and a documentary about a famous Canadian artist. Then the room went dark and the screen lit up; no velvet curtains here.

But first we sang for five minutes to a bouncing yellow ball. It was a sad song about a girl with big feet who looked after ducklings and got drowned:

> O my darlin', O my darlin'
> O my darlin', Clementine,
> You are lost and gone forever,
> Dreadful sorry, Clementine.

While the projectionist rewound Clemmie and threaded the art movie, Teacher briefed us. "Tom Thomson grew up on Georgian Bay, Ontario in the 1880s," she said, "studied commercial art in the States and became a commercial artist in Toronto. In 1912, on a canoe trip north of Lake Superior, he painted his first sketch. While working as a summer guide and fire ranger in Algonquin Park, he brought his Toronto artist friends along to paint with him. Now," she concluded: "their paintings are in galleries and collections across the country. Let's see why."

The opening shot was in black and white. It showed a tall man standing in a canoe. As background music swelled, the photograph dissolved under lush yellows and deep purples and flaming reds. The colours washed over me in swirling buttery brushstrokes. As the camera pulled back, the blobs and smears became clouds and trees and rocks and water. I had seen colour in movies before – *Bugs Bunny* and such – but nothing like this.

In that moment I grasped what painting was. Until then I had thought of it as an adornment for drawings, a sort of elaborate cartoon. Now I realized it was about using colour to express the meaning hidden under surface details, to express one's feelings. I staggered out of that theatre gasping for air. My world would never look the same again.

For next art period she brought a book containing colour prints of some Thomson paintings. We talked about his *Jack Pine*, his *Spring Ice* and, the most famous, his *West Wind*. She quoted his friend and studio mate A.Y. Jackson, who said that Tom, before he drowned in a canoe accident in the park in 1917, was "revelling in paint."

Thomson touched me in another way. He was a woodsman like my father, a guide and canoe-man, a man devoted to forest and stream. But while my father praised my picture-making, I felt sure he thought it was at best a hobby and at worst a waste of time – especially for a boy. Boys were still expected to follow their father's trade, and most did so. I'd certainly intended to – until that week.

He came by this honestly. His father Frank was a practical businessman who dreamed in dollars. His mother Mary, though gifted with words and a sensitive soul, was the daughter of generations of woodsmen and fishers with no time for such foolishness. One of them, Simon Gillingham, had hunted Beothuk for Sunday sport, breaking the sixth commandment and the Sabbath both.

One day, wondering about my father's life on the River, I'd asked him what he thought about during his long passages up and down it. "Oh," he said, "about the rocks and the water and trees and one thing and another." Either, I concluded, he was unable to express what he felt, or he chose not to because it seemed silly or weak. Yet here was Thomson, almost my father's age, as taciturn as he, freely expressing his love of wild woods and waters in paint. And selling his larger paintings for hundreds of dollars.

My mother understood my sudden excitement. As a stymied organist herself, she knew the challenges of creating beauty in a frontier culture, let alone making a living from it. So she had always supported my artistic gropings. Not that she necessarily wanted me to make a *career* of it. "I wants you to get a nice clean job…" She simply understood, and that for me was enough.

Marie Lane's undeserved gift to me that year was her introducing me to art in general and to Canadian art in particular. And just as she helped define painting for me, so Thomson validated it as a career. Another Canadian painter of his era might have served as well – Homer Watson, James Morrice, Maurice Prendergast, David Milne – but I doubt it. Thomson had been a painter after my own heart. Whatever gifts I possessed must, I felt sure, be nurtured at the same woodland springs.

Little wonder, then, that half a century later I'd make a pilgrimage to Toronto to see my childhood hero suitably honoured. On the train from Kingston I recall thinking that, had Tom not died so young, had he lived into his eighties like A.Y. Jackson, I might have met him in the flesh. As it was, I would meet him in the paint.

Spring came in a rush. By May, the February snowbanks were sugary and losing ground. Ditches overflowed with meltwater. Our Balm o' Gilead trees unfurled fat sticky buds, perfuming the rain-washed air with balsam. Their cottony catkins littered the verandah. Unkempt bushes along the paths exploded in mauve and cream and white.

From our goat barn came the bleating of two white baby goats, offspring of poor Billy. They were so beautiful, so frisky, I used to hurry home to play with them before suppertime. If I flopped on the hay, they were soon prancing stiff-legged on my chest. When their tickling made me laugh, they leapt off in mock fright. Under their affectionate nuzzling my worries melted like the dirty snow outside.

Meanwhile, my mother was frantically seeking a new home for her faithful grey Toggenburg. The nanny, having given birth, was now giving milk. But no one in that progressive town wanted a goat, let alone three. They might take the kids. Finally Dad had to slaughter our grey goat. And, because Mom knew goat meat to be delicious, he couldn't bear to toss it out. She made the carcass into roasts and stewing meat. It tasted just like caribou.

My brother kept his promise. One June weekend he said, "'Tis time you stopped walking everywhere." He wheeled out the ancient Raleigh, now refurbished, and faced it up the lane. I doffed my windbreaker and mounted while he held the handlebars. "Just pretend you're the Lone Ranger and this is Silver," he grinned. I managed to wobble a few yards before capsizing into a forest of stinging nettles. Within minutes the skin of my bare arms turned red and scalding hot, as if dipped in boiling water. But overnight the pain and blisters subsided, and the next day I practised on the main road. At some point, once I stopped trying too hard, my wobbling stopped. A cool breeze of my own making began to fan my face and I was riding, riding.

My brother had a new girlfriend. She was the teacher Eileen Simms from my school. Eileen was tall and slim with dark hair. The two of them took me to a movie and she treated me like an adult. I forget what the film was about, but Eileen, I didn't. When they went their separate ways, I missed her.

But not for long. I had my eye on a girl named Emmeline, a grade or two below me. One summer evening at dusk, as Roy and I were driving works, just rough-housing, near the railroad tracks, she happened along with two friends and they joined us briefly. She had clear, blue-grey eyes under delicately arched brows. Her whimsical smile was framed by long black hair that bounced when she ran. As she moved, she had an elfin look, as though she heard the pipes of Pan. She and her friends dallied with us in the dreaming meadow for a space, then she was gone.

Suddenly it was June and school was over. I'd passed my exams. My father was back, he had big plans, he and Mom were packing in earnest. My brother was being transferred to Bowater's Glenwood operation. It was goodbye to the school, to the lonesome train tracks, to the old mansion with its whispering hop vine and musical owl, to elfin Emmeline, to childhood.

EPILOGUE

We are riding Lewis Porter's boat again, steering northeast now into a shining day. We are on course for Chapel Head and Comfort Head and Farewell Head and Victoria Cove and home. I am hunkered in the bow, my usual place, deep in reverie, my usual space. When we came this way last fall, I paid little heed. Now I'm all eyes and ears.

I watch the lift and dip of gulls over our widening wake. I think of my voyages in the *Product of Ceylon.* I study the contours of echoing cliffs, the jade green of grounded ice pans. Like a dog let out, I snuff the warm wind that is resinous with crowberry and var.

The boat is steady, our future turbulent. My father's big plans have to do with opening a tourist lodge on the River. Last summer an American angler named Ben Wright, editor of *Field & Stream,* convinced him to stop working for other people and to start his own outfitting business. Calvin is already thinking of a lodge of his own. Calvin's lodge will be at First Pond, while Dad's and Uncle Don's, to be called Saunders' Camps, will be near Third Pond. No more trapping for Dad, no more fishery patrols; he'll be his own man from now on.

The country has big plans as well. On the boat there's a fellow talking politics. Not just talking, but exhorting, waving his arms. I can hear him shouting above the motor's din. I catch the odd word and phrase: National Convention, Commission of Government, responsible government, referendum, Confederation – especially Confederation. Names I've heard and some I haven't are bandied about: Smallwood, Cashin, Bradley, King and St. Laurent.

To me it is all porridge and crackers. Mom has subscribed to no newspapers and anyway, in our house politics are seldom discussed. However, I'm aware that Newfoundland has just voted to be a country again – which seems a good idea – but that the vote was so close it must be repeated in July. I know Grandpa is against joining Canada, that Dad may be for it. Where Mom stands, I don't know. I'm content to let the grownups take care of it.

As for me, my mind is fixed on home and future. Home is where my friends and kinfolk are, where I've lived most of my young life. It used to be the only place where everything *felt right.* Now, after sojourns in St. John's and Lewisporte, I'm not so sure.

Something has been lost – yet I see better now. And not only because of eyeglasses. It's because I've glimpsed the painter's vision. Where I used to see only surface details, visual information, now I see lights and darks, shapes and contours. Above all I see colour; singing, shouting colour.

"Farewell Head," someone shouts. Slowly the boat swings east and then south into the almost mid-summer sun. Change Islands is a study in olive and ultramarine. Fogo's Hare Bay Head looms behind it all lavender and cobalt. We plunge through the salmon-bright sea. It is a coruscation of light. A hymn comes to mind:

> Immortal, invisible,
> God only wise,
> In light inaccessible,
> Hid from our eyes.

So does one of Calvin's school poems, Bliss Carmen's "The Master of the *Scud*":

> There's a schooner out from Kingsport
> By the morning dazzle gleam,

Snoring down the Bay of Fundy
With a norther on her beam.

We don't exactly have a norther, but the sea breeze that was against us all along The Reach is now, since we've rounded Farewell, on our port quarter. By the time we pass Gander Bay Island, it is fair astern.

A free wind home.

ACKNOWLEDGEMENTS

Memoirs are above all about memories. But since few of us can remember much between birth and five years old, the writer must depend on others' memories, or written records, or both. In this I was fortunate to have some long-lived kin with good recall.

My late parents Brett and Winnifred (Layman) Saunders were both good storytellers. So was the late Kathleen (Torraville) Saunders, who recalled aspects of my birth. Aunt Beatty (Layman) Brown, Mom's younger sister, who often stayed with us as a young woman, wrote long letters answering sundry questions – helped in recent years by her daughter Verna (Brown) Rothberg. My late uncle Harry Layman Jr., himself a writer, provided useful background. My older brother Calvin patiently vetted early drafts and kept me on track with early names and dates.

The going got easier after age seven; I could remember for myself. Still, it was helpful to compare notes with various cousins, among them Frank and David Saunders, and Zena (Gillingham) Baird, who proofed some chapters.

Writing is by nature solitary, sometimes even unsociable. Without the loving forbearance of family and the moral support of friends I might have lost heart. Among the former I owe a special debt to my spouse Beth. Among the latter I especially thank Jane Buss, Boyd Chubbs, Patrick O'Flaherty and David Quinton. Also John Munro, who supplied new information on nineteenth century lumber baron Lewis Miller, founder of Lewisporte.

I thank them all – and my patient editor Clare-Marie Gosse.

Finally – if they're listening out there – my gratitude to past and present memoirists such as Jill Ker Conway, Annie Dillard, Natalia Ginzurg, Paul Johnson, George Orwell, Alfred Kazin and David Macfarlane. Their stories helped me find the courage and the words.

All of the people and places and events in my book are real. Much of the dialogue was re-constructed. Some of the weather was invented. Any mistakes are mine.

G.L.S

Truro Daily News

"I wrote this book," says Gary Saunders, "to find the words to a melody that has haunted me for years. Childhood, after all, is the original score for one's life song. My song, as a child and as an adult, has always been about landscapes, animals and people's stories."

After leaving home at 19, Saunders studied forestry and fine art. His working life was devoted to forest and wildlife conservation programs for the province of Nova Scotia, especially for children. He also lectured in forestry at Memorial University for two years. His freelance nature articles, often self-illustrated, have appeared in a dozen magazines including *Canadian Geographic* and *American Forests.* Four Atlantic Region art galleries carry his paintings.

The author's previous eight books include the folklore/folklife classic *Rattles and Steadies: Memoirs of a Gander River Man* (Breakwater 1986), the best-selling *Doctor Olds of Twillingate* (Breakwater 1994) and *Discover Nova Scotia: The Ultimate Nature Guide* (Nimbus/NS Museum 2001).

Gary and his wife of 48 years, Beth Robertson, live near the Bay of Fundy where they garden and walk – and wish their offspring and grandchildren lived closer.